D-12

Rs. 395/

THE END OF SADDAM HUSSEIN

History through the eyes of the Victims

THE END OF SADDAM HUSSEIN

History through the eyes of the Victims

PREM SHANKAR JHA

Rupa & Co

Copyright © Prem Shankar Jha 2004
Second impression 2004

Published 2004 by
Rupa & Co
7/16, Ansari Road, Daryaganj,
New Delhi 110 002

Sales Centres:

Allahabad Bangalore Chandigarh
Chennai Hyderabad Jaipur Kathmandu
Kolkata Ludhiana Mumbai Pune

All rights reserved.
No part of this publication may be reproduced, stored in a retrieval system, or transmitted, in any form or by any means, electronic, mechanical, photocopying, recording or otherwise,
without the prior permission of the publishers.

Typeset in 11 pt. Classical Garamond by
Nikita Overseas Pvt Ltd
1410 Chiranjiv Tower,
43 Nehru Place
New Delhi 110 019

Printed in India by
Gopsons Papers Ltd.
A-14 Sector 60
Noida 201 301

Contents

	Preface	vii
1.	A Pawn in the Cold War	1
2.	The Clinton Years	29
3.	The Invasion of Iraq	68
4.	Manufacturing Consent	124
5.	The Unravelling of Consent	167
6.	The Real Story	194
	Epitaph for Saddam	212
	Index	219

Preface

The Destruction of a Nation

This book sets out to place on record the way in which the United States, later joined by the United Kingdom, destroyed a modern state and plunged its people into misery and chaos. The world became aware of the destruction when, barely hours after US marines pulled down a statue of Saddam Hussein in Firdous square, in Baghdad, in full view of the world's media, the remnants of the Iraqi army and the police melted away and civil servants simply did not arrive for work. Within hours the central nervous system of the Iraqi state turned into mush and chaos reigned. Rioting and looting broke out immediately. Within hours, every one of the government's 139 public buildings, housing all of its records and files, was swept clean. The poor erupted from the slums and began systematically to ransack the homes of the rich and the middle classes. In a country where they had felt completely safe before, women ceased to go out into the streets. Old scores began to be settled and the murder rate rocketed: even six weeks after the war had ended, Baghdad was witnessing 10 murders a day.

What caught the world's attention was the destruction of the Baghdad Museum of Archaeology, one of the greatest repositories of human antiquities in the world. Ironically, the museum had only been reopened a year earlier after the government decided that the threat of aerial bombardment by the Americans and British had receded! Robert Fisk's description of the destruction epitomises the way in which Iraq itself has been destroyed:

> They lie across the floor in tens of thousands of pieces, the priceless antiquities of Iraq's history... Our feet crunched on the wreckage of 5,000-year-old marble plinths and stone statuary and pots that had endured every siege of Baghdad, every invasion of Iraq throughout history—only to be destroyed when America came to 'liberate' the city.[1]

The official version of the events that led up to the invasion of Iraq on 20 March 2003, puts all the blame upon its leader, Saddam Hussein. Hussein was a bloodthirsty, unpredictable dictator who had killed hundreds of thousands of his own people (the 'official' figure, always unsourced, has risen from 1,00,000 to two 2,00,000 to, most recently, 3,00,000). He had not hesitated to invade neighbouring countries, not once but twice—Iran in 1980 and Kuwait in 1990. Despite the fact that Iraq had signed the chemical weapons convention in 1972, he had used chemical weapons, specifically poison gas, not only against the Iranians, but also against his own people, the Kurds of Northern Iraq. And he had done so not once but at least 40 times.[2] After the first Gulf War, he had suppressed a Shia rebellion in Southern Iraq in the most brutal way, slaughtering at least 1,00,000 Shias. And despite the fact that Iraq had signed the Nuclear Non-Proliferation Treaty, he had been developing nuclear weapons, and had come within months of success in 1991.

After losing the Kuwait War, Hussein accepted Resolution 687 of the UN Security Council, and promised to rid his country of all weapons of mass destruction (henceforth WMD) within 15 days. Once the UN had verified that he had done so, economic sanctions that had been imposed upon Iraq when it invaded Kuwait, would be lifted. Those sanctions remained in force right till after the second Gulf War in 2003, *because Saddam did not disarm*. Instead, he continued to try to manufacture weapons of mass destruction, deceive the inspectors, and when finally they came too close to the truth in 1998, *he threw them out of the country*. He used revenues earned under the UN's Oil for Food programme to build palaces for himself, and to pursue his dreams of power, while his people did not have the drugs they needed to save the lives of children and the aged. By playing cat-and-mouse with the weapons inspectors, Saddam made it impossible for the UN to lift its economic sanctions on Iraq. Therefore it was he, and not the US (which had steadfastly opposed the removal of sanctions), that was the architect of the Iraqi peoples' misery.

After pushing out the UN weapons inspectors, Saddam Hussein re-embarked upon the production of weapons of mass destruction. According to the British Prime Minister, the British joint intelligence committee had come to the conclusion that some of these weapons could be deployed in as little as 45 minutes! Saddam had also built links with Osama bin Laden's al Qaeda. The possibility of Iraq transferring its advanced chemical, biological and nuclear weapons technology to al Qaeda had became very real. Saddam had therefore to be disarmed once and for all. The invasion of Iraq in 2003 was therefore forced upon the US and UK by Iraq.

When Iraq was defeated, Saddam Hussein hounded into hiding, and still no weapons of mass destruction were found, the US and UK quickly shifted the rationale for the invasion to human rights. The invasion had been intended not to *occupy*, much less exploit, Iraq but to *liberate* its people from the clutches of a hated dictator responsible for the deaths of hundreds of thousands of his countrymen and women, and usher in freedom and democracy. At the time of writing, despite a mounting death toll among American soldiers and a devastating suicide bombing of the UN headquarters in Baghdad, the US and UK continue to cling to this fiction. They are in Iraq not as invaders and occupiers, but as liberators. Most Iraqis have welcomed them. The guerrilla attacks upon the 'coalition forces' are being carried out by 'remnants of the old regime,' consisting of 'Saddam loyalists', 'Ba'ath party activists', and foreign Islamist fighters. In the American and British lexicon, these are not members of a 'resistance' or freedom fighters, but simply 'criminals'. Thus have these two would-be dictators of the world reduced invasion into a police action and resistance to criminality, not much different from what they encounter on the streets of London or New York.

This book tells a different story. The destruction of Iraq was not accidental, but cold-bloodedly intentional. It did not happen in 2003. It was not even a response to the terrorist attacks upon the US on 11 September 2001. Planning for it began at least nine years earlier in 1992. It did not arise out of Iraq's defeat in the second Gulf War, but out of the US's indecision over how to deal with Iraq after the first Gulf War and its irrational fear of Saddam Hussein. It was not a product of good intentions gone astray, but of paranoia run amok in Washington. Paranoia alone would not have sufficed to achieve so momentous a feat. But in this case it was allied with awesome military power, built, maintained and constantly added to by a nation that faces no conceivable threat to its existence or its vital economic interests. This combination of unreasoning fear and unchallengeable power proved lethal for Iraq. Before the next decade is out, it could prove lethal to other countries as well. Iran and North Korea have already been warned. Syria has very recently been promoted into their ranks and attacked by the US' surrogate in the Middle East, Israel. Others, like Saudi Arabia and Pakistan could easily follow, if there is a change of government in them that the US does not approve of. The only restraint that the world can apply to the US is moral. The first step in exercising it is to tell the true story of what the US did to Iraq. Only by being forewarned does the world stand a chance of averting a repetition of this tragedy.

A second purpose of the book is to expose the deceit used systematically by the US and UK to persuade the world that what they planned and did was both necessary and moral. That governments frequently lie, is no discovery. Especially when it comes to foreign policy, governments have always been secretive, and have invariably chosen to give their people carefully edited versions of their motives, plans and actions. But in this case deceit was used for a different purpose—to 'manufacture consent' for an action that basically had no precedent and no justification. The compulsion that governments feel to manufacture consent is a relatively new development and is a product of the information age. It has arisen because access to information has given ordinary people the capacity to demand that governments abide by some basic standard of ethics in their dealings with their subjects and with each other. This has gradually, but inexorably, shifted the focus of public attention from the ends of policy to the means that governments use to achieve them. In the past, governments had only to justify the former, and were free to choose the latter. Progressively, in the 20th century, as technology has made the media more versatile, more accessible and more intrusive, they are having to justify the latter as well. States inevitably resist the encroachment. As a result, within them this has given birth to a new function—propaganda.

In foreign policy, the need for propaganda first manifested itself when Woodrow Wilson was elected President of the United States in 1916 on the platform of 'peace without victory' to keep America out of the European war, when in fact he was virtually committed to entering it. Wilson's administration delegated the task of persuading Americans of the need for war to a specially appointed commission, the Creel commission. By selectively planting stories of German atrocities and designs in the media, the Creel commission turned a pacifist American population into one that hungered for war, in as little as six months.

The phrase 'manufacturing consent' can be traced back to the writings of Walter Lippman, one of the great liberal intellectuals who was inordinately impressed by the success of the Creel commission.[3] To Lippman and other liberals, propaganda was an essential bridge between Autonomy and Accountability, between ends and means. It enabled the state to maintain its autonomy, but within the limits placed by the need to convince the public of its righteousness. But for propaganda to be a constructive tool of government, the motives of select few who were at the helm of the state had to be above reproach. For this they had to be seen to be acting in the public, and only the public interest. That is what the British and American public are debating today.

Since the media are the indispensable tools of propaganda, inevitably a large part of any war effort has come to revolve around co-opting them to spread the message of self-righteousness. This book shows how, with rare exceptions, the international, English language media were co-opted. However, the link between the state and the media is not a one-way street. If the state needs the media to spread its message, the state is constrained from acting in ways that it cannot easily explain to the media, and through it to the public. This has led to a constant tussle between the state and the media, and an uneasy equilibrium in which each is constantly on the lookout for new techniques by which to gain an ascendancy over the other. This constant struggle makes it possible for special interest groups to 'infiltrate one or the other to change the constraints within which the state must function". This book describes how the Israeli lobby in the US infiltrated the media and the Iraq National Congress infiltrated the Pentagon, to bring about the destruction of Iraq.

The story of Iraq that follows shows the extent to which the state has been able to use its immense powers of patronage to influence the message that the media sends out and to silence its doubting voices. This too is not new. Philip Knightley and John Pilger are prominent among those who have chronicled the abuse of this power in the 1980s and 1990s. This book adds a much-needed chapter on Iraq after 1991.

In theory, the constraint that the media are able to exercise on the autonomy of the state should improve decision-making. Sadly in the case of Iraq, it has almost certainly done the opposite. This is not deliberate, but a byproduct of the transition from the unconstrained sovereignty of the state in the pre-information age to the constrained sovereignty of today. US–Iraq relations became a victim of the change because they were forged in the early 1980s before the information technology revolution suddenly tilted the balance of power in favour of the media in relation to the state. As a result, the Reagan administration had not armed itself with a publicly acceptable rationale for the connection. By the end of the 1980s when a succession of embarrassing stories began to appear in a now much more powerful media about Iraq's human rights record, and the oppressiveness of Saddam's regime, Washington could not withstand the criticism of its Iraq connection that followed, and began to pull out of the tacit commitments it had made to Iraq in the previous decade. The resulting misunderstanding played a key role in catapulting Iraq into Kuwait in 1990.

The counter-offensive of the state, to co-opt the media, has been fierce. Since 1990, more or less co-terminous with the end of the Cold War, propaganda—now re-labelled 'spin'—has gained an undreamed-of importance. Much of the world's media has succumbed to the resulting pressures. But, as this story shows, many journalists, especially print journalists, have remained immune to the pressures and inducements they have been subjected to. The co-optation process, moreover, can never be complete. There are simply too many journalists, asking too many questions, at too many different times, of too many people, to permit the news givers to keep their stories 'straight'. Thus, in bits and pieces, at different times and in different newspapers and TV talk shows, the truth has leaked out. Internet has made the collation of this information infinitely easier than it had been before. The story that follows is constructed painstakingly, therefore, from the very sources that the American and British propaganda machines tried hardest to control. It is not a pretty story.

Notes

1. "A Civilisation Torn to Pieces". *The Independent* 13 April 2003.
2. US Department of State. "International Information Programs: The lessons of Halabja—An Ominous Warning".
3. Noam Chomsky. *Media Control. The Spectacular Achievements of Propaganda*. 2nd Edition. New York Seven Stories Press, 2002.

1

A Pawn in the Cold War

In the Arab world, especially the Mediterranean littoral which is its heartland, the Iraqis have always been considered a violent people. In the early 1960s, long before Saddam Hussein came to power, intellectuals in Damascus or Beirut would roll up their eyes in resignation as they discussed the latest story of a political murder, a pogrom or a public hanging in Baghdad. What else could one expect of the Iraqis?

A large part of the violence stems not from any innate characteristic of the 'Iraqi people' but from the conditions of the country's birth. Iraq was born out of the betrayal of a promise made by a previous global hegemon, the United Kingdom. The promise had been made to Arab leaders chafing to throw off the yoke of a decaying Ottoman Empire by T.E Lawrence, who worked as a cartographer for the Military in London and later was transferred to Military Intelligence in Cairo. In 1916 he was sent on a fact-finding mission behind Turkish lines, to acquire information and establish contact with the Arab nationalist movement. Lawrence reported that the Arabs could be galvanised by making Sharif Husain, of Medina, a direct descendant of the Prophet, its leader. The quality of his reports and his rapport with Husain and his sons led to an assignment as a British liaison officer in the Arab Revolt. After the war, Lawrence promoted Arab independence in England and at the Paris Peace Conference where he served as a British delegate. The idea of Arab independence was, however, anathema to France, which was determined to rule Syria, while the British government had similar ambitions in Iraq. These were fuelled by the discovery of oil in the region. Despite US objections, the three provinces of the Ottoman empire which had become the seat of the Arab revolt were duly allocated to France and Britain as mandated territories—colonies in all but name. The British also hived off Kuwait, which had been a part of the Basra province of the Ottoman empire, to rule it directly from India. An exhausted and defeated Lawrence returned to Oxford where he had been awarded a research fellowship at All Souls College.

However, by the end of 1920, British attempts to impose colonial government in Iraq had provoked open rebellion. Winston Churchill was appointed to find a solution. Churchill persuaded Lawrence, who was campaigning against British policy in the press, to become an advisor. Lawrence was instrumental in the accession of the Emir Feisal to the throne of Iraq, and in the foundation of the Kingdom of Trans-Jordan (modern Jordan). Although still under British rule, both countries thereafter enjoyed a greater degree of self-government.

Iraq's problems did not however end. As any map of the Middle East shows, the British and French did not exactly respect ethnic boundaries when they carved Arabia up between them. As in Africa, in several places the boundaries between Iraq and Trans-Jordan, or Iraq and Syria, were straight lines drawn on the map with a ruler. These cut straight across ethnic divides. This complicated the task of nation-building, because it denied the rulers of Iraq, Syria and Jordan the advantage of a traditional ethnic identity and loyalty upon which to graft a modern national consciousness. Iraq was the worst affected of the three countries, for it contained not only Arab Sunnis and Arab Shias, but also Kurds, who were a completely separate nation with a strongly articulated ethnic consciousness. Even the solution that was later adopted by India, of creating a federation of ethnic nationalities, was not really open to Iraq, because most of the

Arabs were divided into nomadic tribes that moved over large areas in search of pasturage. There were thus no traditional ethnic boundaries of the kind that existed in India when the government of Jawaharlal Nehru decided, in 1957, to reorganise provincial boundaries inherited from the British to coincide with major ethnic faultlines.

Nation building in Iraq therefore, had perforce to be based upon coercion. This explains some of the violence that seems inherent in that country. Of its seven rulers before Saddam Hussein, only one died in harness. One was exiled, and five were killed or died in mysterious accidents. This helps to explain the paranoia that underlay the repressiveness of Saddam Hussein's regime and his penchant for suppressing even the shadow of dissent in the most public way possible.

When the Iraqi monarchy fell in 1958, it did not succumb to the forces of traditional ethnicity, but to a new wave of Arab nationalism that had begun to sweep the Arab countries of the Mediterranean littoral in the 1950s. In Egypt its leader was Gamal Abdel Nasser. In Syria and Iraq its leaders were Salah Bitar and Michel Aflaq, who founded the Ba'ath (Arab Socialist) party. Aflaq was a Christian who retained close ties with the Iraqi regime till his death in the 1980s. Both Nasserism and Baathism were products of western education. They imbued generations of students with a modern sense of nationalism, a deeply secular and socially reformist outlook. Not surprisingly after Germany's defeat at the hands, mainly, of the Russians, both movements professed an admiration for Socialism and centralised planning.

In every respect, therefore Nasserism, and Baathism were the Arab counterparts to Nehruvian socialism and secularism in India. But as in British India, western education fostered not only modernity, but also a heightened awareness of ethnic and religious identity. In Iraq this sharpened two contradictions. The first was between the modern, urbanised sector of society and the traditional, mainly rural, Sheikhs and Imams who owed allegiance to the monarch. The second was between competing ethnicities, broadly the Shias, Sunnis and Kurds. The first conflict led to the overthrow of the monarchy. But this laid bare the second conflict, and made it inevitable that the successor regime would be authoritarian and would seek to consolidate

Iraqi nationalism by suppressing other ethnicities in the state. Ba'ath socialism fitted the bill because it was secular and therefore determined to suppress the religious divisions between Sunni Arabs and Shia Arabs in the country.

Whichever way one looked at it, therefore, Iraq's nation building was going to be violent. But the violence was deepened and prolonged by several factors, two of which were the US intervention in its internal affairs, and its choice of Saddam Hussein as one of its tools for the intervention.

The US intervention arose because Iraq, like Egypt before it, set out to nationalise strategic assets owned by foreign companies in its territory. In Nasser's case it was the Suez Canal. In Iraq it was the oil industry. Had the threat these movements been directed only at the economic assets of the former colonial powers, the US would in all probability have stayed aloof from inter-Arab and intra-Arab affairs. When Nasser nationalised the Suez Canal, the Eisenhower administration intervened to get Britain and France to call off their invasion of Egypt in 1956. But the wave of Arab nationalism that Nasser set off, and the merger of Egypt and Syria to form the United Arab Republic in 1958, heightened Israel's perception of threat. Israel had more to fear from modern than from traditional regimes in the Middle East, because the former embodied Arab Nationalism. The US therefore grew to distrust Nasserism.

A new threat rose in Iraq when Gen. Abdel Karim al Kassem led a successful coup against the monarchy in 1958. Iraq was then regarded as a key buffer and strategic asset in the Cold War with the Soviet Union. For example, in the mid-1950s, it had been quick to join the anti-Soviet Baghdad Pact which was to defend the region and whose members included Turkey, Britain, Iran and Pakistan. This began to change after the 1958 coup against the monarchy that brought Brigadier Abdel Karim al Kassem to power. Richard Sale, the intelligence correspondent of United Press Internatonal (UPI) described the forging of the Saddam–CIA connection in the following words:

> Little attention was paid to Kassem's ...regime until his sudden decision to withdraw from the pact in 1959, an act that

"freaked everybody out" according to a former senior US State Department official. Washington watched in marked dismay as Kassem began to buy arms from the Soviet Union and put his own domestic communists into ministry positions of "real power". In 1961 Kassem also threatened to annex Kuwait, and partly nationalised the foreign owned Iraq Petroleum Corporation[1]. He therefore became a 'communist' and had to go. The domestic instability of the country prompted CIA Director Allan Dulles to say publicly that Iraq was "the most dangerous spot in the world."[2]

One of the instruments chosen by the CIA to get rid of Kassem, was the 20-year-old 'thug', Saddam Hussein. The following account by Sale, describes the close relations that had existed between Saddam and US intelligence agencies in the two decades before he became its arch enemy, in painstaking detail:

> In the mid-1980s, Miles Copeland, a veteran CIA operative, (had) told UPI (that) the CIA had enjoyed "close ties" with Kassem's ruling Ba'ath Party, just as it had close connections with the intelligence service of Egyptian leader Gamal Abdel Nasser. In a recent public statement, Roger Morris, a former National Security Council staffer in the 1970s, confirmed this claim, saying that the CIA had chosen the authoritarian and anti-communist Ba'ath Party "as its instrument."
> According to another former senior State Department official, Saddam, while only in his early 20s, became a part of a US plot to get rid of Kassem. According to this source, Saddam was installed in an apartment in Baghdad on al-Rashid Street directly opposite Kassem's office in Iraq's Ministry of Defense, to observe Kassem's movements.
> Adel Darwish, author of *Unholy Babylon,* said the move was done "with full knowledge of the CIA," and that Saddam's CIA handler was an Iraqi dentist working for CIA and Egyptian intelligence. US officials separately confirmed Darwish's account.

Darwish said that Saddam's paymaster was Capt. Abdel Maguid Farid, the assistant military attaché at the Egyptian Embassy who paid for the apartment from his own personal account. Three former senior US officials have confirmed that this is accurate.

The assassination was set for Oct. 7, 1959, but it was completely botched. Accounts differ. One former CIA official said that the 22-year-old Saddam lost his nerve and began firing too soon, killing Qasim's driver and only wounding Qasim in the shoulder and arm. Darwish told UPI that one of the assassins had bullets that did not fit his gun and that another had a hand grenade that got stuck in the lining of his coat.

"It bordered on farce," a former senior US intelligence official said. But Kassem, hiding on the floor of his car, escaped death, and Saddam, whose calf had been grazed by a fellow would-be assassin, escaped to Tikrit, thanks to CIA and Egyptian intelligence agents, several US government officials said.

Saddam then crossed into Syria and was transferred by Egyptian intelligence agents to Beirut, according to Darwish and former senior CIA officials. While Saddam was in Beirut, the CIA paid for Saddam's apartment and put him through a brief training course, former CIA officials said. The agency then helped him get to Cairo, they said.

In Cairo, according to Darwish and former US intelligence officials, Saddam was installed in an apartment in the upper class neighborhood of Dukki and spent his time playing dominos in the Indiana Café, watched over by CIA and Egyptian intelligence operatives.

During this time Saddam was making frequent visits to the American Embassy where CIA specialists such as Miles Copeland and CIA station chief Jim Eichelberger were in residence and knew Saddam, former US intelligence officials said.

According to Darwish, Saddam's US handlers even pushed Saddam to get his Egyptian handlers to raise his monthly allowance, a gesture not appreciated by Egyptian officials since they knew of Saddam's American connection,. His assertion was confirmed by former US diplomat in Egypt at the time.

In February 1963 Kassem was killed in a Baath Party coup. Morris claimed recently[3] that the CIA was behind the coup, which was sanctioned by President John F. Kennedy, but a former very senior CIA official strongly denied this[4]....

But the agency quickly moved into action. Noting that the Baath Party was hunting down Iraq's communist, the CIA provided the submachine gun-toting Iraqi National Guardsmen with lists of suspected communists who were then jailed, interrogated, and summarily gunned down, according to former US intelligence officials with intimate knowledge of the executions.

Many suspected communists were killed outright, these sources said. Darwish told UPI that the mass killings, presided over by Saddam, took place at Qasr al-Nehayat, literally, the Palace of the End.

A former senior US State Department official told UPI: "We were frankly glad to be rid of them. You ask that they get a fair trial? You have to get kidding. This was serious business."

A former senior CIA official said: "It was a bit like the mysterious killings of Iran's communists just after Ayatollah Khomeini came to power in 1979. All 4,000 of his communists suddenly got killed.

Saddam, in the meantime, became head of Al-Jihaz -e-Khas, the secret intelligence apparatus of the Baath Party. In 1968 an internal Baath party coup brought Ahmed Hassan al-Bakr to power. Al-Bakr was Saddam's mentor. Eleven years later, power passed from Al-Bakr to Saddam Hussein. Saddam declared war on Iran only months later.[5]

US cooperation with Iraq during the Iran-Iraq war, 1980-1990

The weakest point of the policies followed by the Clinton and Bush administrations towards Iraq is, "If Saddam was such a demon, if he was so power-hungry, brutal and unpredictable, why did the US maintain a close military and economic relationship with him throughout the 1980s?

Of the depth of these relations there can be little doubt. Sale describes the development of an intelligence link as follows:

> The CIA/Defense Intelligence Agency relation with Saddam intensified after the start of the Iran-Iraq war in September of 1980. During the war, the CIA regularly sent a team to Saddam to deliver battlefield intelligence obtained from Saudi AWACS surveillance aircraft to aid the effectiveness of Iraq's armed forces, according to a former DIA official, part of a US interagency intelligence group. This former official said that he personally had signed off on a document that shared US satellite intelligence with both Iraq and Iran in an attempt to produce a military stalemate. "When I signed it, I thought I was losing my mind, (he) told UPI. A former CIA official said that Saddam had assigned a top team of three senior officers from the Estikhbarat, Iraq's military intelligence, to meet with the Americans...According to Darwish, the CIA and DIA provided military assistance to Saddam's ferocious February 1988 assault on Iranian positions in the al-Fao peninsula by blinding Iranian radar for three days.[6]

But intelligence was not the only area in which the USA helped Iraq. Throughout the war, the US (and UK) supplied food, loans, dual use technology for the manufacture of weapons of mass destruction. The germ cultures that Iraq used in order to develop its stores of anthrax, botulism, *e.coli* and a host of other deadly bacteria and toxins came from a US firm, the American Type Culture Collection, based not far from Washington, D.C. in Rockville, Maryland. This company exported 36 stains of ten deadly pathogens to Iraq in the 1980s with the approval of the US government. Some of these stains had come from the US biowarfare research centre at Fort Detrick.[7] It continued to do so even after it got to know that Iran and Iraq were using chemical weapons and Iraq had used poison gas against the Kurds in 1988. The following excerpts from the conclusion of a report on what came to be called 'Iraqgate', compiled for the Digital National Security Archive, USA, exposes the depths of the US' commitment to Iraq during the Iran-Iraq war and afterwards till Iraq's invasion of Kuwait.[8]

> US involvement with Iraq in the 1980s developed from decisions taken by the Reagan and Bush administrations to pursue cooperative arrangements with Iraq because of perceived common interests between Baghdad and Washington. As noted above, these arrangements included providing Iraq with economic assistance and intelligence information both during and after the Iran-Iraq war. Officials sometimes preferred to characterize the programs that were utilized for Iraq's benefit as vehicles to help US exporters by making their products more competitive in the international marketplace—and they did indeed serve that purpose. However the available documentation, some of which appears in this collection, attests that they were used, with respect to Iraq, primarily to cement closer relations and to help that country cope with its financial problems. The US provided assistance despite its awareness of Iraq's active programs to develop indigenous production capabilities for missiles and chemical and biological weapons—and perhaps nuclear weapons as well. Despite controls governing US exports of dual-use (civilian and military) technology, a considerable range of militarily useful material was legally exported from the US, including some that could be utilized in nuclear weapons development programs.[9]

The Iraqgate report also referred to an affidavit submitted by a former National Security Council official, Howard Teicher, as part of a trial involving allegations of export law violations. In that affidavit he had indicated that during the Iran–Iraq war, high-level CIA officers had ensured that Iraq was provided with weapons, including cluster bombs, pursuant to a National Security Decision Directive signed by

Ronald Reagan authorising US military re-supply of Iraq. The report also showed that the US was not the only country to do so. The British government also approved the sale of machinery that it knew was destined for the production of weapons of mass destruction.[10]

Did the US encourage Iraq?

What the critics of US policy fail to ask is, 'did the US only support Iraq after the Iran-Iraq war began, or did it, however indirectly, encourage Iraq to declare war on Iran?'. If it was the latter, then the reasons for such a comprehensive engagement with Iraq become self-evident. One reason for suspecting collusion is the US' fulminating anger over the hostage crisis in Iran in 1980. That crisis could only have strengthened its belief that an Iran under the Ayatollahs, full of revolutionary fervour, was a serious threat to the conservative Arab regimes in that area that were the US' principal allies. There is, however, more direct evidence that the US did indeed give an 'orange light' to Iraq's invasion of Iran. This greatly strengthens the possibility that the US encouraged Iraq to invade Iran.

Officially, Iraq reestablished relations with the US only in 1984. But in an Iraqi official transcript of Saddam Hussein's talks with US Ambassador April Glaspie on 25 July 1990, Saddam reminded Glaspie that "The decision to establish relations with the US were (sic) taken in 1980 during the two months prior to the war between us and Iran".

His next sentence gave away the reason for the concealment: "When the war started, and *to avoid misinterpretation*, we postponed the establishment of relations hoping that *the war would end soon*".[11] In short, it was precisely to avoid giving the impression that the US was siding with Iraq in the war that the official resumption of diplomatic relations was postponed. *This decision was taken two months before Iraq invaded Iran.*

Saddam's prepared speech to Ambassador April Glaspie, which he described as a message for President Bush, contains numerous references to the burden Iraq shouldered on behalf of its Arab neighbours, to contain the expansionist Iran in the first flush of its revolutionary zeal. Although Saddam never said so explicitly, many references made it clear that he believed that in this Iraq's and the US' interests were identical. For instance at one point he said:

> But you know you are not the ones who protected your friends during the war with Iran. I assure you, had the Iranians overrun the region, the American troops would not have stopped them, except by the use of nuclear weapons.....Is this Iraq's reward for its role in securing the stability of the region and for protecting it from an unknown flood?[12]

Why did Iraq invade Kuwait?

Why, after having been fought to a stalemate by Iran did, an exhausted Iraq turn its guns on Kuwait? In all the recent writing on Iraq, there is an inexplicable lack of curiosity about Saddam Hussein's motives for waging a second war so close on the heels of the first. For the general public, the explanation that he was a power-hungry, bloodthirsty demon was sufficient. His preparedness to plunge his country into war not once but twice was cited by President Bush (J.) and Prime Minister Tony Blair as the clearest evidence that conventional policies of deterrence would not work on Iraq and the only course open to the 'world' was to disarm him, if necessary by force.

The Iraqgate investigation ascribed the invasion to the rupture of Iraq's relationship with the US, but laid the blame for this on Saddam Hussein. In 1982 the Reagan administration had cleared Iraq for participation in US Commodity Credit Corporation Loans. These were intended to boost sales of American agricultural products abroad. In the years that followed, Iraq became one of the major recipients of that aid. However, after the Iran–Iraq war ended, it became more and more difficult for the Bush (Sr.) administration to continue providing this assistance in the face of complaints and persistent media reports of Iraq's human rights violations and allegations that it had been diverting some of this aid into the purchase of weapons and weapon, making machinery. The Iraqgate investigation identified the breaking point of that relationship as the trigger for Saddam's attack on Kuwait.

In May 1990, the US had extended $1 billion worth of credit guarantees to Iraq. Just two months later, however Saddam Hussein made a decision that destroyed the relationship between Iraq and the US that had been so carefully cultivated during the preceding decade. Iraq's leadership had grown increasingly frustrated over its failure to obtain additional funding from either the US, or from other sources. In mid-July, the Iraqi government informed the US Embassy that Iraq would cease all imports from the US unless it received new CCC credit guarantees by the end of September. The Embassy noted Iraq's increasingly severe economic problems, and reported that recent threats Iraq made against Kuwait reflected its realisation that it would have to cut back drastically on civilian "and perhaps even military projects" unless it received desperately needed funds.[13] At a 25 July OPEC ministerial council meeting in Geneva, Iraq accused Kuwait of violating its oil production quotas, and of stealing Iraqi oil, and suggested that Kuwait forgive the debts Iraq owed to it (accumulated during the Iran-Iraq war). On 1 August negotiations between the two countries to resolve their differences broke down. Deciding that direct action was necessary to save his country from its economic dilemma, and greatly miscalculating the international response to his action, Saddam Hussein ordered an invasion of Kuwait on 2 August 1990.[14]

The Saddam transcript confirms that the threat to Kuwait was also an ultimatum to the US, but one given out of a sense of increasing isolation and desperation, caused by the US government's gradual retreat from the close relationship it had built with Iraq during the Iran–Iraq war. In it, Saddam put the ultimate blame for the breakdown of the relationship on the barrage of criticism and embarrassing disclosures the Bush administration faced in the media. The US–Iraq relationship had been free from hiccups, Saddam pointed out, so long as it was a secret one. Trouble began only after it became official, and therefore publicly known, in 1984. In 1986, Iraq learned, from exposés in US media, that the Reagan administration had been selling weapons clandestinely to Iran since August 1985, in what came to be known as the Iran-Contra scandal. The middleman in the deal, and possibly also its originator, given its visceral fear of Iraq, was Israel.[15] (Saddam probably did not know then that the US was also passing intelligence on Iraqi troop movements to Iran). When the scandal erupted, the US Ambassador to Iraq tendered an apology to Iraq. Iraq accepted this apology despite its misgivings and 'wiped the slate clean'.

He would not have raised this issue again, Saddam said, had "new events (not) remind(ed) us that old mistakes were not just a matter of coincidence". He went on to say that

> Our suspicions increased after we liberated the Fao peninsula (the eastern bank of the Shatt el Arab). The (US) media began to involve itself in our politics. And our suspicions began to surface anew, because we began to question whether the US felt uneasy with the outcome of the war when we liberated our land.
> It was clear to us that certain parties in the United States—and I don't say the President himself—*but certain parties who had links with the intelligence community* and with the State Department—and I don't say the Secretary of State himself—I say that these parties did not like the fact that we liberated our land. Some parties began to prepare studies entitled: "Who will succeed Saddam Hussein?" They began to contact Gulf states to make them fear Iraq, to persuade them not to give Iraq economic aid. *And we have evidence of these activities.* (emphasis added)

What Saddam was referring to was obvious to Glaspie, for she made no comment and did not demur. While the US feared Iran, Israel feared Iraq. Iraq's conquest of the whole of the Fao peninsula would leave it more powerful than ever before. It had to be undone. Since the White House and the State Department were then committed to containing Iran, Israel according to Saddam, had resorted to leaks in the media to discredit the US–Iraq relationship and weaken Iraq.

As the war dragged on, Iraq went deeper and deeper into debt. By 1988 this amounted to $40 billion, excluding Iraq's debts to various Arab countries. But in 1986 oil prices had crashed to a low point of $12 a barrel, in real terms barely above what they were in 1973. Iraq found itself facing insolvency. Saddam hinted that Iraq had for some time been trying to persuade its Arab debtor nations to waive the debt.

> Iraq came out of the war burdened with $40 billion debts, excluding the aid given by Arab states, *some of whom consider that too to be a debt although they knew—and you knew too—that without Iraq they would not have had these sums and the future of the region would have been entirely different.*

He also urged them to work together to raise the price of oil. When Glaspie said that high oil prices would hurt consumer countries, he said that he did not want the price to be too high and believed that $25 a barrel was an appropriate price. Glaspie concurred. Most economists would have done the same. However, he received no support from the other oil producers. Saddam was especially bitter about the unhelpful attitude of Kuwait and the UAE. These were the countries that had benefited most, in terms of security from Iraq's war on Iran, but were not prepared to lift a finger to help Iraq when it faced economic distress. Saddam also accused the US of being behind the policy of forcing down oil prices.

What tipped Saddam over the brink into contemplating the invasion of Kuwait, however, was his belief that the oil prices had been forced down by deliberate, concerted policy.

> But when planned and deliberate policy forces the price of oil down without good commercial reasons, then that means another war against Iraq. Because military war kills people by bleeding them, and economic war kills their humanity by depriving them of their chance to have a good standard of living. As you know, we gave rivers of blood in a war that lasted eight years, but we did not lose our humanity. Iraqis have a right to live proudly. We do not accept that anyone could injure Iraqi pride or the Iraqi right to have high standards of living.
> Kuwait and the U.A.E. were at the front of this policy aimed at lowering Iraq's position and depriving its people of higher

> economic standards. And you know that our relations with the Emirates and Kuwait had been good.

Saddam chose to pressurise Kuwait because it had established oil installations at the very edge of the boundary with Iraq, and had been tapping Iraqi oil.

> On top of all that, while we were busy at war, the state of Kuwait began to expand at the expense of our territory. You may say this is propaganda, but I would direct you to one document, the Military Patrol Line, which is the borderline endorsed by the Arab League in 1961 for military patrols not to cross the Iraq–Kuwait border. But go and look for yourselves. You will see the Kuwaiti border patrols, the Kuwaiti farms, the Kuwaiti oil installations—all built as closely as possible to this line to establish that land as Kuwaiti territory.

By July 1990, with interest on its loans mounting steadily, Iraq was in desperate financial straits. Saddam had failed to get other OPEC countries to raise the price of oil, and failed to get his Arab neighbours to waive Iraq's debt. He had obtained another $1 billion of CCC loans from the US in the teeth of media opposition, but as he complained to Glaspie, the list of products that Iraq could not buy had been expanded till all it could use the money for was to buy wheat. At the OPEC meeting on 25 July, he threatened Kuwait (not for the first time) and asked it to waive Iraq's debt to it in exchange for wiping the slate clean on Kuwait's theft of Iraqi oil. He also tried to get the US to put pressure on Kuwait by making a thinly veiled threat that he would otherwise acquire the whole of Iraq, i.e. annex Kuwait. It was in this context, and as a way of telling him that the US would not oblige him, that Glaspie told him: "*We have no opinion on the Arab–Arab conflicts*". One month after Iraq invaded Kuwait, on 2 September 1990 a tape and a transcript of the meeting was leaked by unknown sources to British journalists in Baghdad. A comparison of this transcript with the official transcript of the conversation made by the Iraqis, shows that it was severely distorted. In particular this remark was pulled out of its context by the those who leaked the tape, to support the contention that the US had shown Saddam an 'orange light' to invade Kuwait.[16]

The furore that ensued made the State Department turn Glaspie into a scapegoat, and ruined her career. But the full text of what she actually said, reads as follows:

> I know you need funds. We understand that and our opinion is that you should have the opportunity to rebuild your country. *But* we have no opinion on the Arab–Arab conflicts, like your border disagreement with Kuwait (emphasis added). I was in the American Embassy in Kuwait during the late 60's. The instruction we had during this period was that we should express no opinion on this issue and that the issue is not associated with America. James Baker has directed our official spokesmen to emphasize this instruction. We hope you can solve this problem using any suitable methods via Klibi or via President Mubarak. All that we hope is that these issues are solved quickly.

It was in the context of Saddam's desperate hunt for funds that she made her disclaimer and not his barely veiled warning that he might have to reclaim 'the whole of Iraq'. Glaspie came directly and pointedly to that threat later:

> But you, Mr. President, have fought through a horrific and painful war. Frankly, we can see only that you have deployed massive troops in the south. Normally that would not be any of our business. But when this happens in the context of what you said on your national day, then when we read the details in the two letters of the Foreign Minister, then when we see the Iraqi point of view that the measures taken by the UAE and Kuwait is, in the final analysis, parallel to military aggression against Iraq, then it would be reasonable for me to be concerned. And for this reason, *I received an instruction*

to ask you, in the spirit of friendship—not in the spirit of confrontation—regarding your intentions.

Saddam's answer was detailed and anything but irrational:

> We want to find a just solution which will give us our rights but not deprive others of their rights. But at the same time, we want the others to know that our patience is running out regarding their action, which is harming even the milk our children drink, and the pensions of the widow who lost her husband during the war, and the pensions of the orphans who lost their parents.
>
> As a country, we have the right to prosper. We lost so many opportunities, and the others should value the Iraqi role in their protection. Even this Iraqi [the President points to their interpreter] feels bitter like all other Iraqis. We are not aggressors but we do not accept aggression either. We sent them (Kuwait and UAE, presumably) envoys and handwritten letters. We tried everything. We asked the Servant of the Two Shrines—King Fahd—to hold a four-member summit, but he suggested a meeting between the Oil Ministers. We agreed. And as you know, the meeting took place in Jidda. They reached an agreement which did not express what we wanted, but we agreed.
>
> Only two days after the meeting, the Kuwaiti Oil Minister made a statement that contradicted the agreement. We also discussed the issue during the Baghdad summit. I told the Arab Kings and Presidents that some brothers are fighting an economic war against us. And that not all wars use weapons and we regard this kind of war as a military action against us. Because if the capability of our army is lowered then, if Iran renewed the war, it could achieve goals which it could not achieve before. And if we lowered the standard of our defenses, then this could encourage Israel to attack us. I said that before the Arab Kings and Presidents. Only I did not mention Kuwait and UAE by name, because they were my guests.

> Before this, I had sent them envoys reminding them that our war had included their defense. Therefore the aid they gave us should not be regarded as a debt. We did not more than the United States would have done against someone who attacked its interests.
> I talked about the same thing with a number of other Arab states. I explained the situation to brother King Fahd a few times, by sending envoys and on the telephone. I talked with brother King Hussein and with Sheik Zaid (of the UAE) after the conclusion of the summit. I walked with the Sheik to the plane when he was leaving Mosul. He told me, "Just wait until I get home." But after he had reached his destination, the statements that came from there were very bad—not from him, but from his Minister of Oil.
> And after the Jidda agreement, we received some intelligence that they were talking of sticking to the agreement for two months only. Then they would change their policy. Now tell us, if the American President found himself in this situation, what would he do? I said it was very difficult for me to talk about these issues in public. But we must tell the Iraqi people who face economic difficulties who was responsible for that.

Not fully satisfied with Saddam's answers, Glaspie asked him a second time what he intended to do. It was only then that Saddam told her that if Kuwait simply did not see reason, he would be left with no option but to adopt other means. Glaspie's reaction was what one would have expected from any Ambassador given such momentous news. She said that she would convey it personally to the US President. The precise text of this exchange was as follows:

> **Glaspie:** Mr. President, it would be helpful if you could give us an assessment of the effort made by your Arab brothers and whether they have achieved anything.
> **Hussein:** On this subject, we agreed with President Mubarak that the Prime Minister of Kuwait would meet with the deputy chairman of the Revolution Command Council in

Saudi Arabia, because the Saudis initiated contact with us, aided by President Mubarak's efforts. He just telephoned me a short while ago to say the Kuwaitis have agreed to that suggestion.
Glaspie: Congratulations.
Hussein: A protocol meeting will be held in Saudi Arabia. Then the meeting will be transferred to Baghdad for deeper discussion directly between Kuwait and Iraq. We hope we will reach some result. We hope that the long-term view and the real interests will overcome Kuwaiti greed.
Glaspie: May I ask you when you expect Sheik Saad to come to Baghdad?
Hussein: I suppose it would be on Saturday or Monday at the latest. I told brother Mubarak that the agreement should be in Baghdad Saturday or Sunday. You know that brother Mubarak's visits have always been a good omen.
Glaspie: This is good news. Congratulations.
Hussein: Brother President Mubarak told me they were scared. They said troops were only 20 kilometres north of the Arab League line. I said to him that regardless of what is there, whether they are police, border guards or army, and regardless of how many are there, and what they are doing, assure the Kuwaitis and give them our word that we are not going to do anything until we meet with them. When we meet and when we see that there is hope, then nothing will happen. But if we are unable to find a solution, then it will be natural that Iraq will not accept death, even though wisdom is above everything else. There you have good news.
Aziz: This is a journalistic exclusive.
Glaspie: I am planning to go to the United States next Monday. I hope I will meet with President Bush in Washington next week. I thought to postpone my trip because of the difficulties we are facing. But now I will fly on Monday.[17]

The most striking feature of the above conversation is that it was between allies whose purpose was to clear misunderstandings, express each others' concerns and chart out an agreed course of action. But by the time the first, doctored version of the conversation appeared in the media on 2 or 3 September the US had embarked upon the effort to mobilise a coalition against Saddam and had begun to demonise him. The tone of the 2 September tape and, even more unambiguously, of the official version released to the *New York Times* three weeks later, was totally incompatible with Bush's descriptions of Saddam as evil, and 'another Adolf Hitler'. The Bush administration therefore had no option but to disown the conversation and sacrifice the Ambassador who had participated in it.

The transcript helps one to fill out the part of the story that the Iraqgate report did not deal with. While the latter outlines Saddam's mistakes, the former explains not only why Iraq made those mistakes but also the role that revelations in the American media played in disrupting the US–Iraq relationship and creating a sense of betrayal, isolation and desperation in Iraq. Saddam's invasion of Kuwait was not irrational or unpredictable, just based upon a profound miscalculation. Saddam did have reason to feel let down and isolated. He had had the full backing of the US, of Kuwait and of the UAE, in his war against Iran, for they gave him the arms, the intelligence, the technology and the resources with which to wage war. They therefore did have a moral responsibility to help Iraq recover from the effects of a war that it had fought, at least partly, on their behalf. They might not have been able to do as much as Saddam wanted them to do. But at the end he was not asking for much more than a gesture of support. Kuwait and the UAE denied even this to him, while the US sanctioned a billion dollars—one fortieth of Iraq's debts, with innumerable caveats on how it could be used. In these circumstances he did not have to be 'another Adolf Hitler' to consider Kuwait's refusal to make restitution even for the oil it had pumped out from under Iraqi soil sufficient ground for taking some punitive action. Where he went wholly wrong was in attempting to annex Kuwait.

Had the US prevailed upon Kuwait and the UAE to write off some of Iraq's debts; had it used its influence with Saudi Arabia and Kuwait to support Iraq's bid to push up oil prices; or had it been more generous with its own aid to Iraq, it is virtually certain that the invasion of Kuwait would never have taken place. But the US could do none of those things because by then a barrage of stories in the media had roundly pilloried Iraq for its human rights record, and thoroughly frightened the American public into believing that it was channelling US aid into building nuclear and other weapons of mass destruction that threatened US hegemony and could pose a threat to the country itself. The Bush administration had to justify support for Iraq on the grounds of realpolitik. This would have been relatively easy at the height of the Cold War but became difficult after the fall of the Berlin Wall. It chose therefore to dissociate itself from Iraq and leave it to fend for itself.

The tragedy that engulfed the people of Iraq in the succeeding 13 years can therefore be traced back to the constraint imposed upon the autonomy of the US administration in foreign policy by the rise of a new power in the land, the American media.

Notes

1. Andrew and Patrick Cockburn. *Out of the Ashes, The Resurrection of Saddam Hussein.* London: Verso, 2000.
2. Richard Sale. *Saddam Was key in early CIA plot. Information Clearing house (e-newspaper)* 11 April 2003. UPI interviewed almost a dozen former US diplomats, British scholars and former US intelligence officials to piece together the above account. The CIA declined to comment on the report.
3. David Morgan: Former CIA official says CIA aided Iraqi Baathists: www.rense.com. 21 April 2003. The official, Wayne Morris, is quoted saying the following:

   > "This takes you down a longer, darker road in terms of American culpability," said Morris, a former State Department foreign service officer who was on the National Security Council staff during the Johnson and Nixon administrations.
   > In 1963, two years after the ill-fated US attempt at overthrow in Cuba known as the Bay of Pigs, Morris says the CIA helped organize a bloody coup in Iraq that deposed the Soviet-leaning government of Gen. Abdel-Karim Kassem.

> "As in Iran in '53, it was mostly American money and even American involvement on the ground," said Morris, referring to a US-backed coup that had brought the return of the shah to neighboring Iran.
>
> Kassem, who had allowed communists to hold positions of responsibility in his government, was machine-gunned to death. And the country wound up in the hands of the Baath Party. At the time, Saddam was a Baath operative studying law in Cairo, one of the venues the CIA chose to plan the coup, Morris says. In fact, he claims the former Iraqi ruler castigated by President Bush as one of history's most "brutal dictators," was actually on the CIA payroll in those days.
>
> "There's no question," Morris told Reuters. "It was there in Cairo that (Saddam) and others were first contacted by the agency."

4. Morris' conclusion is also shared by authors Andrew and Patrick Cockburn op. cit. The relevant pages of the book read as follows:

> On February 8, a military coup in Baghdad, in which the Baath Party played a leading role, overthrew Qassim. Support for the conspirators was limited. In the first hours of fighting, they had only nine tanks under their control. The Baath Party had just 850 active members. But Qassim ignored warnings about the impending coup.
>
> What tipped the balance against him was the involvement of the United States. He had taken Iraq out of the anti-Soviet Baghdad Pact.
>
> In 1961, he threatened to occupy Kuwait and nationalized part of the Iraq Petroleum Company (IPC), the foreign oil consortium that exploited Iraq's oil.
>
> In retrospect, it was the CIAs favorite coup. "We really had the 'ts' crossed on what was happening," James Critchfield, then head of the CIA in the Middle East, told us. "We regarded it as a great victory."
>
> Iraqi participants later confirmed American involvement. "We came to power on a CIA train," admitted Ali Saleh Sa'adi, the Baath Party secretary general who was about to institute an unprecedented reign of terror. CIA assistance reportedly included coordination of the coup plotters from the agency's station inside the US embassy in Baghdad as well as a clandestine

radio station in Kuwait and solicitation of advice from around the Middle East on who on the left should be eliminated once the coup was successful. To the end, Qassim retained his popularity in the streets of Baghdad. After his execution, his supporters refused to believe he was dead until the coup leaders showed pictures of his bullet-riddled body on TV and in the newspapers.

5. Sale; op. cit.
6. Sale. op. cit.
7. Digital National Security Archive. *Iraqgate: Saddam Hussein, US Policy and the Prelude to the Persian Gulf War*, 1980–1994. For a detailed analysis of the credibility and importance of the Iraqgate story see article in the Columbia Journalism Review March April, 1993. at http://www.cjr.org/year/93/2/iraqgate.asp.

   One company, the American Type culture Collection, was given permission by the US department of commerce to sell to Iraq, for 'research' purposes, Anthrax, E coli, Botulinum toxin, and a number of other pathogens and toxins. See Karl Vick: *Man Gets Hand on Bubonic Plague Germs, But That's No Crime.* Washington Post December 30, 1995.p. D1. Also Associated Press; *Report Links Gulf War Expert to US supplier of Germs to Iraq.* The New York Times. November 28, 1996. P. A 19. See also William J. Broad and Judith Miller: The Deal on Iraq: Secret Arsenal: The Hunt for the germs of War- A Special Report. The New York Times February 26 1998. See also Phyllis Bennis and Dennis Halliday: *Iraq: The Impact of Sanctions and US policy.* Interviewed by David Barsamian in *Iraq Under Siege.* op. cit. P. 35.

8. *Iraqgate: Saddam Hussein, US Policy and the Prelude to the Persian Gulf War*, 1980-1994. op. cit.
9. The following is a list of the documents that the investigators consulted to prepare DNSA report on the 'Iraqgate' story. As can be seen, these are all US government documents. To prepare the report they made extensive use of the Freedom of Information Act.

   1. Commerce Department List "Approved Licenses to Iraq," 1212/90.

2. Senate Banking Committee Hearing: Testimony of David Kay, 10/27/92, pp. 37-43.
3. State Department Memorandum: "Iraq Use of Chemical Weapons," 11/1/83.
4. State Department Memorandum: "Iraqi Use of Chemical Weapons," 11/21/83.
5. State Department Memoranda: "Swan Song for Iraq's Kurds?," 9/2/88; "US Policy Toward Iraqi CW Use," 9/13/88.
6. State Department Memorandum: "Export Import Financing for Iraq," 12/29/88.
7. State Department Memorandum: "Export-Import Financing for Iraq," 12/29/88.
8. State Department Paper: "Guidelines for US-Iraq Policy," ca. 1/20/89.
9. State Department Memorandum: "Meeting with Iraqi Under Secretary Nizar Hamdun," 3/23/89.
10. State Department Memorandum: "Export-Import Financing for Iraq," 4/10/89.
11. Letter from James A. Baker, III to Clayton Yeutter, 6/9/89.
12. The White House: "US Policy Toward the Persian Gulf," 10/2/89.
13. CIA Memorandum: "Iraq-Italy: Repercussions of the BNL-Atlanta Scandal," 11/6/89.
14. State Department Memorandum: "SNEC Cases of Interest," 11/21/89.
15. "Atlanta Group Weekly Report," ca. 11/22/89.
16. Agreement, 1/20/90.
17. Letter from Patrick Leahy to Clayton Yeutter, 2/12/90.
18. Waas, Murray and Douglas Frantz. "New Documents Show Bush Aides Favored Helping Iraq." *Los Angeles Times*, 9/4/92.
19. State Department Cable: "DAS Gnehm Call on Minister of Trade- CCC and BNL," 12/10/89.
20. State Department Memorandum: "Second Tranche of CCC Credits for Iraq," 1/4/90.
21. State Department Memorandum. "Statue of Iraq CCC Program," 2/28/90.
22. Handwritten Notes, 3/1/90.
23. State Department Memorandum: "NAC Meeting on Iraq CCC Program," 3/5/90.

24. US Attorney's Office: "Notice to USDA of Iraqi Complicity in Criminal Violations," 5/4/90.
25. State Department Memorandum: "Possible Indictment of Iraqi Officials," 5/22/90.
26. State Department Memorandum: "Weekly Report," 5/18/90.
27. Senate Select Committee on Intelligence (SSCI): "The Intelligence Community's Involvement in the Banca Nazionale del Lavoro (BNL) Affair," 2/5/93, p. 68, citing a memorandum from Nicholas Rostow.
28. State Department Cables: "CCC: Iraqi Grain Policy," 7/18/90; "Iraqi Threats to Kuwait and UAE," 7/18/90.
29. Agriculture Department Memorandum: "Freedom of Information Act (FOIA)—National Security Archives," 11/19/93. See also, R. Jeffrey Smith, "US to Pay $400 Million to Cover Iraq's Bad Debt," *Washington Post*, 2/17/95.
30. State Department Memoranda: "US Policy Toward Iraqi CW Use," 9/13/88; "Administration Position on Proposed Iraq Sanctions," 11/18/88; Senate Committee on Foreign Relations: Statement of William H. Webster, 3/1/89, pp. 29-45

10. Ibid.
11. *The New York Times* Sunday, 23 September 1990.
12. Ibid.
13. State Department Cables: "CCC: Iraqi Grain Policy," 7/18/90; "Iraqi Threats to Kuwait and UAE," 7/18/90.
14. *Iraqgate: Saddam Hussein, US Policy and the Prelude to the Persian Gulf War,* 1980-1994. op. cit.
15. 'What we now know as the Iran arms sales, or the Iran initiative, was actually a series of related but distinct events that began in the summer of 1985 and continued through 1986. Israel sent US-supplied weapons to Iran on three occasions in 1985. These shipments took place with US approval, and, in one instance, with US participation. They led to the release in September 1985 of one American held hostage in Lebanon. The United States delivered missiles and missile parts to Iran on five occasions in 1986, after President Reagan signed an intelligence ``Finding'' authorizing such shipments. These 1986 shipments led to the release of two more US hostages, though terrorists seized two additional Americans in September 1986. The first shipment of US-made weapons from Israel to Iran took place August 20, 1985. But discussion and debate within the US Government as to the desirability of arms sales to Iran had been

going on for months at the time of the first Israeli shipment'. *Iran/Contra Report of Indep. Counsel :GPO Access . Federal Bulletin Board File Libraries. Part 1.*

16. The precise text of this exchange was as follows:

    Glaspie:Mr. President, not only do I want to say that President Bush wanted better and deeper relations with Iraq, but he also wants an Iraqi contribution to peace and prosperity in the Middle East. President Bush is an intelligent man. He is not going to declare an economic war against Iraq.

    You are right. It is true what you say that we do not want higher prices for oil. But I would ask you to examine the possibility of not charging too high a price for oil.

    Hussein: We do not want too high prices for oil. And I remind you that in 1974 I gave Tariq Aziz the idea for an article he wrote which criticized the policy of keeping oil prices high. It was the first Arab article which expressed this view.

    Tariq Aziz: Our policy in OPEC opposes sudden jumps in oil prices.

    Hussein: Twenty-five dollars a barrel is not a high price.

    Glaspie: We have many Americans who would like to see the price go above $25 because they come from oil-producing states.

    Hussein: The price at one stage had dropped to $12 a barrel and a reduction in the modest Iraqi budget of $6 billion to $7 billion is a disaster.

    Glaspie: I think I understand this. I have lived here for years. I admire your extraordinary efforts to rebuild your country. I know you need funds. We understand that and our opinion is that you should have the opportunity to rebuild your country. *But we have no opinion on the Arab-Arab conflicts, like your border disagreement with Kuwait.*

    I was in the American Embassy in Kuwait during the late 60's. The instruction we had during this period was that we should express no opinion on this issue and that the issue is not associated with America. James Baker has directed our official spokesmen to emphasize this instruction. We hope you can solve this problem using any suitable methods via Klibi or via President Mubarak. All that we hope is that these issues are solved quickly."

In the above context, Glaspie's reference to 'border disagreement with Kuwait', can have only one meaning. It was a reference to Iraq's claim that Kuwait had been pumping out its oil by digging wells laterally. Glaspie was simply informing Saddam that the US would not intervene in a border dispute *over oil*. By no stretch of imagination could this be interpreted as indifference to the elimination of Kuwait as a nation. At this point Kuwait had been an ally of the US for several years. Its ships had been plying through the Red Sea under the protection of the American flag. The very idea that Glaspie was capable of giving Saddam a go ahead on annexation was absurd, and it was only slightly less absurd to think that Saddam was not aware of this.

But on September 2, British journalists in Baghdad got a very different version of the interview, in the form of both a tape and a transcript. According to an internet site (APRIL GLASPIE.html), this tape ran as follows:

US Ambassador Glaspie – I have direct instructions from President Bush to improve our relations with Iraq. We have considerable sympathy for your quest for higher oil prices, the immediate cause of your confrontation with Kuwait. (pause) As you know, I lived here for years and admire your extraordinary efforts to rebuild your country. We know you need funds. We understand that, and our opinion is that you should have the opportunity to rebuild your country. (pause) We can see that you have deployed massive numbers of troops in the south. Normally that would be none of our business, but when this happens in the context of your threat s against Kuwait, then it would be reasonable for us to be concerned. For this reason, I have received an instruction to ask you, in the spirit of friendship – not confrontation – regarding your intentions: Why are your troops massed so very close to Kuwait's borders?
Saddam Hussein – As you know, for years now I have made every effort to reach a settlement on our dispute with Kuwait. There is to be a meeting in two days; I am prepared to give negotiations only this one more brief chance. (pause) When we (the Iraqis) meet (with the Kuwaitis) and we see there is hope, then nothing will happen. But if we are unable to find a solution, then it will be natural that Iraq will not accept death.
US Ambassador Glaspie – What solutions would be acceptable?
Saddam Hussein – If we could keep the whole of the Shatt al Arab - our strategic goal in our war with Iran - we will make concessions (to the Kuwaitis). But, if we are forced to choose between keeping half of

28 • The End of Saddam Hussein

the Shatt and the whole of Iraq (i.e., in Saddam s view, including Kuwait) then we will give up all of the Shatt to defend our claims on Kuwait to keep the whole of Iraq in the shape we wish it to be. (pause) What is the United States' opinion on this?
US Ambassador Glaspie – We have no opinion on your Arab - Arab conflicts, such as your dispute with Kuwait. Secretary (of State James) Baker has directed me to emphasize the instruction, first given to Iraq in the 1960's, that the Kuwait issue is not associated with America. (Saddam smiles).[16]

No one knows who released this tape and transcript. Nor is it apparent how anyone saw Saddam smile on an audiotape.

17. Excerpts From Iraqi Document on Meeting with US Envoy. *The New York Times* Sunday, 23 September 1990.

2

The Clinton Years

Iraq invaded Kuwait on 2 August 1990. In doing so, Saddam Hussein exposed not only his naivete but also the way in which, by surrounding himself with 'yes' men during more than a decade of dictatorial rule, he had lost touch with the real world and committed a fatal error. For there was no way in which the US and the rest of the world could have accepted Iraq's annexation of Kuwait. Kuwait was a member of the United Nations. In invading it, Iraq had violated Article 2 of the UN Charter. The UN could hardly ignore so direct an assault upon the international order it was designed to sustain. Action against Iraq under Chapter 7 of the Charter was therefore inevitable. All that remained to be decided was what shape it would take.

On 6 August 1990, the Security Council imposed comprehensive economic sanctions on Iraq under Resolution 661. But very soon the Bush administration decided that this would probably not be enough to force Iraq out of Kuwait, and that force would have to be used. The driving preoccupation behind this was almost certainly the need to control, or at least prevent others from controlling, the supply of oil to the world market. The annexation of Kuwait would give Iraq, already in possession of the second largest proven oil reserves in the world, a dominant position in the market. But the US faced an even more daunting prospect. If Iraq was allowed to get away with annexing Kuwait, would it stop there or would it start eyeing the reserves of Saudi Arabia? Nothing that Saddam had said to Glaspie even remotely hinted at an animus against Saudi Arabia. But an easy annexation of Kuwait could have easily encouraged him to enlarge his ambitions. Between them, Iraq, Kuwait and Saudi Arabia controlled 65 per cent of the proven oil reserves of the world. The possibility that a somewhat unpredictable dictator like Saddam Hussein could control all of it was one that Washington could not stomach. To preempt it, Iraq's military machine needed to be crippled. That meant a war to liberate Kuwait.

In the weeks that followed, Bush Sr. embarked upon a skillfully planned campaign to build a coalition of UN member-nations to invade Kuwait. But he also needed to mobilise support for a war, within the US. Less than a year after the fall of the Berlin Wall, this was no easy task. Bush therefore embarked upon a campaign to demonise Saddam Hussein. Saddam became, overnight, 'another Adolf Hitler' and 'the Butcher of Baghdad'. Here was an unpredictable, bloodthirsty dictator who had twice declared war upon his neighbours within a decade, and used proscribed chemical weapons not only against his adversaries but also his own nationals, the Kurds of Northern Iraq. Tales of Saddam Hussein's purges and summary executions swamped the media. He had to be stopped from becoming even more powerful. Bush also exaggerated the threat of an Iraqi invasion of Kuwait. He warned Americans that Saddam Hussein had hundreds of tanks and 300,000 troops in Kuwait poised on Saudi Arabia's borders when, as an independent analysis of Soviet satellite imagery suggested, there were less than 100,000 soldiers in Kuwait with only a small number of tanks.[1]

Bush thus turned the campaign to evict Iraq from Kuwait into a moral crusade. 'Nothing of this moral importance,' the president proclaimed, 'had occurred since World War II.'[2] This was the same man that the *New York Times* had praised in 1975, when he was vice-president but effectively the man in command, for his 'personal strength' in seeing to the 'pragmatic' and 'cooperative' nature of the burgeoning Ba'athist regime of Iraq.[3]

When Saddam Hussein refused to vacate Kuwait, war became inevitable. The UN gave it its blessings in Security Council Resolution 678 of 2 November 1990 which authorised member states to use "all necessary means"—the official jargon for military action—if Iraq failed to vacate Kuwait by 15 January 1991. In the war that followed, the UN forces launched 48,000 air strikes against 1,200 targets and used 85,500 tons of explosives. 22,000 of these sorties were aimed at the Iraqi army, which was literally knocked senseless and fled without offering a fight to the 500,000 ground troops that the coalition had assembled for the war.[4] By the time the war finished, Iraq's oil refineries had been blown up, and most of its power plants, sewage and water facilities bombed into ruins.

The UN Security Council resolutions, especially 660 and 679, had asked only that Iraq be driven out of Kuwait and not that the government in Baghdad be overthrown. Consequently, President Bush resisted fervent appeals from the American right-wing that US troops should continue to chase Iraqi soldiers all the way to Baghdad, capture the city and either kill or depose President Saddam Hussein. Bush pointed out that there was no UN mandate for doing so and any such attempt would fracture the UN coalition. In the weeks that followed the defeat of the Iraqi army, the US stood by while Saddam Hussein's government crushed rebellions among the Kurds in Northern Iraq and the Shias in the South-east. Its goal was to maintain a strong united Iraq, but without Saddam Hussein.[5] This restraint was to come back and haunt the Clinton and George W. Bush administrations in the twelve years that followed and to lead to the eventual destruction of Iraq.

Iraq had to be disarmed, and its capacity to embark on yet another costly and dangerous misadventure eliminated. This was the reasoning behind the UN Security Council's Resolution 687 of 3 April 1991. The Security Council laid down elaborate conditions for Iraq to comply with. It had to declare all of its stocks of nuclear, chemical and biological weapons, materials and facilities within 15 days, and unconditionally accept the destruction of all such weapons, components, subsystems, research and development, manufacturing and support facilities under UN supervision. This included all missiles with a range of more than 150 kms. A UN Special Commission (UNSCOM) was to be set up to supervise the destruction.

But the resolution also had two carrots for Saddam. The preamble reminded all member states of their commitment 'to the sovereignty, territorial integrity and political independence of Kuwait and Iraq'. And paragraph 22 said that economic sanctions would be lifted once Saddam had complied with the resolution and all weapons of mass destruction had been destroyed. The plan for the UN Special Commission set up to oversee the destruction also required it to respect Iraq's concern for its sovereignty and national security, when doing its work. These provisions became the centre of a protracted struggle that devastated Iraq and eventually pushed the US into a unilateral and unprovoked military invasion actions that has severely damaged the post-World War II international order.

The cat-and-mouse game over inspection

Although Iraq accepted the demands made in UNSC Resolution 687, it did not do so willingly. Resolution 687 had given Iraq till some time in July to destroy its weapons of mass destruction unilaterally. As subsequent disclosures were to show, Iraq tried its level best to conceal some at least of these weapons and programmes. Within days of agreeing to comply with Resolution 687 the Iraqi government set up an informal 'high level concealment' committee to minimise the amount of weapons and weapon-making capabilities that Iraq would have to declare.[6] The task of ferreting out information from the Iraqis therefore became a long drawn out and bitter one. To do this, UNSCOM found itself depending more and more heavily upon the intelligence agencies of 'co-operative countries', notably Israel.[7]

UNSCOM's Success

Under the constant pressure of pinpointed UNSCOM questioning, Iraq's declarations became progressively more accurate and explicit. Between 1991 and 1998, it revised its declaration on nuclear weapons and facilities four times within a period of 14 months and submitted six different declarations on its biological weapons capabilities.[8]

As the revelations multiplied, it became clear that Iraq had been much further advanced in the development of nuclear weapons and missiles than the CIA and other intelligence agencies had suspected. Iraq was attempting to enrich uranium to weapons grade by three routes, including not only the gas centrifuge method initially used by Pakistan, but also an older but very slow process which had been abandoned in the West based upon electromagnetic isotope separation.

These efforts had not, however, got very far by the time of the Gulf War. This was revealed by Iraq's attempt to initiate a crash programme to separate enriched uranium from IAEA-safeguarded Soviet and French reactors, when the American troop buildup began. However that programme too did not yield the uranium that Iraq needed to improve its bargaining power before the Gulf War.[9]

The IAEA's findings were particularly disturbing because they suggested that Iraq's scientists had already succeeded in developing, or were close to developing, the trigger for a nuclear bomb and had been stymied mainly by the lack of sufficient fissile material. The enrichment facilities that Iraq grudgingly declared to the IAEA during the course of inspections showed that it had been two or three years away from developing nuclear weapons, and not ten years away as the CIA had originally estimated.[10]

Iraq's chemical weapons capability was better known partly because these had been extensively used in the Iran–Iraq war against Iranians and Kurds before the Gulf War. By 1991, according to its own declarations, it had produced at least 2,850 tonnes of mustard gas, 795 tonnes of Sarin and Cyclosarin, and 3.9 tonnes of VX nerve gas.[11] All this was duly destroyed at UNSCOM's behest.

Iraq's biological weapons capability, by contrast, came as another unpleasant surprise to UNSCOM and the Americans. In 1972, Iraq had signed the Biological and Toxin Weapons Convention which had been signed by the US, the USSR and more than 100 other countries. But some years later, the Iraqi government deliberately embarked upon research into and production of biological weapons. In the 1980s, the American intelligence and military officials[12] came to know that Iraq was trying to develop weapons that could deliver anthrax, a disease that kills within two weeks. In 1988, the US was able to stop a Swiss company from selling a 1325 gallon fermentation tank that it believed was destined for the biological weapons programme.[13] However before the Gulf War, there was only one suspected bio-weapons plant in Iraq at Salman Pak. This was bombed into ruins during the War.[14] After the war, for four years, from 1991 till 1995, Iraq maintained that it had only 'small scale research facilities'.[15] But in January 1995, an Australian UNSCOM inspector, Rod Barton, confronted four Iraqi generals with two memos that showed that Iraq had purchased 10 tonnes of nutrients for growing germs in the 1980s and demanded to know where it had gone. This began a cascade of declarations which showed, among other things, that Iraq had begun a crash programme to produce germs and toxins before the Gulf War and had even tested one pilotless Mig-21 with simulated germ warheads. In all, Iraq admitted having produced 19,000 litres of Botulinum toxin; 8,500 litres of Anthrax and 2200 litres of Aflatoxin.[16]

UNSCOM embarked upon a thorough destruction programme. President Clinton testified to its success in February 1998, on the eve of bombing Iraq, when speaking at the Pentagon. He confirmed that

> despite Iraq's deceptions, UNSCOM has nevertheless done a remarkable job. Its inspectors...have uncovered and destroyed more weapons of mass destruction capacity than was destroyed during the Gulf War. This includes nearly 40,000 chemical weapons, more than 100,000 gallons of chemical weapons agents, 48 operational missiles, 30 warheads specifically fitted for chemical and biological weapons and a massive biological weapons facility at Al Hakam equipped to produce Anthrax and other deadly germs.[17]

An accounting of Iraq's Scud-type missiles purchased or manufactured, used and destroyed, presented by Prime Minister Tony Blair to the British Parliament in September 2002 also confirmed UNSCOM's success, albeit indirectly.[18] According to Blair's report Iraq had purchased or built an unknown number of Scud and Scud-type missiles in the 1980s. It had fired more than 500 out of them at Iran and 93 at Israel, Saudi Arabia and Bahrain during the Gulf War. Since the CIA's report on Iraq's WMD placed the number of Scud-type missiles at 819, this meant that Iraq was left with 226 missiles or thereabouts in April 1991. UNSCOM, according to the same report had destroyed 'very large quantities of chemical weapons and ballistic missiles and associated production facilities by 1998'. By implication, therefore, Blair conceded that not many could have survived this and the subsequent bombing raids. In fact, his report was disingenuous and had fudged facts that were already in the public domain in order to give the impression that Iraq still retained some missiles. UNSCOM's last report to the UN Security Council, dated 25 March 1999, carried the following table on the acquisition and disposal of the scud missiles:

Table 1

Summary of the material balance of the 819 proscribed combat missiles imported by Iraq.

Expenditure/disposal event quantity	Declared	Accounting status
Pre-1980 expenditures, such as in training	8	Accounting is based on documentation provided by Iraq.
Expenditure during the Iran-Iraq war (1980-1988), including the War of the Cities in February-April 1988	516	Accounting is based on documentation provided by Iraq. Iraq's data on some of these missile firings, in particular during the War was corroborated by independent sources.
Testing activities for development of Iraq's modifications of imported missiles and other experimental activities (1985-1990)	69	Accounting is based on documentation provided by Iraq. Iraq's data on a number of these test firings was corroborated by independent sources.
Expenditures during the Gulf War (January-March 1991)	93	Accounting is based on documentation provided by Iraq. Iraq's data on nearly all of these firings was corroborated by independent sources. A discrepancy in the accounting of a small number of fired missiles exists between Iraq's data and data provided by other sources.
Destruction pursuant to Security Council resolution 687 (early July 1991)	48	UNSCOM verification during the destruction.
Unilateral destruction by Iraq (mid-July and October 1991)	85	Accounting is based on documentation provided by carried out laboratories in Iraq. The Commission analysis of remnants of the unilaterally destroyed missiles excavated in 1996-1997. The Commission identified remnants of engines from 83 out of the 85 missiles declared.

UNSCOM had, in short, accounted for all the Scud-type missiles Iraq had acquired. There were none left to convert into the 20 Al-Husayn rockets that British and American Intelligence claimed Iraq still possessed. It was no surprise, therefore, that after the occupation of Iraq no such missiles were found.

UNSCOM also discovered and destroyed suspected bio-weapons production, or dual-use equipment, at two more biological products plants at Al Dawrah and Al Hakam. UNSCOM unearthed and dismantled production and research facilities at 13 Iraqi plants devoted to the production of missiles, guidance systems and propellants.[19]

Overall, UNSCOM's mission was a success. Scott Ritter, an American member of UNSCOM entrusted with countering Iraq's concealment activities, concluded, in a book written before the invasion of Iraq, that by the time the UNSCOM inspectors left Iraq in December 1998, they had destroyed 90 to 95 per cent of all Iraqi weapons of mass destruction.[20] As it turned out, this too proved far too conservative.

Important discrepancies remained, however, between what it was known to have produced or purchased and what it or UNSCOM was known to have destroyed. According to American sources, UNSCOM still did not know where 132 out of 157 germ bombs that Iraq had acknowledged building for its air force had gone. Nor could it account for about 25 germ warheads it believed had been built for the 650 km missile, the Al Huseyn.[21] The main reason for the discrepancies was Iraq's decision to destroy a large amount of its CBW unilaterally before the July 1991 deadline given under Resolution 687. Although it was known that Iraq had indeed destroyed a substantial amount of proscribed weaponry, in the case of biological and chemical weapon agents in particular, it was very difficult to determine precisely how much had been destroyed.

In April 1997, these discrepancies were not considered sufficiently important to prevent UNSCOM from submitting a report to the Security Council that foreshadowed the lifting of economic sanctions., Two months before stepping down from the executive chairmanship of UNSCOM, Rolf Ekeus was able to report that "the accumulated effect of the work that has been accomplished over six years since the cease-fire went into effect between Iraq and the coalition is such that *not much is unknown about Iraq's retained proscribed weapons capabilities"*. The report did however underline that the discrepancies in the accounting for the missiles and chemical and biological materials could not be ignored.

> What is still not accounted for cannot be neglected. Even a limited inventory of long-range missiles would be a source of deep concern if those missiles were fitted with warheads filled with the most deadly of chemical nerve agents, VX. If one single missile warhead were filled with the biological warfare agent, Anthrax, many millions of lethal doses could be spread in an attack on any city in the region. With that in mind, the Special Commission has undertaken extraordinary efforts to bring to a satisfactory conclusion the full accounting of Iraq's weapons of mass destruction and long-range missiles, in order to be able to make sure that all the proscribed items have been disposed of.[22]

By 1997, Iraq was desperate to have the sanctions lifted. Its per capita income had fallen by two thirds. A large part of the population had been pushed below the poverty line. Thanks to the destruction of its urban infrastructure, up to two thirds of its population did not have safe drinking water or sanitation. Its infant mortality rate had jumped from 50 per 1,000 in 1990 to 117 per 1,000 in 1995. Ekeus' report allowed its government to begin seeing light at the end of the tunnel.

It was soon disappointed. While the USSR, France and China were disposed to lift the sanctions, the US and UK remained adamant upon maintaining them. Iraq's inability to provide sufficient proof of the destruction it claimed it had undertaken, became their pretext for continuing the economic sanctions upon it, and eventually for the invasion of 2003. The reason for this cruel and ultimately self-defeating policy was the US' own confusion over its goals in Iraq.

When the work of UNSCOM began to wind down, the US found that it could no longer postpone facing the central dilemma of its policy towards Iraq. This was that even if UNSCOM succeeded in destroying every last WMD or missile, and every single associated component, production and research facility, so long as Iraq's universities and professors continued to function, it could not destroy Iraq's *capability* to rebuild its weapons of mass destruction at some future date. Paragraph 22 of Resolution 687 committed the UN to lifting economic sanctions as soon as UNSCOM certified that Iraq was free of weapons of mass destruction. Once sanctions were lifted, Iraq would have both the technical capacity and the resources to rebuild its war machine. Peace in the Middle East would depend thereafter upon the Iraqi government's *intentions* and not its *capabilities*. This would pose no problem for policy if Saddam Hussein could be considered a 'normal' head of state. Once it was declared free of WMD, Iraq could be reintegrated into the world community and constrained from embarking upon further adventurism with the normal tools of threat and inducement. The alternative was to remove him from power before rehabilitating Iraq.

The first course soon became unthinkable. The US had spent almost a decade in convincing the world that Saddam Hussein was anything but rational, and could not therefore be trusted to behave like a normal head of state. To lift sanctions and resume normal relations with Iraq, it would either have to repudiate everything it had said about the dictator since Iraq's invasion of Kuwait, or admit that the US, like other nations, did not allow the nature of a regime to dictate relations with it. During the Cold War, this would not have posed a problem because the end, of containing the Soviet Union, could always be invoked to justify the means. But in the media-driven politics of the 1990s, without the excuse of the Cold War, no American government had the courage to either rehabilitate Saddam or assert the need to divorce international relations from domestic politics. It was therefore left with no option but to try and topple Saddam Hussein's government.

The dilemma surfaced within weeks of the end of the first Gulf War. A growing number of critics, mostly from the far right wing of the Republican party, began to criticise George Bush (Sr.) for not having "finished the job by eliminating Saddam Hussein" and then having stood by while Saddam crushed the Shia and Kurdish revolts against his regime.

The Clinton administration inherited the dilemma but could not find a satisfactory solution. Unable to face the first, it chose the second alternative. Between 1991 and February 1998, the Central Intelligence Agency made four covert and spectacularly unsuccessful attempts to dislodge Saddam Hussein. These included everything from radio propaganda to paramilitary plots. Undaunted by failure, the CIA was cobbling together a fifth and even more ambitious attempt when the *New York Times* broke the story in 1998.[23]

Its failure to oust Saddam forced the Clinton administration to consider other ways of preventing the re-emergence of Iraq as a power centre in the Middle East. The first signal that the US had no intention of allowing the sanctions to be lifted came in April 1994 when Secretary of State Warren Christopher unilaterally withdrew the promise contained in paragraph 22 of UNSC resolution 687 to lift sanctions when UNSCOM's work was over.[24] Three years later, the new Secretary of State Madeleine Albright insisted that sanctions would not be lifted so long as Saddam remained in power.[25] In the Security Council, the US refused to brook any discussion of a quid pro quo—the lifting of sanctions in exchange for Iraq's full co-operation in destroying its weapons of mass destruction.[26] From 1994 till 2002, not a single UN resolution reiterated the promise contained in paragraph 22 of Resolution 687.

The US' dilemma became acute when Ekeus presented his last report. From 1997 onwards, support for the economic sanctions began to erode rapidly. Russia and France both began to insist that they should be lifted as soon as possible as part of a coherent medium-term strategy that combined the lifting of sanctions with the installment of a long-term monitoring mechanism in Iraq.[27] To prevent this, the US was forced to resort to more and more underhand ways of prolonging the sanctions. It did so by the simple expedient of making sure that UNSCOM never proclaimed itself satisfied with Iraq's compliance with Resolution 687, and brought up fresh inspection demands whenever it seemed that the work was drawing to a close.

The brinkmanship that led to destruction

Iraq soon realised that the US had no intention of ever lifting the sanctions upon it while Saddam remained in power. It therefore resorted to the last weapon in its armoury: in a dangerous game of brinkmanship, it began to withdraw co-operation from UNSCOM in the hope of forcing the US and UK to put a time limit on the sanctions. This inevitably sharpened the differences between the five permanent members of the Security Council. These surfaced at a meeting of the Security Council on 23 October 1997 when France, Russia, China, Egypt and Kenya abstained from a resolution that threatened to put travel restrictions upon Iraqi officials if they continued to impede weapons inspections. This emboldened Iraq in October 1997 to bar American inspectors from the inspection teams on the grounds that they were spying on Iraqi defence facilities and feeding the information to the US Air Force to enable more accurate targeting of Iraqi installations. It also threatened to shoot down U-2 planes assisting UNSCOM by accusing them of spying from the air.

In particular, Iraq accused Scott Ritter, a senior American weapons inspector entrusted with looking for concealed sites relating to weapons of mass destruction, of being an American intelligence agent, and insisted that he should be withdrawn. The US denied that Ritter was any such thing.[28] When Iraq expelled Ritter, the US responded by threatening to bomb Iraq. But this met with still more resistance in the Council. On the basis of a compromise suggested by the British, it was decided to send a three-man UN mission to Baghdad to make Iraq climb down.[29] The mission failed to persuade Iraq to allow the inspections to continue, but nine days later, following a Russian request, Iraq backed down and agreed to let the inspectors resume work. America too backed down from its threat to attack Iraq, but its representative on UNSCOM, Charles Duelfer, claimed that during the interregnum Iraq had moved a lot of equipment out of the sensitive sites that it had reopened for inspection.[30]

In November 1997, possibly also as a part of its new strategy, Iraq declared a number of sites to be Presidential palaces and put them out of bounds for the inspectors. The next crisis therefore erupted in February when the head of UNSCOM demanded access to various Presidential palaces that the Iraqis had declared off limits. The US again assembled its forces for an attack. In preparation for the bombing, the US massed 32 ships, 28,000 personnel and 300 aircraft in the Persian Gulf[31]—a move that cost it $1.6 billion—and embarked upon an unprecedented public relations campaign to persuade the American public of the need to go to war. Following a last minute intervention by UN Secretary-General Kofi Annan, who went personally to Baghdad after ten days of discussions with the members of the Security Council, the Iraqis once more caved in and agreed to let the sites be inspected. The only condition Baghdad placed was that in deference to Iraq's sovereignty, the inspectors should be accompanied by members of the diplomatic corps. Annan agreed to the request.

The US made no secret of its lack of enthusiasm for Annan's mission. But Annan was determined to try and avert war, and had the full support of other key members of the Security Council as well as of virtually all the Arab states, so the US concurred. However it insisted that Annan's mission was to make Iraq agree to comply 'fully' with all UN resolutions. It expressly forbade him from making any deal that involved a quid pro quo to Iraq. In short, Annan was to offer no relief from sanctions, and no time frame for their removal, in exchange for complying fully with the UN resolutions. Annan apparently did not agree to these terms, insisting that he was not prepared to go to Baghdad solely as a messenger.[32] The Clinton administration eventually relented. At a two-hour meeting with Annan on 15 February, Secretary of State Madeleine Albright laid down a series of 'red lines' that Annan was not to cross. Chief of these was that Iraq had to comply fully and that UNSCOM would be the judge of its compliance.

What the US offered in exchange can be surmised from its actions over the course of the next six months. The most important concession was to allow Annan to offer some kind of assurance to Iraq that the sanctions could be lifted by the end of the year if it complied fully with UNSCOM's inspection requests. Annan offered this in a personal meeting with Saddam Hussein intended to clear roadblocks to the resumption of inspections, hours before his departure from Baghdad.³³ His agreement also committed UNSCOM to respecting Iraq's sovereignty and dignity. This was no more than a reiteration of what had been conceded implicitly in Resolution 687, but was seen by US officials³⁴ as a concession that could hinder UNSCOM's work.³⁵ It also seems likely, in view of what happened during the next few months, that the US tacitly accepted the validity of some at least of Iraq's complaints against UNSCOM's inspectors—that they were gathering intelligence on Iraq's defences and passing it to Israel; that they were too brusque and intrusive, and that the UNSCOM chief, Butler, in particular, had to be more restrained.³⁶

Then followed a honeymoon period of two months—the only honeymoon that Iraq and UNSCOM had known. On 14 March, upon his return from Iraq, Butler praised the Iraqi government for the new spirit of co-operation it was displaying: "We were given access of a kind we've never had before, both in terms of places we got into and in terms of the number of inspectors and the way we got into those places," he told the *New York Times*.³⁷ During the visit the Iraqis agreed to the inspection of 1038 structures in eight Presidential sites. UNSCOM was allowed to choose at random which ones it would inspect, in order to minimise the advance warning that Baghdad would receive. The UN Undersecretary for Disarmament, Sri Lankan diplomat Jayantha Dhanapala, was to supervise the inspection of the Presidential sites and enlist diplomats who would accompany the inspectors.³⁸

Three months later, Butler said, during a visit to Baghdad from 11–13 June, that "Iraqi cooperation on the new 'road map' of remaining disarmament steps would lead him to present an unprecedented favourable report to the UN Secretary-General in October". Butler said that only a small though not unimportant amount of work remained for UNSCOM to do.³⁹ The road map was designed to obtain confirmation that Iraq had indeed destroyed 45 chemical and biological missile warheads, and obtaining more information on Iraq's long-range ballistic missile and biological warfare programmes. While Butler expected corroboration of the first, he felt that UNSCOM needed more information on the second to complete its job. The UN

Secretary-General's Special Representative, Prakash Shah, echoed Butler's optimism: "The expectation is the next six-month report will be very important and a crucial one in the activities of UNSCOM. Both Butler and the Iraqis have expressed that they want to finish the work in the coming few months".[40]

Butler's second visit to Iraq was successful. UNSCOM and the government drew up a two-month work schedule to clear up 'remaining disarmament issues'. Tariq Aziz, the Iraqi deputy prime minister, called the agreement a breakthrough because it was 'very specific in nature'. "We have always complained", he said to the *Financial Times*, "that UNSCOM did not specify exactly, precisely, what are, in their view, the few remaining issues before closing all files".[41] Butler himself said that he hoped the deal on what he called a speedy work program would allow him to present a final report on Iraq's disarmament to the Security Council for its October review.[42]

Annan's intervention seemed, therefore, to have broken the stalemate over weapons inspections and bridged the yawning gap between UNSCOM and the Iraqi government. But the terms he hammered out with the Iraqi President only made the American dilemma more acute. For the first time a date had been at least tacitly set for the lifting of economic sanctions, if Iraq co-operated fully with UNSCOM. The Secretary General now had his own special representative in Baghdad to prevent abrasive confrontations between the Iraqi government and UNSCOM. Iraq was, therefore, on its way to reintegration with the international community *but without the regime change that the US would have liked.*

This was not at all to Washington's liking. It may not, therefore, have been pure coincidence that on 24 June, six days after Butler and the Iraqi government set a time limit and established a detailed agenda for completing the weapons inspections, *The Washington Post* disclosed that a US army laboratory had found traces of the nerve gas VX on fragments of destroyed warheads recovered by UNSCOM inspectors from a destruction pit at Taji in March. This, US spokesmen claimed, was a very serious development as Iraq had steadfastly claimed that while it had produced experimental quantities of VX gas, it had never succeeded in mating it to a warhead to create a usable weapon.⁴³ This deception meant that Iraq was still trying to hide some elements of its WMD programme and therefore was still violating its commitments to the UN Security Council.

Butler made this disclosure at a closed-door meeting of the UN Security Council on 24 June. The analysis, he claimed, had been completed two weeks earlier on 10 June. Iraq reacted with an angry outburst that this was nothing more than an attempt by the US to prevent the lifting of sanctions, and demanded that the tests be carried out in more 'neutral' countries.⁴⁴ Fragments of the warheads were therefore sent to laboratories in France and Switzerland. However, far from waiting for a confirmation, Butler repeated his allegations to the press. He told *The Washington Post*: "I explained to the Council that this was very serious because Iraq always insisted it never weaponised VX". "Facts are facts," he added. "Iraq has been deceiving the international community with weaponsiation of nerve gas". The US was very quick to respond. "This is a very serious violation," said the US Ambassador to the UN, Bill Richardson. "It means *Iraq won't have the sanctions lifted*"⁴⁵ (emphasis added).

A number of features of this disclosure suggest that Iraq's accusation was not far from the truth. First, *The Washington Post*'s story was not based upon hearsay. It obtained a full copy of the report from the Aberdeen Proving Ground of the US army in Maryland from, of all sources, the Iraqi National Congress, an exile group based in Washington, that is opposed to Saddam Hussein and has close ties to the US administration.⁴⁶ This makes it virtually certain that the US leaked the document deliberately.

Second, the report was deliberately leaked to *The Washington Post* on the same day as Butler addressed the UN. If the Aberdeen Proving Ground concluded its tests on 10 June, then the US sat on the report for a full 14 days before leaking it. This synchronised disclosure was obviously meant to create as much distrust of the Iraqi government as possible in order to hustle the Security Council and American public opinion into prolonging the sanctions on Iraq.

But the most puzzling feature of the entire smear operation—for that is what it was—is that although Butler must have known about the Aberdeen test results when he departed for Baghdad on the evening of 10 June or been informed about them as soon as he arrived the next day, he did not once bring up Iraq's alleged duplicity during the two days of his meetings in Baghdad. On the contrary he described his talks with the Iraqi government as highly successful and went on to draw up the last portion of his "road map" for the completion of weapons inspections and the lifting of economic sanctions. In view of the importance that he later ascribed to this 'concealment', how does one explain his silence in Baghdad?[47]

There is only one answer that fits all the facts: it is that the results of the test did not come as a surprise to him because *they confirmed what he already knew*. The Iraqis had already disclosed that they had been trying to make nerve gas warheads and had failed. What is more, UNSCOM had already obtained preliminary confirmation from its destruction pit excavations that these had been destroyed and was looking for confirmation that these were indeed the warheads that had been destroyed.[48] Thus, when the US informed him that traces of nerve gas had been found on the missile warhead shards, Butler, who had sent the shards to Aberdeen in March, doubtless took it as further confirmation that the Iraqis had lived up to their promises. That is the most plausible explanation for why he did not raise the issue in Baghdad.

The US, however, saw in the results an opportunity to derail the completion of inspections, so it decided to withhold the information till it could be released in such a manner that it would have the maximum impact. Worse still, Butler fell in with the US' plan.[49] Not only did he never mention that UNSCOM had sent the shards for testing only to confirm that Iraq had kept its part of the bargain but, having made not even a murmur about the test results while he was in Baghdad, Butler also made the first disclosure at the place where he knew it would do the most damage. To maximise the impact, Butler went public and spoke extensively to the press the very same day, immediately after the Council meeting.[50] There are few better examples of the abuse of media power by an unscrupulous government in a democratic state.

The key issue here was not whether Iraq had not fully disclosed the extent of its effort to marry chemical weapons to warheads but whether all the warheads that it had acquired for this purpose had been destroyed. Iraq had told the Commission that it had unilaterally destroyed the 45 warheads. UNSCOM's function was to verify that it had done so. The Amorim report on the status of weapons inspection when the UNSCOM inspectors were pulled out of Iraq in December 1998 just six months later, shows that the commission was satisfied on the basis of the shards and other parts that it had recovered from the destruction pits, and that 43 to 45 special warheads imported for the purpose of making chemical weapons had indeed been destroyed. In December 1999, UNSCOM had doubts only about the fate of about 25 imported and 25 indigenous *non-special* warheads.[51]

In retrospect, the reason why the US, and the now-complaisant Butler, made such a fuss about Iraq's not disclosing the nature of its tests fully, was to heighten suspicion of its willingness to comply with the inspection regime, and thereby justify their raising the goalposts and demanding still higher standards of compliance and accounting from Iraq.

It may not therefore come as a surprise that the French and Swiss scientists who examined the missile warhead fragments came to very different conclusions from those obtained by the US army. The Swiss did not find any traces of nerve gas. The French test found residues that were compatible with the presence of not only VX but also two other deadly gases, Sarin and Soman, but said that these residues could also have come from detergents used to clean the missiles. A second set of tests by the US army also turned up negative for VX.[52] But by the time these results came in, the damage had been done. Butler had given his damning report to the UN Security Council, and the question mark over the lifting of economic sanctions was once again as large as ever.

UNSCOM found fresh grounds for scepticism in July when it discovered a letter at Air Headquarters, Baghdad, which suggested that Iraq had overstated the number of chemical weapon bombs that it had used in the war against Iran by 6,000. As pointed out earlier, these could have been part of another list, and might by 1998 have been discovered and destroyed anyway. But it gave Butler another pretext for going back on his tacit commitment to complete

UNSCOM's work by August, and submit a report that could pave the way for the lifting of sanctions, and demand a fresh batch of inspections, this time with no restrictions and no time limit.

To this UNSCOM added a third ground for continuing the inspections: it claimed that it had reason to suspect that Iraq had built at least three implosion devices which only needed to be filled with enriched uranium to be converted into nuclear bombs. This charge was specifically refuted by IAEA, which said that it had 'no indication of prohibited nuclear material or activity in Iraq'. David Kyd, IAEA's spokesman, specifically denied any knowledge or suspicion of Iraq's possession of implosion devices. But such is the power of disinformation that four years later, this became one of the principal reasons cited by the US and UK for deciding to declare war on Iraq.[53]

When the two-month period agreed to by Butler and the Iraqi government came to an end in August, Butler again went to Baghdad and demanded a long list of fresh documents and site inspections. The already thoroughly incensed Iraqis refused to give him either and accused him of simply playing out a part assigned to him in a US-scripted drama to prolong sanctions. The talks failed completely and Butler came back to the UN complaining that the Iraqis had withdrawn co-operation from UNSCOM.

Butler's complaint, broadcast worldwide through the press and putting all the blame on the Iraqis, gave the US precisely the pretext it was looking for. "Saddam's decision to suspend co-operation with the...UN special commission is a violation of the agreement he reached with U.N.Secretary General Kofi Annan less than six months ago, and is a direct challenge to the authority of the Security Council", wrote Madeleine Albright in a bylined article.[54] However, she went on to expose, inadvertently, not only that the confrontation had been deliberately provoked by Butler, but also that he had done so in consultation with the US and with it's explicit support.

"This month, UNSCOM had intended to follow up with some *particularly intrusive* inspections, *which we supported*. However, when Iraq suspended all inspections on 3 August, we understood that Saddam had done something that *even*

> *his backers in the Security Council could not defend.* It was in this context that *I consulted with Butler,* who came to *his own* conclusion that *it was wiser to keep the focus on Iraq's open defiance of the Security Council"* (emphasis added).[55]

No single admission by the US government so completely exposes the depths of its anxiety over Iraq's revival and its determination to prevent it, as this essay by Albright. First, the Secretary of State takes time off to write an article aimed at discrediting and vilifying a single head of state. Second, Butler consults with the US *before* he asks for 'particularly intrusive' inspections, in order to seek its support.[56] There has to be a particularly fine line between 'consultation' and taking orders, when the other party is the world's sole superpower with a publicly declared stake in preventing the sanctions from being lifted. Third, Butler presents the demand for a new set of 'particularly intrusive' inspections at a meeting where the Iraqis are expecting him to work out a timetable for lifting economic sanctions. This must have come like a douche of ice water to the Foreign Minister, Tariq Aziz and looked dangerously like provocation. Finally on his return from Baghdad, Butler, by Albright's admission, advises the US government on the best way to discredit Iraq in the Security Council and neutralise "Iraq's friends on it". This is hardly the behaviour one expects of a dispassionate UN civil servant.

Albright once more spelt out the goals of the US:

> What Saddam really wants is to have sanctions lifted while retaining his residual weapons-of-mass-destruction capabilities. We will not allow it. ...If the Council fails to persuade Saddam to resume co-operation, then *we will have a free hand to use other means* to support UNSCOM's mandate.

Albright's threat differed only in her choice of words from the one that President George W. Bush was to brandish before the entire world at the UN in 2002. This was the first hint the US gave that it was already contemplating Operation "Desert Fox" and it was three years before the destruction of the World Trade Center.

Why did the US stoop to such underhand ways of discrediting Iraq? The reason is that by June 1998, support for the sanctions had all but vanished in the Security Council. Instead, the majority of the members openly supported the initiative launched by Kofi Annan in March which involved trading full compliance with weapons inspection for a lifting of sanctions in October or shortly thereafter. In sharp contrast to the US, Annan's approach was cooperative and not confrontational. Having reaffirmed respect for Iraq's national sovereignty and security, he quietly went about reigning in the inspectors, and preventing the inspection process from getting derailed by what the Iraqis probably justifiably saw as attacks upon their sovereignty. Butler's confrontational tactics were out of line with this approach. The first time this came to light was in April, a month after his first highly satisfactory talks with Iraq. Diplomats in Baghdad were surprised to find that the tone of Butler's report to the Security Council was in marked contrast to the optimism Butler had exuded in Baghdad.[57] From then on, Butler's reports began to be treated with increasing scepticism by the other members of the Security Council. One diplomat bluntly told the *Financial Times*, "UNSCOM has lost credibility. Now we rush to hear the Iraqi side as well".[58]

The US went along with Annan's soft approach, but for reasons of its own. The more UNSCOM was made to defer to Iraqi sensibilities, the easier it became for Washington to claim that the weapons inspection process had not been satisfactorily concluded. This brought it into conflict with some of its own hard line inspectors. One of these was Scott Ritter, the controversial American inspector whose intelligence-gathering activities had led to the February crisis. Ritter resigned in August after charging the US and UK governments with abandoning intrusive inspections because they were excessively keen to respect Iraq's sensibilities. Ritter's accusations proved highly embarrassing to the two governments because contrary to his naïve belief, by August the US was, through Butler, using UNSCOM not to complete the inspections but to prevent their completion.

Two examples given by Ritter illustrate the lengths to which a by now thoroughly co-opted Butler was prepared to go to prevent the inspections from being completed. In 1998, the head of UNSCOM's biological inspection section was a former biological weapons officer with the US army named Richard Spertzel. Throughout 1998, Spertzel refused to allow the inspection of Iraq's Presidential palaces, the very same palaces to gain entry into whom the US had almost gone to war. When the Iraqis confronted him, demanding to know why he was not permitting their inspection he said that he had never expected to find any biological weapons in them and hadn't wanted to give them the benefit of a negative reading.[59] Butler knew what Spertel was up to, at the very least because of Ritter's vigorous protests but did nothing.

The second episode occurred in September 1997. An UNSCOM biological weapons inspector who did a surprise inspection of the Iraqi National Standards Laboratory saw two gentlemen with a briefcase trying to sneak away. When after a chase and several gunpoint confrontations she managed to obtain the briefcase, it turned out to contain documentation from Iraq's Special Security Organisation, Saddam Hussein's personal security group. When a quick survey revealed words like '*botulinum toxin* reagent test kits' and '*clostridium perfingen* reagent test kits,' UNSCOM was sure that it had made a major breakthrough: Saddam Hussein was using his personal bodyguard units to move sensitive documents around and away from the inspectors. However, when the documents were translated, they turned out to contain painstakingly detailed test reports on each and everything that Saddam Hussein ate, wore and touched. What UNSCOM had stumbled upon was Saddam Hussein's elaborate precautions for keeping himself alive. Despite that, Butler continued to cite this discovery on American National Radio and television as proof of Iraq's continued work on biological weapons.[60]

Whatever the motives may have been, the resulting soft approach resulted in a two-month hiatus in which there were no intrusive inspections. UNSCOM continued to monitor existing sites and facilities but did not enter any new sites. As a part of this continuing effort, in the beginning of October, Tariq Aziz, Iraq's deputy Prime Minister, met Kofi Annan and forged another deal with him. According to this deal, the Security Council and not UNSCOM would decide what more Iraq needed to do to get the sanctions lifted. In contrast to the latter, the Security Council would make its decisions on a determination of what Iraq needed to do in order to cease being a threat to its neighbours. Implicitly, therefore, it involved an acceptance by the members that it was unrealistic to expect to be able to account for each and every last weapon that Iraq possessed. A more realistic goal was to reduce Iraq's remaining arsenal to the point where it could no longer pose a threat to anyone.[61] This change in approach was made explicit by Kofi Annan in a face-to-face meeting with the editors of *The Washington Post*.[62]

For Washington, the message of Annan's meetings was clear. Support for continuing the sanctions was almost gone. What is more, the UNSCOM's credibility had now been seriously dented. Three weeks later, on 26 October, in what was almost a replay of the June episode, a panel set up by UNSCOM, of 10 inspectors drawn from seven countries, announced that it had accepted the US army's finding that Iraq had loaded its missile warheads with VX nerve gas. It based its finding upon the fact that all the laboratories had found residues of degraded detergents upon the warhead shards. By October, the media blitz about the enormity of Iraq's crime in having tried to make chemical warheads had completely erased from public memory the fact (hidden from all but a few newspaper correspondents) that UNSCOM had already known of these attempts when it resumed work in March, and had sent shards of destroyed warheads to Aberdeen to make sure that these were the ones that had been destroyed. Instead, the campaign convinced people that Iraq had hidden the fact that it had loaded (or tried to load) warheads with chemical weapons from UNSCOM. The 'discovery' by the US army, therefore, proved how deceitful Saddam Hussein was and therefore the need to continue inspections with full rigour.

Iraq had no illusions about what the 26 October 'revelations' meant for the economic sanctions. So it went back to playing the only card that a weak and isolated country had left to play: on 31 October, it banned even the monitoring of existing sites by UNSCOM. Tariq Aziz explained that his country was not gambling or seeking a confrontation, but had been left with no choice when it realised that co-operating with UNSCOM would not get the sanctions lifted.[63] But it must also have hoped that by provoking another crisis it would be able to get the issue reopened and the friendlier Security Council members into the act again.

The Iraqi action did set off a crisis but it did not go the way Iraq had wanted. The Security Council met on 5 November and condemned its action, demanding that it resume full co-operation immediately. When Iraq did not immediately comply, it walked neatly into the US' trap. The very next day, US officials let the press know that the Clinton administration had lost faith in weapons inspection because Iraq would never allow one to be completed, and was thinking of other ways to contain Iraq including the continuation of economic sanctions and military action.[64] The State Department's spokesman, James P. Rubin, also insisted that the US did not need any additional authorisation (from the UN) to use force. This was a reference to the Security Council's 2 March resolution which had warned Iraq that it would face 'the severest consequences' if it failed to give unrestricted access to UNSCOM.[65] To underline the message, UNSCOM pulled 26 out of its 140 inspectors out of Baghdad on 6 November.[66]

After a week of trying to stick to its stand that it would allow the inspectors to resume work only if there was a clear response to its 'legitimate demand to lift the unjust embargo', on 14 November, even as American bombers loaded with cruise missiles were in the air, Iraq caved in.[67] It agreed to open any and all sites targeted by UNSCOM and to hand over two documents that UNSCOM had demanded, without getting any reassurance on the lifting of sanctions in exchange for compliance, from the Security Council.

Inspections were immediately resumed but Butler was, by then, working accordingly to a script that had already been written in Washington. Within days of Iraq's capitulation, he sent a request for access that was virtually impossible to comply with. It contained not only a request for 12 specific documents, but also a general authorisation to inspect any defence and other ministerial archives that it chose to examine. Iraq had no objections to turning over two of the documents. These were the letter (or document) UNSCOM had found in the Air Headquarters in July on chemical bombs, and records of a brigade that was being equipped as a missile unit. But Butler also asked for the Iraqi government's report on the 1995 defection of Saddam's son-in-law, Hussein Kamel, additional documents on the attempts to create VX gas, documents to prove that Iraq had destroyed all of its stock of Scud missile propellants, and two diaries of persons involved in the missiles program. Iraq said that it could not comply because there had been no investigation of Kamel's defection (only a summary execution) and that the two diaries had been destroyed. Without refusing to turn over the files on propellants, it asked UNSCOM to be satisfied with its earlier verification that all or nearly all missiles and warheads had been destroyed.[68]

However, in addition to these documents and access to archives, Butler made an even more provocative request. This was for the minutes of the meetings of the 'High level concealment committee' that had been set up in 1991 to hide proscribed materials. The Iraqi Deputy Foreign Minister Riad-al-Qaysi responded that since instructions on concealment had been given orally, there were no records of its meetings.[69]

Iraq made a determined bid to live up to its promise. According to Richard Butler himself, between 15 November and 17 December when Clinton finally unleashed American and British bombers on Iraq, UNSCOM carried out 400 site inspections, all but six of which were done with full Iraqi co-operation. In the remaining six, Iraq allowed inspections but made some conditions.[70]

Butler's efforts to fulfil the Security Council's 5 November mandate lasted just three weeks. On 17 December, these six sites, and Iraq's inability, or reluctance, to furnish all the documents Butler had asked for, became the base for a report by him to the UN Security Council, that "Iraq's conduct insured that no progress was able to be made in the fields of disarmament. In the light of this experience, and in the absence of full cooperation from Iraq, it must regrettably be recorded again that the commission is not able to conduct the substantive work mandated to it by the UN Security Council, with respect to Iraq's prohibited weapons programs."

Armed with this report, the US and UK began four days of intense bombing of Iraqi installations in an operation code-named 'Desert Fox', that left most of its painfully reconstructed infrastructure once more in ruins. Just how much this was the pre-ordained end of a prescripted charade was made clear by the fact that the bombing began two hours *before* the Security Council had even received Butler's report.

Iraq had been bombed frequently after 1991. It was bombed as a punishment for planning the assassination of former President Bush in Kuwait, and again in 1994. Indeed, minor reprisals for Iraq's transgression of the no-fly zones imposed upon it by the US and its allies occurred almost daily. But the bombing of Iraq in December 1998 was qualitatively different. Not only was it far more intense than anything it had suffered since the Gulf War, but it was also done without the sanction of the United Nations Security Council.

The US and UK claimed that the sanction existed in the mere fact that Iraq was defying Chapter 7 resolutions of the Security Council. They specifically claimed authority from the 2 March Resolution. 1154, which had warned Iraq that further violations of UN resolutions would entail "the severest consequences for Iraq". But one has only to compare the wording of Resolution 1154 with that of Resolution 679 of 29 November 1990 which did explicitly authorise the use of forces, to conclude that 1154 did no such thing. For 679 authorised "member states to use *all necessary means* to uphold and implement resolution 660". 660 thus devolved the responsibility for further action upon member states acting individually or in concert. And it left the choice of means upon them. Resolution 1154, by contrast, warned Iraq of severe penalties but did not even hint at anyone having the right to inflict them without another authorisation, perhaps similar to 679, from the Security Council.

On 17 December, the US and UK thus crossed a meridian in the development of the international state system. For the first time since the end of the Second World War and the setting up of the United Nations, two countries that, by virtue of their power, pre-eminence and special status within the Security Council, had a special duty to uphold the charter of the United Nations, knowingly violated its most important clause. This is the obligation of member states not to wage war upon one another except in pursuit of an explicit resolution of the Security Council authorising them to do so. The 17 December attack was thus not simply an attack on Iraq but on the United Nations itself. Nor is this all. Since the UN charter enshrined the basic principles of the Westphalian state system, it was an attack upon that system too. What is more, as the events that followed were to show, this was not an aberration, but a giant first step into a new world.[71]

Did Iraq's transgression justify such a huge step into the unknown? The contents of Butler's report showed, as Kofi Annan noted in his forwarding letter to the Council, that UNSCOM did not enjoy 'full co-operation' from Baghdad. But they do not come even close to suggesting that the scope for inspections was over, or that there was enough left out of them to justify the unprecedented step of bombing the country without any further authorisation from the UN. Clinton's justification for doing so was that "in four of five categories set forth, Iraq has failed to cooperate. Indeed it has placed new restrictions on inspections". Here are some of the particulars:

> Iraq repeatedly blocked UNSCOM from inspecting suspect sites. For example it shut off access to the headquarters of its ruling party...even though UN resolutions make no exception for them and UNSCOM *has inspected them in the past* (emphasis added).
>
> Iraq repeatedly restricted UNSCOM's ability to obtain necessary evidence. For example...to photograph bombs related to the chemical weapons program. It tried to stop an UNSCOM biological team from videotaping a site and photocopying documents and prevented Iraqi personnel from answering UNSCOM's questions.
>
> Prior to the inspection of another site, Iraq actually emptied out the building, removing not just documents even the furniture and the equipment.

Iraq has failed to turn over virtually all the documents requested by the inspectors. Indeed we know that Iraq ordered the destruction of weapons-related documents in anticipation of an UNSCOM inspection'.[72]

If all this could have been taken at face value, it would have provided ample grounds for a further resolution by the Security Council, possibly authorising the use of force. But by then UNSCOM's objectivity was already being seriously questioned other diplomats at the Security Council. To begin with, by far the most important document that Butler asked for was shown to the inspectors in the presence of Prakash Shah, Kofi Annan's Special Representative in Baghdad. This was the letter or document discovered by inspectors in the Air Headquarters in July. Its demand for the other documents listed above, especially to view documents that related to the Iran–Iraq war of the 1980s, was little more than a fishing expedition. While such investigative tactics are justified in the early phases of an investigation when the investigators are looking for leads, they made little sense after an investigation has gone on for 90 months and at least 95 per cent of Iraq's WMD capability had already been destroyed.

As for access to the Ba'ath party headquarters, an enterprising journalist disclosed that what had been objected to was not the inspection but the very large number of inspectors that Butler was insisting upon. The Iraqi authorities pointed out that the number had been fixed by an agreement with UNSCOM in 1996. Butler responded that the numbers had been revised repeatedly since then. The journalist Roula Khalaf of the *Financial Times,* found out from another senior Western diplomat in Baghdad that the numbers, and other modalities for site inspection had been revised for large military installations and not for the typical Baghdad house in which the Ba'ath party headquarters was located.[73]

Finally, Butler himself noted in his report that Iraq had largely cooperated with monitoring teams that inspected dual-use facilities. What it had objected to was the photographing of the bombs, citing concern for its national security.[74]

Butler's report, and particularly its bleak conclusion, surprised the entire diplomatic community, which had been closely monitoring the inspections. "We did not consider that the problems reported during the one month of inspections were major incidents", said a diplomat. Such differences were unavoidable. "UNSCOM's mandate says it should have full access but take into account Iraq's sovereignty, dignity and national security concerns. This leaves room for questions and will always give rise to problems".[75]

Had completing the weapons inspection been the real goal of UNSCOM, Butler would have submitted his list of tasks, accomplished and remaining, with an analysis of the obstacles to the Security Council. The Council would then have given Iraq a specific set of instructions on which of these tasks had to be completed and by when. Only if Iraq had refused to abide by the Council's directive would the question of using 'other means' have arisen. But as Madeleine Albright's article had inadvertently exposed, that the Clinton administration was already preparing to bomb Iraq was the foregone conclusion of the charade that had been enacted ever since June. And Butler was a willing accomplice. Whatever doubts he had raised among the members of the Security Council and the diplomatic community in Baghdad, were confirmed by the way in which he prepared and submitted his final report.

Butler's final report

At around 2.00 PM on 14 December, while Butler was still finalising the draft of his report to the Security Council, the White House Chief of Staff, John Podesta, was informing Congressional leaders that US forces would launch an attack on Iraq the next day. Butler did not submit his report to Annan till around 6.00 PM that evening, but by then, aboard Air Force One, Clinton had already ordered the attack on Iraq.[76] The conclusion was unavoidable: Butler had informed the US administration of his conclusions even before he had finalised his report, and long before Kofi Annan had had a chance to add his comments to it before sending it to the members of the Security Council. This led the Russian Ambassador, backed by China and some of Annan's senior advisers to accuse Butler of drafting his stark conclusions to serve Washington's war aims.[77]

Other evidence, although still circumstantial, strengthened the suspicion. On 14 December, before drafting his report, Butler made four visits to the United States' permanent mission to the UN across the plaza from the UN building.

Butler also ordered the UNSCOM inspectors to evacuate Baghdad on Tuesday night (probably Iraq time) when most members of the Security Council had still not seen the report. In short, Butler, like Clinton and John Podesta, knew that the US was going to attack Iraq when Annan and the Security Council were still in the dark about its contents.

When taxed to explain these 'coincidences', Administration officials admitted that they had advance knowledge of the language Butler would use in his report, and had influenced it, as one official said, "at the margins".[78]

To sum up then, Iraq did not comply fully with UNSCOM's demands. It placed some restrictions on access to sites, albeit minor ones which could be justified on the grounds of national sovereignty or security. It did not furnish most of the documents Butler had asked for. While some of these had undoubtedly been destroyed earlier or did not exist, some were probably destroyed on the government's orders specifically because Butler had asked for them. But in the final analysis, how important were the documents and the restricted sites themselves?

So far as the Ba'ath party's headquarters were concerned, they were housed in an ordinary house that *had been searched before*.[79] As for the documents that Iraq did not furnish, according to Scott Ritter, they were of almost no value anyway and had been asked for only to create a pretext for declaring that Iraq had failed to cooperate with UNSCOM.[80] One is therefore forced to the conclusion arrived at by Ritter, that the weapons inspections and documents asked for were intended mainly to provoke the Iraqis.

The close cooperation between Butler and the US administration achieved the desired end. Sanctions were not lifted. But support for them had dwindled within the UN and the New York-based diplomatic community. UNSCOM had become somewhat discredited. The US therefore knew that the policy of procrastination had run its course.

Determined not to rehabilitate Saddam, and still unable to topple him, it switched to the only other 'policy' that remained open—the use of force.

The air strikes were designed to degrade Iraq's capacities even further.[81] The Clinton administration knew that a renewed attack on Iraq would give Baghdad the excuse to end all weapons inspection and prevent UNSCOM from returning to Iraq. But by the end of October, coincidentally around the time that the confrontation between Baghdad and UNSCOM took a final, decisive turn for the worse, it was fully reconciled to this eventuality. Senior American officials began to give background briefings to journalists that the US had concluded that 'the United Nations inspection regime is no longer an effective instrument for restraining President Saddam Hussein'. Instead the administration was turning to other forms of 'traditional containment', including sanctions and the use of force.[82]

Operation Desert Fox finished UNSCOM, as it turned out, forever. But war proved a far less effective and far more expensive way of containing Saddam. With UNSCOM's inspectors no longer there to tell them what they had hit and what to aim at, they found that they had no idea how effective they were being in 'degrading' Iraq's military capability. As a result the US and UK found that once they had started down this road, they could not stop. In the year that followed the December 15–18 bombings, they bombed Iraq virtually every other day. By August they had hit 359 targets in Iraq in eight months. This was three times the number of targets hit during 'Desert Fox'. By October 1999 they found that they had run out of targets. By the end of the year the US and UK had flown more than 6,000 sorties, dropped more than 1800 bombs and hit more than 450 targets. This was the longest sustained US air operation since the Vietnam War.[83] During the next four years they had only the vaguest idea of what Saddam Hussein was up to. Thus after the terrorist attacks on America on 11 September 2001,the fear that a resurgent Iraq might pass on its technological expertise to the likes of Al Qaeda, came back to haunt the US again. All that the drama of 1998 achieved was to give its paranoia a hard new edge.

Notes

1. Peter D. Zimmerman. "Bush's deceit". *The Washington Post* 13 August 2003. Zimmerman writes: "In September 1990 his father's administration claimed that Iraq had hundreds of tanks and 300,000 troops in Kuwait massed on the Saudi border. But independent analysis by me and a colleague, using extremely sharp Soviet satellite photos, showed no evidence whatever of a significant Iraqi force in Kuwait. Nonetheless, in 1990 the American people were told that an attack on Saudi Arabia was imminent".
2. Rick Atkinson. "Murky ending fogs end of Desert Storm Legacy". In Fog of War. *Washington Post* 1998.
3. Wadood Hamad. "Iraq's tragedy: Waiting for Godot! Eclipse". The Anti *war review*. Vol 12. 23 November 2002.
4. Atkinson op. cit.
5. In July, Thomas L. Friedman, then the chief diplomatic correspondent of the New York Times, wrote that the best dispensation in Iraq from the US' point of view, would be "an iron-fisted junta" that would rule Iraq just the way Saddam Hussein had done, but without him to head it. *New York Times* 7 July 1991. p.4. "A Rising Sense that Iraq's Hussein must go".
6. Roula Khalaf. "UN inspectors play for high stakes in Iraq paper chase". *Financial Times*, 23 November 1998. In July-August 1998 Richard Butler, the head of UNSCOM asked the Iraqi Deputy Foreign Minister Riad-al-Qaysi, to hand over the minutes of a 'High Level Concealment committee, set up in 1991, to his organisation. Al-Qaysi apparently told him that the decision to hide materials had been conveyed orally and that "in a technical sense" the committee had never existed. Iraq cited this as one of several examples of Butler's pre-determined decision to prevent a closure of UNSCOM's work and therefore of the lifting of economic sanctions.
7. Ibid. See under 'Discussion- Iraq's weapons of Mass Destruction Programme'. Israel's involvement was revealed explicitly when it became known that Scott Ritter, the senior American member of UNSCOM, whom the Iraqis wanted expelled because he was a member of an American intelligence agency, had indeed been an officer of America's Marine Intelligence Service, and had maintained close links with Israel's secret service. He had in fact travelled frequently to and from Israel while a member of UNSCOM. Ritter revealed Israel's close links with UNSCOM in an interview to the Israeli newspaper Haaretz, published on September

9, 1998. In an article written for an Israeli newspaper, possible also Haaretz, about theree weeks later, he acknowledged that he would not have been able to carry out his work as an inspector had it not been for the information fed to him by the Israelis.(Roula Khalaf in The Financial Times, London 10 October 1998).
8. William Jefferson Clinton. "Address to the Joint chiefs of Staff and the Pentagon staff". 17 February 1998.
9. CIA report on Iraq's WMD, op.cit.
10. The details of Iraq's nuclear weapons programme were revealed to the US by a defecting Iraqi nuclear scientist, Khizr Abdul Abbas Hamza. Judith Miller and James Reisen: Tracking Baghdad's arsenal: Inside the arsenal: A special report; "Defector Decribes Iraq's Atom Bomb Push. The New York Times, 15 August 1998. Hamza claimed when he defected that he was the head of the bomb-makingprogramme, but Scott Ritter has pointed out that he was only a middle level functionary, who had actually been fired before he defected. Pitt and Ritter: op.cit.
11. "Iraq's Weapons of Mass Destruction: The assessment of the British Government". Report presented to the British parliament by Prime Minister Tony Blair in September 2002. Pp. 12-13.
12. Then helping Saddam against Iran.
13. William J. Broad and Judith Miller. "The Deal on Iraq: Secret Arsenal: The Hunt for the Germs of War—A special Report". *The New York Times*, 26 February 1998.
14. Ibid.
15. CIA report October 2002. op. cit.
16. Iraq's Weapons of Mass Destruction: The assessment of the British Government Presented by Tony Blair to the British parliament in September 2002. Pp15 and 16.
17. Clinton's 17 February address, op.cit.
18. "Iraq's weapons of mass Destruction: The assessment of the British Government op cit.
19. CIA October 2002. op. cit. According to Blair's report to the British parliament 500 were fired at Iran and 93 during the Gulf War. This meant that Iraq was left with 298 missiles or thereabouts in April 1991. UNSCOM, according to the same report destroyed 'very large quantities of chemical weapons and ballistic missiles and associated production facilities by 1998'. Despite this UNSCOM concluded in its october 1998 report that it had been unable to fulfil its mandate. Op.cit. p. 16.
20. William Rivers Pitt and Scott Ritter. *War on Iraq*. New York: Context Books, 2002. P.29. In a face-to-face session with the editors of

The Washington Post sometime in October 1998, the UN Secretary-General, Kofi Annan had admitted that it would probably not be possible to rid Iraq of all its WMD potential and that UNSCOM and the Security Council would have to setle for a determination that such weapons (as remained) in the hands of Baghdad did not pose a threat to its neighbours. This wise counsel went unheeded: "Iraq suspends co-operation". *The Hindu,* Chennai, India 2 November 1998: Also available on the FT intelligence wire.

21. Broad and Miller: op. cit.
22. Report of the Executive Chairman of the Special Commission, established by the Secretary-General pursuant to paragraph 9 (b) (i) of Security Council resolution 687 (1991). 11 April 1997. Doc. No. S/1997/ 301
23. Tim Weiner". "The Deal on Iraq: The CIA; CIA Drafts Covert Plans to Topple Hussein". *The New York Times* 26 February 1998. A sixth attempt was being planned in October 2002 even as President George W. Bush prepared America to go to war against Iraq. See Julia Preston and Eric Schmitt: US split with France deepens. But Bush team explores options short of war in Iraq. The New York Times 16 October 2002.
24. George Monbiot. "Inspection as Invasion". *The Guardian* 8 October 2002.
25. Ibid. This was reported at the time and later. See Philip Shenon. "Rebuking ex-arms inspector, Albright defends US Role". *The New York Times:* 10 September 1998.
26. Barbara Crossette. "With new inspection setup a new Annan-Iraq link". *The New York Times* 10 March 1998.
27. Steven Erlanger: Gulf War alliance: six years later seams fray. *The New York Times* 5 November 1997.
28. Roula Khalaf: *Financial Times* October 8. See endnote 8 above. The US did this despite the fact that Ritter, as he himself confessed later, was a member of American Marine Intelligence and had maintained a constant, close relationship with Israeli intelligence that UNSCOM knew about and encouraged. There was nothing intrinsically wrong in Ritter, of UNSCOM for that matter obtaining help from the intelligence agencies of member nations of the United Nations. Once Iraq had decidedto conceal as many of its weapons as possible, UNSCOM had no option but to rely upon help from member states' intelligence agencies.
29. Ibid.
30. Barbara Crossette. "UN's Envoys fail to budge the Iraqis on Inspection Issues". *The New York Times,* 7 November 1998.
31. Mark Suzman. "Washington takes wary line on UN deal". *Financial Times* London, 23 February 1998.

32. Elaine Sciolino: Standoff with Iraq: For the UN chief, scarcely room for Negotiating. *The New York Times*, 18 February 1998.
33. Michael R. Gordon and Elaine Sciolino: Fingerprints on Iraqi accord belong to Albright. *The New York Times*, 25 February 1998.
34. Unnamed sources quoted in the American press who were in all probability unaware of the discussions that had taken place between Albright and Annan.
35. Steven Erlanger: Th deal on Iraq: the Overview: Clinton Says Iraq is promising unconditional access to sites. *The New York Times*, 24 February 1998.
36. These concessions can be deduced from what Annan and the US administration subsequently did. Some highly intrusive inspections were discouraged by the US and UN. Scott Ritter's liaison with Israeli intelligence was terminated. This was almost certainly one of the reasons for his resignation from UNSCOM in August. And he was charged with spying for Israel by the FBI. When Butler made a public statement that Iraq was not cooperating with the UN, the Secretary general banned him from making public statements in the future.
37. Christopher S. Wren: Chief UN Inspector says Iraq is granting much wider access. *The New York Times*, 14 March 1998.
38. Ibid.
39. Roula Khalaf: Butler sees progress on Iraq. *The Financial Times* 12 June 1998.
40. Roula Khalaf: UN envoy warns on impact of Iraqi sanctions. *The Financial Times*, London. 15 June 1998.
41. Roula Khalaf: Iraq hails deal with UN to close 'All Files'. *The Financial Times*, London, 17 June 1998.
42. Ibid.
43. John M. Goshko: Iraqi nerve gas Tests confirmed; UN Chief Inspector briefs Council. *The Washington Post* 25 June 1998.
44. Ibid. See also Associated press story datelined November 28, 1998 'Iraq responds to UN requests'. In November Riad al Qaysi, Iraq's deputy Foreign Minister, went on record accusing the US of planting the nerve gas on the warhead fragments taken for testing. It insisted that it had never succeeded in producing stable VX gas, and therefore that the question of being able to load warheads with it did not arise. It accused the US of planting the nerve gas on the warhead fragments taken for testing. *The Star Tribune* Minneapolis.

45. Ibid.
46. Ibid
47. Letter from Executive Charirman of UNSCOM to the Security Council 17 june 1998. The relevant paras read as follows:
'The discussions were held in a cordial and professional manner, which reflected the new spirit of cooperation between both sides following the signature of the Memorandum of Understanding between the Secretary-General and the Government of Iraq on 23 February 1998 (see S/1998/208).
As a result of the talks, the Deputy Prime Minister and I agreed on a schedule for work to be carried out by both sides during the next two months in order to try to resolve most of the priority disarmament issues.
I believe that if the Government of Iraq provides the full cooperation it undertook to provide, in the Memorandum of Understanding between the United Nations and Iraq, it should be possible for the Commission to resolve remaining issues and begin to formulate reports on its work pursuant to paragraph 22 of resolution 687 (1991)'. S/1998/529. 17 June 1998. Para 22 referred to the lifting of sanctions.
48. Roula Khalaf: UN envoy warns on impact of Iraqi sanctions. The *Financial Times*, London. 15 June 1998.
49. This may not have been the first time he did so, and it certainly was not his last. Diplomats in the Security Council remembered, when interviewed in June, that after praising Iraq's cooperation when he was in Baghdad, Butler had come back to New York and reported to the UN Security Council that 'no progress had been achieved in the previous six months' Roula Khalaf' *The Financial Times* June 18, 1998: op.cit.
50. John M. Goshko: Iraqi nerve gas Tests confirmed; UN Chief Inspector briefs Council. *The Washington Post* 25 June 1998.: Goshko's precise words are, " Butler spoke after giving a closed-door briefing to the 15-member council....." By speaking out immediately in public he defeated the entire purpose of closing the session to the public. Thus was Kofi Annan and the UN outmaneuvered.
51. Amorim report to UN security Council, 25 March 1999. The key paragraph is reproduced below.

Table 4 provides a summary of the assessment of recovered warheads remnants relevant to the material balance.

Table 4

Category of warheads destroyed	Declared quantity	Recovered or otherwise as accepted accounted for
Special warheads destroyed unilaterally (modified imported and indigenously produced)	45	43-45
Imported conventional warheads (Iraq's unilateral and UNSCOM—supervised destruction)	107	83
Indigenous warheads of all types (accounting method is by imported rings, as key elements in a warhead structure)	196-200	170-180

Issues related to remnants of warheads that have not been recovered, but which have been declared by Iraq as unilaterally destroyed (some 25 imported warheads and some 25 Iraqi manufactured warheads), remain outstanding in the accounting of proscribed warheads that Iraq claimed to have destroyed unilaterally. The full and verifiable accounting for proscribed missile conventional warheads remains essential for the verification of the premise that Iraq has not retained any proscribed missiles and that all proscribed missiles and their warheads indeed have been destroyed."

52. Youssef .M. Ibrahim: "Panel studying Iraq missiles is of two minds on Nerve Gas". *The New York Times*, 27 October 1998. What the three countries' experts agreed upon was that the missile fragments had been washed before being sent. This suggested that Iraq had something to hide. What no one could explain was how the US army was able to find traces of VX on shards washed in detergent when the others could not. Nor does it explain why the same laboratory could not find these traces a second time.
53. Roula Khalaf: Baghdad to cut deal on weapons inspections. *The Financial Times*, London, 2 October 1998. The suspicion that Iraq already has the trigger device for a bomb also permeates the CIA and British Intelligence

report on Iraq's WMD, which were released in September and October 2002. It is not voiced explicitly but is implied by the concern with which both the US and Britain view Iraq's alleged attempts to obtain enriched uranium from Africa.
54. Madeleine K. Albright. "Saddam rattling his cage, but he cannot break out of it". *The Houston Chronicle*. 18 August 1998.
55. Ibid.
56. Albrights statement shows that some reports that were put out in American news papers by American officials who were not identified, the US did not put pressure on Butler not to embark upon intrusive inspections, and that he took all his decisions by himself, was another piece of disinformation designed to portray the US as respecting Annan's initiative and co-operating with the UN security Council in its bid to make it work. See Steven Erlanger: US Urged Arms Monitors to Back Off From Clash With Iraq. New York Times 15 August 1998.
57. Diplomats in Baghdad were surprised by the report because 'Positive points that they were told would be included in the reports were nowhere to be found'. 'Roula Khalaf *FT* 18 June 1998: op.cit.
58. Ibid.
59. Scott Ritter, as told to William Pitt *War on Iraq*. Context books. New York, 2002. P. 43.Ritter claims in the book that he got into shouting matches with Spertzel on this issue in the morning staff meetings, but Butler did nothing. P44.
60. Ibid. p. 45-6.
61. Khalaf, *FT* 2 October 1998. op.cit.
62. In a face-to-face session with the editors of *The Washington Post* a few days after his meeting with Aziz, Kofi Annan said that it would probably not be possible to rid Iraq of all its WMD potential and that UNSCOM and the Security Council would have to settle for a determination that such weapons (as remained) in the hands of Baghdad did not pose a threat to its neighbours. The Hindu, Chennai, India 2 November 1998: Iraq suspends co-operation. Also available on the FT intelligence wire.
63. Roula Khalaf, Tension Rises as Iraq Bans UN inspectors. *The Financial Times* London, P.2.
64. Steven Erlanger: US set to give up Arms Inspection for Curbing Iraq. *The New York Times*, 8 November 1998.
65. Steven Lee Myers: US Works to win Allies' support for Using Force against Iraq. The New York Times, 5 November 1998.
66. Roula Khalaf: Cohen berates Iraq on weapons checks. *Financial Times* 7 November 1998.

67. R.W. Apple Jr.: Crisis with Iraq: (News Analysis) Who backed down? *The New York Times*, 16 November 1998.
68. Roula Khalaf: UN Inspectors play for high stakes in Iraq paper chase. *The Financial Times*, London. 23 November 1998.
69. Ibid.
70. Butler's December 17 report to the UN Security Council. Quoted by James Bone and Michael Binyon: UN arms inspector faces the bombing backlash. *The Times*, London. 22 December 1998.
71. The UN was bypassed again in the attack on Serbia to liberate Kosovo in 1999, and yet again in George Bush's war (or near-war) against Iraq in 2002. See below.
72. Transcript of President Clinton's address to the nation published by the *New York Times*. 17 December 1998.
73. Khalaf: UNSCOM report UN inspectors encountered serious problems but notfatal blow to their work'. *FT* 17 December 1998.
74. Ibid.
75. Ibid. Diplomats were equally surprised. See David Usborne: How Iraq yet again broke its promises to the UN'. *The Independent*, London. 17 December 1998.
76. Barton Gellman: Top Inspector denies aiding US war aims. *The Washington Post*. 18 December 1998
76. Gellman op. cit.
77. Ibid.
78. Ibid.
79. Roula Khalaf: op. cit *FT* December 18.1998. The modalities for entering this site were fixed in 1996, which is when it was first inspected.
80. Ritter told BBC's Radio 4 Today, "I can guarantee you that every piece of information used to support this most recent inspection was of a dated nature". "Butler", he said, had " allowed the US to manipulate the work of UNSCOM in such a fashion as to justify an air strike". Attack Data Old, claims expert; Ex-Inspector criticises strikes. *The Herald* , Glasgow 24 December 1998.
81. David Gardner quotes Blair as explaining:" our objections in this military action are clear. (They are) to degrade (Mr. Saddam's) capability to build and use weapons of mass desruction: Shots in the dark. The Financial Times, London, 18 December 1998.
82. Steven Erlanger: US set to give up Arms inspection to curb Iraq. *The New York times* 7 November 1998.
83. Anthony Arnove in Arnove (ed.) *The War Against Iraq* p.9. London: Pluto Press.

3

The Invasion of Iraq

Operation Desert Fox, and the ten months of relentless bombing that followed, did nothing to resolve the dilemma that was driving US policy or, to be more precise, lack of a policy towards Iraq. The bombing had further alienated Saddam Hussein without overthrowing him. It had destroyed much of Iraq's painfully rebuilt infrastructure. But the Anglo-Saxon duo had no idea of the extent to which they had succeeded in 'degrading' its weapons of mass destruction. They also did not know whether it had any such weapons left. All that the bombing eventually achieved was to ensure that UNSCOM could not return to Iraq. Without UNSCOM to act as their eyes and ears in Iraq, the US' and UK's paranoia deepened.

This situation could not last forever. Iraq was desperate to get the economic sanctions lifted. One third of its people were living below the poverty line, and two thirds no longer had access to safe drinking water or sanitation. The infant mortality rate had climbed from 50 per 1,000 in 1991 to over 125 per 1,000 by 1998, and 70 per cent of the deaths could be traced to respiratory and gastro-intestinal diseases.[1] This meant that by the middle of 2002, close to one million children had died, mostly because of malnutrition, gastro-intestinal diseases and a lack of timely medication. 60 per cent of the population, moreover, was living on food handouts from the World Food Programme and voluntary organisations.² Sooner or later, Iraq was bound to return to the negotiating table and try once again for the deal that it thought it had obtained in February 1998—the return of weapons inspectors in exchange for assurances that the sanctions would be lifted once the inspectors were satisfied that there were no weapons of mass destruction left.

The Clinton administration remained determined not to allow sanctions to be lifted while Saddam Hussein remained in power, but was willing to use the UN to provide the justification for not doing so. Security Council Resolution 1284 of 17 December 1999 therefore appointed a new weapons inspection commission, the UN Monitoring and Verification Commission (UNMOVIC) to resume weapons inspection and demanded that Iraq agree to their return. Till July 2002, Iraq resisted their return, bargaining for a reciprocal commitment to end sanctions.³

Initially the Bush administration followed its predecessor's policy.⁴ Shortly after assuming office it initiated a review of the US' policy on Iraq, but this yielded no new initiatives. The National Security Council had completed a review of Iraq's possible links with Al Qaeda and found none.⁵ The CIA was primarily concerned by the 'stateless' nature of the new terrorism, which called for a new set of responses from the US and other affected states. The State Department was veering towards the crafting of 'smart sanctions' which would ease the restrictions on the supply of food and medicines to Iraq while bearing down hard on the smuggling of equipment for his rearmament programmes. Till the terrorist bombing of the World Trade Center in New York and the Pentagon on 11 September 2001 (henceforth 9/11), Iraq was not high on the Bush administration's list of priorities.

The situation changed radically after 9/11. Terrorism was not a new phenomenon. Attacks on civilians had been an integral part of attempts to destabilise and eventually overthrow established regimes. But till the 1990s, terrorism had been used to promote a political agenda mainly within the bounds of a nation state.⁶ The goal of the terrorists was to overthrow the regime of a country to which they belonged. Indeed most such movements resented being labelled terrorist, and insisted that they were freedom movements forced to adopt violent methods because of unrelenting persecution by the state.

The terrorist attack on 11 September 2001 was entirely different. It was carried out in America but not by Americans. Nor was its aim to overthrow a regime or political system in the USA.[7] Its target was a particular set of values and a society that embodied them. This was 'the West', 'Western culture,' 'Westernisation' and everything that these loose terms represented to people in traditional societies. The US was chosen as the principal target because it was the hegemonic power that was driving the changes that these terms encapsulated. The purpose of this new terrorism was to register a protest against the way in which the world was changing and to prevent the changes from invading the Islamic world. It was, therefore, the first armed rebellion against the economic, political and cultural integration of the world being brought about by globalisation.

9/11 had its precursors. There had been similarly motivated terrorist attacks on US personnel and property in the 1990s, and these had grown both in frequency and effectiveness. The early 1990s had seen attacks on American armed forces personnel in Saudi Arabia, on CIA operatives in front of its headquarters at Langley Virginia, and an attempt to blow up the World Trade Center in 1993 that had cost six lives.[8] The mid-1990s had seen attacks on American airmen in Riyadh and Dhahran in Saudi Arabia, and an attempt to blow up a number of American civilian airliners in the Far East in the spring of 1994. These attacks had culminated in the bombing of the US embassies in Nairobi and Dar-es-Salaam in 1998 and the suicide bombing of the American destroyer, the *USS Cole* in Yemen's waters in 1999 that claimed 14 lives.

But those attacks had been either abortive[9], of minor importance, or had taken place outside the country. None of them had therefore punctured the cocoon of security in which Americans were living after the end of the Cold War. By contrast, the 9/11 attacks occurred on American soil, were launched upon two of the key symbols of American global hegemony, and proved successful beyond the expectations even of their planners.[10] Three thousand of the best and brightest in the new global economy lost their lives. The simplicity of the methods used to carry out the attack, the sophistication of the planning that had gone into it and, above all, the unflinching resolve of the hijackers of the four aircraft, to sacrifice their lives, created a stark new awareness of their own vulnerability in all Americans. All of a sudden, a country that had believed that it had no enemies and was militarily invulnerable, found itself confronted by a deadly and implacable foe that did not operate from any identifiable geographical base and was therefore invulnerable to attack by conventional military means. The vulnerability was heightened by the realisation that America was being attacked not for anything it had done, but for what it was; not for something it could change, but for something over which it had no measurable degree of control. This ruled out the option that nation states facing conventional terrorism or insurgency enjoy, of mixing political accommodation with coercion to restore peace. For the US, in the war that had been forced upon it, force remained the only option.

The Impact of 9/11

President Bush responded to the attack by declaring a war on terrorism. Although he used the term 'war' to describe what the United States was embarking upon, it was apparent from the beginning that what he had in mind was something very different. Throughout human history, the word had referred to armed conflicts between territorially defined states or societies. Although US spokesmen often referred to it as a war against communism, even in the Cold War the real adversary had been another modern state. The war that Bush declared on 15 September was not against a state but against individuals who subscribed to a feeling—hostility to the changes that the world was undergoing. If international terrorism was a rebellion against the way the world was changing, then a war upon it was no more than an unthinking defence of those changes. If terrorism was a protest against the perceived injustice of the emerging international political and economic system, then the war against it was designed to stamp out the protest instead of addressing its causes. And if the protest was coming from people in many countries, then a war designed to stamp it out would have to be fought in many countries. Since these were sovereign states, the US had to seek their cooperation. When it was not forthcoming, or when the state was too weak to offer effective cooperation, the war on terrorism required the US to step in and do the job of crushing the terrorists directly.

The concept of national sovereignty was therefore the first casualty of 9/11 and the American response to it. This assault had three components: first, the rejection of the military doctrine of *deterrence* in favour of a doctrine of *'preemption'*. Second, the subtle, stage-by-stage elimination of the difference between *'preemption'* and *'prevention'* as a justification of military action; and third, the abrupt overthrow of the UN as the emerging seat of international authority and legitimacy, by the US. Deterrence had been the lynchpin of peace in the Westphalian state system. It yielded a stable international order, because it required the aggressor—the nation that wanted to change the status quo—to make the first move and relied upon raising the cost of that move to him, to preserve peace. But deterrence worked best when the aggressor was also a territorially defined nation state. Preemption, by contrast, allowed a nation to anticipate a threat and prevent it from materialising. But to be acceptable as a justification for war the threat had to be imminent, visible and emanating from another state. Terrorism did not fit this bill. Thus the only way to deal with it was to *prevent* a terrorist threat from emerging. This meant that the US had to establish control over, and reshape, any state that *could become* a base, or haven, for terrorists even if that state showed no aggressive intentions towards the US, and was doing its best to apprehend terrorists operating from its soil. 9/11 thus gave the US a pretext for declaring war on the Westphalian state system. Since this system had been re-consecrated after World War II by the charter of the United Nations, the US also declared war on the United Nations.

The first country against which the US used its still embryonic doctrine of preemption was Afghanistan. But its origins predated the Afghan war by a full nine years. It was formulated by Paul Wolfowitz, and its target was Iraq.

Iraq's potential as a 'troublemaker' in the Middle East had been highlighted by a small group set up in the Pentagon as early as 1977. In a secret assessment of threats to the US, the group highlighted Iraq's outsized armed forces and unresolved territorial disputes, and raised the possibility that it might one day attack Kuwait or Saudi Arabia. The group had been convened by Paul Wolfowitz, then a relatively new arrival at the Department of Defense.[11] When Iraq attacked Iran instead, these fears were put aside as the US entered into its covert alliance with Iraq. However, when Saddam occupied Kuwait in 1990 he revived all these dormant fears. The fear lay coiled at the root of the pressure that George Bush (Sr.) came under from members of his own administration to send the US army all the way to Baghdad in order to depose Saddam Hussein in 1991. In 1992, Wolfowitz presided over the writing of a "Defense Planning Guidance" paper which not only foresaw another war against Iraq, but did so on the basis of a broader policy proposal that envisioned waging preemptive war on any country that was bent upon acquiring nuclear, biological or chemical weapons.[12]

Wolfowitz was then the Under Secretary for Policy in the Defense Department. Dick Cheney was the Secretary for Defense. This 46-page paper, which spelt out America's mission in the post-Cold War years circulated among senior levels in the Bush (Sr.) administration for several weeks till it was leaked to the *New York Times* and *The Washington Post*. The White House then instructed Cheney to rewrite it. This may have had the opposite effect, because its key ideas became part of bipartisan thinking on foreign policy in the coming years. The following are some key excerpts from the paper.

> Our first objective is to prevent the re-emergence of a new rival. This is a dominant consideration underlying the new regional defense strategy and requires that we endeavor to prevent any hostile power from dominating a region whose resources would, under consolidated control, be sufficient to generate global power. These regions include Western Europe, East Asia, the territory of the former Soviet Union, and Southwest Asia.

There are three additional aspects to this objective: First the U.S must show the leadership necessary to establish and protect a new order that holds the promise of convincing potential competitors that they need not aspire to a greater role or pursue a more aggressive posture to protect their legitimate interests. Second, in the non-defense areas, we must account sufficiently for the interests of the advanced industrial nations to discourage them from challenging our leadership or seeking to overturn the established political and economic order. Finally, we must maintain the mechanisms for deterring potential competitors from even aspiring to a larger regional or global role.

Another major US objective should be to safeguard US interests and promote American values. The US should aim "to address sources of regional conflict and instability in such a way as to promote increasing respect for international law, limit international violence, and encourage the spread of democratic forms of government and open economic systems."[13]

The draft outlined several scenarios in which US interests could be threatened by regional conflict: "access to vital raw materials, primarily Persian Gulf oil; proliferation of weapons of mass destruction and ballistic missiles, threats to US citizens from terrorism or regional or local conflict, and threats to US society from narcotics trafficking."

The draft relied on seven scenarios in potential trouble spots to make its argument—with the primary case studies being Iraq and North Korea. In such situations it emphasised that "if necessary, the United States must be prepared to take unilateral action".

There was no mention in the draft document of taking collective action through the United Nations. Instead the document stated that coalitions "hold considerable promise for promoting collective action," but it also stated that the US "should expect future coalitions to be ad hoc assemblies" formed to deal with a particular crisis and which may not outlive the resolution of the crisis.

The document stated that what was most important was "the sense that the world order is ultimately backed by the US" and that "the United States should be postured to act independently when collective action cannot be orchestrated" or in a crisis that calls for quick response. In 1993, when the Clinton administration continued Bush senior's policy of non-intervention in Iraq, Wolfowitz, now no longer in the administration, launched a blistering attack on the policy in an article in the *Wall Street Journal* entitled 'Clinton's Bay of Pigs'. In it he derided the US' policy of "passive containment and inept covert operations" and clearly implied that the right course was to oust Saddam Hussein. By 1994 Wolfowitz was explicitly proposing a military invasion of Iraq.[14]

In January 1998, Wolfowitz along with Donald Rumsfeld, and William Kristol, the editor of a highly influential periodical started in 1997, *The Weekly Standard*, were among 18 co-signatories of a letter addressed to Clinton urging him to take all necessary diplomatic and military measures to depose Saddam Hussein:

> We are writing to you because we are convinced that current American policy toward Iraq is not succeeding, and that we may soon face a threat in the Middle East more serious than any we have known since the end of the Cold War. In your upcoming State of the Union Address, you have an opportunity to chart a clear and determined course for meeting this threat. We urge you to seize that opportunity, and to enunciate a new strategy that would secure the interests of the US and our friends and allies around the world. That strategy should aim, above all, at the removal of Saddam Hussein's regime from power.
> We urge you to turn your Administration's attention to implementing a strategy for removing Saddam's regime from power. This will require a full complement of diplomatic, political *and military efforts*. Although we are fully aware of the dangers and difficulties in implementing this policy, we believe the dangers of failing to do so are far greater. We believe the US has the authority under existing UN resolutions to take the necessary steps, including military steps, to protect our vital interests in the Gulf. In any case, American policy

cannot continue to be crippled by a misguided insistence on unanimity in the UN Security Council[15] ...As recent events have demonstrated, we can no longer depend on our partners in the Gulf War coalition to continue to uphold the sanctions or to punish Saddam when he blocks or evades UN inspections. It hardly needs to be added that if Saddam does acquire the *capability* to deliver weapons of mass destruction, as he is almost certain to do if we continue along the present course, the safety of American troops in the region, of our friends and allies like Israel and the moderate Arab states, and a significant portion of the world's supply of oil will all be put at hazard. The only acceptable strategy is one that eliminates the *possibility* that Iraq will be able to use or threaten to use weapons of mass destruction. In the near term, this means a willingness to undertake military action as diplomacy is clearly failing. *In the long term, it means removing Saddam Hussein and his regime from power.*[16] (emphasis added)

The stress on words like 'capability' and 'possibility' showed that the authors no longer considered it necessary for the US to be actually threatened first, let alone attacked. Just the capacity of some state or government to pose a threat was sufficient cause for a 'preemptive' military attack. The authors sent a similar letter to senate majority leader Trent Lott and former Speaker of the House of Representatives Newt Gingrich on 29 May.[17] When George Bush (Jr.) became President, this group moved from the fringes of foreign policy making to its dead centre. Eight out of the 18 signatories to the letter went on to occupy senior positions in the Department of Defense.[18]

The coming together of these eight was not a coincidence. In the Bush (Sr.) administration Wolfowitz had been part of a tight-knit far right neo-conservative group that also included the then Defense Secretary, Dick Cheney, his wife Lynn Cheney, and Donald Rumsfeld. This group, which is overwhelmingly Jewish, stayed together during the eight Clinton years and became a part of the American Enterprise Institute, a conservative think tank founded in 1943, that became the home base of the neo-conservative movement during the Clinton years. In 1998 they became part of a neo-conservative think tank, *The Project for the New American Century*. The PNAC had been set up by William Kristol. It was, and is, housed in the same Washington, D.C. office building as the American Enterprise Institute. The two share far more than an address: the PNAC was set up under the New Citizenship project, which is also headed by William Kristol and is also an offshoot of the AEI. This project received $1.9 million from a right wing foundation, The Bradley Institute, which is also a substantial contributor to the John M. Olin Institute for Strategic Studies at Harvard University which was, till 2000, headed by Samuel Huntington. A large number of the participants in the PNAC are fellows of the AEI. A similar overlap is found among all the neo-conservative think-tanks—Hudson Institute, Center for Security Policy, Washington Institute for Near East Policy, Middle East Forum, and Jewish Institute for National Security Affairs. The main organ of the neo-conservatives is Kristol's *Weekly Standard*, which has a circulation of 55,000, but an influence far greater than its circulation suggests. The *Weekly Standard* is funded by Rupert Murdoch, owner of the *Fox News* TV network in the US, which set a record for jingoism during the invasion of Iraq. Murdoch contributed $10 million or thereabouts towards the setting up of the journal. These close interconnections give the agenda of a relatively small clique of influential thinkers the appearance of widespread consensus.[19]

From the time it was set up, the PNAC has argued vigorously for untrammelled unilateralism in foreign policy, for a sharp increase in defence spending from the then 2.8 per cent of the GDP to 3.5 to 3.8 per cent, and for giving the American armed forces the capacity to fight multiple, simultaneous major theatre wars. The arguments used by the authors of the report were eerily similar to those of the Reaganite right wing in the early 1980s when it was arguing for a sharp increase in defence spending in order to confront a resurgent Soviet threat. Years of cuts in defence spending, the report claimed, had 'eroded American military combat readiness, and put in jeopardy the Pentagon's plans for maintaining military superiority in the years ahead'.[20] The only difference was that the Cold War was over and America, which already accounted for 37.5 per cent of the defence spending of the entire world, had no discernible rivals. Kristol's think tank was, in fact, laying out a blueprint for the total and unfettered domination of the world by the US in the 21st century.

When George W. Bush came to power in 2000, and appointed Donald Rumsfeld his Secretary for Defense, Kristol's think tank finally acquired the power to shape American foreign policy that it had craved for so long. Paul Wolfowitz, the father of the war, became Deputy Secretary of Defense, No. 2 to Rumsfeld in the Defense Department. Another friend of Perle's, Douglas Feith, headed the Pentagon Planning Board. Other prominent neo-conservatives in key places were John Bolton, an Undersecretary in the State Department, and Eliot Abrams, responsible for the Middle East in the National Security Council. Abrams was connected with the Iran-Contra-Israel scandal. Other prominent neo-conservatives are Oliver North, the hero of that scandal, who, together with Michael Ledeen, another of its heroes, belongs to the Jewish Institute for National Security Affairs. He advocated total war not only against Iraq, but also against Israel's other enemies, Iran, Syria, Saudi Arabia and the Palestinian authority. Yet another member of the group, Dov Zakheim, became Comptroller for the Defense Department.

9/11 gave its members the pretext they had needed to sell their vision of American dominance to the American public. But their strategy needed a target. Iraq, their old *bete noir*, was all too conveniently at hand. Not surprisingly, most of the eight found themselves in a newly established 'Office of Plans', one of whose main functions was to prepare a case for the invasion of Iraq.

Their infallible weapon was paranoia. Till 9/11 the US had had one inveterate enemy in the Middle East—Saddam Hussein. Now it had a second in Osama bin Laden and Al Qaeda. Having seen what Al Qaeda could do and having found out, from documents captured in Afghanistan, how determined it was to acquire weapons of mass destruction, they posed the very simple question, "Can the US afford to take the chance that the two enemies will not unite their effort and capabilities one day?"

In the grief, shock and disorientation that followed the attack on the Pentagon and the Trade Towers, the neo-conservatives were the only group with a ready explanation and a solution. Only nine days after the outrage, William Kristol published an Open Letter to President Bush, in the *Weekly Standard,* asserting that it was not enough to annihilate the network of Osama bin Laden, but that it was also imperative to "remove Saddam Hussein from power" and to "retaliate" against Syria and Iran for supporting Hizbullah.

It was signed by 41 leading neo-cons, including Norman Podhoretz, a Jewish former leftist who has become an extreme right-wing icon, editor of the prestigious *Encounter* magazine, and his wife, Midge Decter, also a writer, Frank Gaffney of the Center for Security Studies, Robert Kagan, also of the *Weekly Standard,* Charles Krauthammer of *The Washington Post,* and Richard Perle.[21] That Open Letter was, in effect, the beginning of the Iraq war.

The neo-conservative argument was presented cogently by Wolfowitz to Bush and his top advisers, in the presence of Donald Rumsfeld, at a 'war council' held at Laurel Lodge in Camp David during the weekend after the attacks on the Trade Center and the Pentagon. While accounts of precisely what happened there vary, it seems that Bush did hear Wolfowitz out and was attracted to his ideas. For Wolfowitz not only stressed the threat that an unreformed Iraq posed, but suggested that a democratised Iraq could become the launchpad of democracy throughout the Arab world and a counterweight to Islamic extremism in the Middle East. This vision of the future apparently appealed to the evangelist in Bush.[22]

Since both the CIA and the State Department were against any military action in Iraq, the invasion of Iraq did not immediately become a part of the US' new war strategy. What therefore followed was a relentless campaign by the neo-conservative 'cabal' in the Defense Department to tilt the balance in favour of a military invasion. In a special issue of the *Weekly Standard,* published after 9/11, Gary Schmitt, who was by then the executive director of the *Project for the New American Century,* laid out the case for invading Iraq in an article titled 'Why Iraq?'. From beginning to end, this essay consisted of no more than a string of uncorroborated assertions about the extensive links that Al Qaeda had with Iraq's intelligence apparatus.

> Shortly before getting on a plane to fly to New Jersey from Europe in June 2000, Mohammed Atta, the lead hijacker of the first jet to slam into the World Trade Center and, apparently lead conspirator in the attacks of September 11, met with a senior Iraqi intelligence official. This was no chance encounter. Rather than take a flight from Germany, where he had been living, Atta traveled to Prague almost certainly for the purpose of meeting there with the Iraqi Intelligence official, Ahmed Samir Ahani... US officials have responded to reports of this meeting (and others between Atta and Iraqi intelligence operatives) by denying that they provide a 'smoking gun' tying Iraq to the attacks of September 11. That might be true by the standards of a court of law, but the United States is now engaged not in legal wrangling but in a deadly game of espionage and terrorism. In the world where we now operate the Prague meeting is about as clear and convincing as evidence gets—*especially since our intelligence service apparently has no agents in place of its own to tell us what was in fact going on.*
>
> This much, however, is beyond dispute: Regardless of the differences between their visions for the Middle East, Saddam Hussein and Osama bin Laden share an overriding objective—to expel the United States from the Middle East. *Alliances have been built on less.* (emphasis added)

Schmitt went on to cite much more of what he considered evidence of the Iraq–Al Qaeda link. He claimed, for instance, that the anthrax that was sent in letters to members of the American media and Senator Tom Daschle in September 2001 came from Iraq; that Ramzi Youssef, the mastermind behind the bombing of the World Trade Center in 1993, was linked to Iraq via a passport and other details, and that Saddam's intelligence had set up a special terrorist training site in Iraq. He strongly implied that this was for the use of Al Qaeda. Lastly Schmitt repeated the bald assertion that Iraq was continuing to build weapons of mass destruction. He concluded by citing German intelligence, which he said believed that it was not only pursuing a nuclear weapons programme but was within three years of having its first bomb.

In retrospect, it is apparent that Schmitt's article was little more than an outpouring of paranoia. His so-called evidence consisted of low grade reports of the kind that intelligence agencies all over the world get every day and routinely discard. That is how the CIA and the National Security Council had treated it. This was obviously the case with the crucial Prague meeting on which he had built most of his case for invading Iraq was built. US intelligence sources said that the information had come from Czech officials. It was used by Vice President Dick Cheney in NBC's 'Meet the Press' in late 2001. But the 2003 summer Congressional Report on the 9/11 attacks stated that "The CIA has been unable to establish that [Atta] left the United States or entered Europe in April under his true name or any known alias."[23]

Several other allegations by Schmitt were proved to be false by subsequent investigations. For instance, the anthrax was shown to have originated in the US. Ramzi Youssef, the mastermind behind World Trade Center 1993, is a Baluch from Pakistan. The allegation that he was in reality an Iraqi agent who stole the identity of a deceased Pakistani boy, was made by journalist Laurie Milroie, in a book titled *The War Against America.* Milroie had been commissioned or at the very least wholly subsidised, during the writing of the book by the American Enterprise Institute, the parent think tank of the neo-conservatives.[24] The Clinton administration had dismissed her as a 'nut case'[25], but in 2002 Milroie was able to get an endorsement for her book from none other than Paul Wolfowitz.[26]

Lastly the allegation that Iraq had a nuclear weapons programme in 2001, was conclusively disproved by the International Atomic Energy Agency's weapons inspectors in March 2003.[27]

But for those who were neither prepared to rehabilitate Saddam Hussein nor continue to depend upon Osama bin Laden's supposed animosity towards him, Schmitt's main argument remained irrefutable. The US simply could not gamble on Saddam not building links with

Al Qaeda in the future, for too much was at stake. Schmitt summed up the threat as follows:

> There is no question that Iraq has been involved in terrorism in the past.... But the far more important justification for extending the war on terrorism to toppling Saddam's regime is the terrorist threat he will pose in the near future when his effort to acquire still deadlier weapons comes to fruition."[28]

A short while after this article appeared, on 5 December 2001, nine members of the US Senate wrote to President Bush to remove Saddam Hussein from power. Citing unsourced reports that Saddam's "biological, chemical and nuclear weapons programs continue apace and may be back to pre-Gulf War status" the letter concluded that "in our own national interest Saddam Hussein must be removed from power".[29] The very next day, William Kristol attached the letter and circulated it with his own covering letter to 'Opinion Leaders'. His purpose was to underscore the fact that the proposed war on Iraq already had bipartisan support in the Senate, for the nine signatories were drawn from both the Republican and Democratic parties.

While the senators had only hinted at a possible connection between Iraq and terrorism, Kristol spelt it out in unambiguous terms.

> In recent weeks the President had made it clear that the war on terrorism is made even more urgent by the fact that terrorist states such as Iraq are actively developing nuclear, biological and chemical weapons. The nexus between terrorism and weapons of mass destruction makes the removal of Saddam Hussein key to success in the overall war against terrorism and a matter of considerable national urgency.[30]

By December 2001, as the President's speeches were indicating, and as Kristol noted, President Bush was more or less convinced of the need to invade Iraq to depose Saddam. All that remained was to convince the American public and Congress, and the US' allies in NATO. This was not likely to prove easy. As *New York Times* writer Bill Keller conceded, "a preemptive strike against an uncertain threat is perhaps the most radical new security notion of the post-Cold War era". But what Bush was contemplating went beyond even that. For in 2002 Iraq was too worn out by war and 12 years of sanctions to threaten anyone. By the US' army's own estimates, its armed forces were only a third of their pre-1991 size, and most of their weapons had been destroyed by attrition. Iraq did not thus have the capability to attack either its neighbours, or the US, or Israel. The war the far right was proposing was to prevent the development of that capability. This was not simply a preemptive action but an action to prevent the need for preemptive action in the future. Such a war was about as far away from Grotius' definition of a just war, as anyone could get.[31]

The Bush administration's campaign over the next twelve months to familiarise the world with a wholly novel idea was brilliantly constructed. In his State of the Union address in January 2002, Bush gave the nation and the world its first inkling that America had a new security doctrine that no longer relied upon deterrence to maintain the security of the United States, but would in future rely upon prevention (later renamed 'preemption') to do so.

> Our nation will continue to be steadfast and patient and persistent in the pursuit of two great objectives. First, we will shut down terrorist camps, disrupt terrorist plans, and bring terrorists to justice. And, second, we must *prevent* the terrorists and regimes who seek chemical, biological or nuclear weapons from threatening the United States and the world.....
> Our second goal is to *prevent* regimes that sponsor terror from threatening America or our friends and allies with weapons of mass destruction. Some of these regimes have been pretty quiet since September the 11th. But we know their true nature. North Korea is a regime arming with missiles and weapons of mass destruction, while starving its citizens. Iran aggressively pursues these weapons and exports terror, while an unelected few repress the Iranian people's hope for freedom.
> Iraq continues to flaunt its hostility toward America and to support terror. The Iraqi regime has plotted to develop anthrax, and nerve gas, and nuclear weapons for over a decade. This is a regime that has already used poison gas to murder thousands

of its own citizens—leaving the bodies of mothers huddled over their dead children. This is a regime that agreed to international inspections—then kicked out the inspectors. This is a regime that has something to hide from the civilized world. States like these, and their terrorist allies, constitute an *axis of evil*, arming to threaten the peace of the world. By seeking weapons of mass destruction, these regimes pose a grave and growing danger. They could provide these arms to terrorists, giving them the means to match their hatred. They could attack our allies or attempt to blackmail the United States. *In any of these cases, the price of indifference would be catastrophic"* (emphasis added).[32]

Bush took this a step further in his Graduation Day speech at the US Military Academy at West Point on 1 June 2002.

> The gravest danger to freedom lies at the perilous crossroads of radicalism and technology. When the spread of chemical and biological and nuclear weapons, along with ballistic missile technology—when that occurs, even weak states and small groups could attain a catastrophic power to strike great nations. Our enemies have declared this very intention, and have been caught seeking these terrible weapons. They want the capability to blackmail us, or to harm us, or to harm our friends—and we will oppose them with all our power.
> For much of the last century, America's defense relied on the Cold War doctrines of deterrence and containment. In some cases, those strategies still apply. But new threats also require new thinking. *Deterrence—the promise of massive retaliation against nations—means nothing against shadowy terrorist networks with no nation or citizens to defend. Containment is not possible when unbalanced dictators with weapons of mass destruction can deliver those weapons on missiles or secretly provide them to terrorist allies.*
> We cannot defend America and our friends by hoping for the best. We cannot put our faith in the word of tyrants, who

solemnly sign non-proliferation treaties, and then systemically break them. *If we wait for threats to fully materialize, we will have waited too long* (emphasis added).

The full doctrine of prevention, now re-labelled 'preemption' to claim for it the shelter of international law, emerged in the document entitled "The National Security Strategy of America", released by the White House on September 17. This was the first comprehensive review of America's security policy after the terrorist attacks of 9/11:

In the Cold War, especially following the Cuban missile crisis, we faced a generally status quo, risk-averse adversary. Deterrence was an effective defense. But deterrence based only upon the threat of retaliation is less likely to work against leaders of rogue states more willing to take risks, gambling with the lives of their people, and the wealth of their nations.

- In the Cold War, weapons of mass destruction were considered weapons of last resort whose use risked the destruction of those who used them. Today, our enemies see weapons of mass destruction as weapons of choice. For rogue states these weapons are tools of intimidation and military aggression against their neighbors. These weapons may also allow these states to attempt to blackmail the United States and our allies to prevent us from deterring or repelling the aggressive behavior of rogue states. Such states also see these weapons as their best means of overcoming the conventional superiority of the United States.
- Traditional concepts of deterrence will not work against a terrorist enemy whose avowed tactics are wanton destruction and the targeting of innocents; whose so-called soldiers seek martyrdom in death and whose most potent protection is statelessness. The overlap between states that sponsor terror and those that pursue WMD compels us to action.

For centuries, international law recognized that nations need not suffer an attack before they can lawfully take action to defend themselves against forces that present an imminent danger of attack. Legal scholars and international jurists often conditioned the legitimacy of preemption on the existence of an imminent threat—most often a visible mobilization of armies, navies, and air forces preparing to attack.

We must adapt the concept of imminent threat to the capabilities and objectives of today's adversaries. Rogue states and terrorists do not seek to attack us using conventional means. They know such attacks would fail. Instead, they rely on acts of terror and, potentially, the use of weapons of mass destruction—weapons that can be easily concealed, delivered covertly, and used without warning.

The targets of these attacks are our military forces and our civilian population, in direct violation of one of the principal norms of the law of warfare. As was demonstrated by the losses on September 11, 2001, mass civilian casualties is the specific objective of terrorists and these losses would be exponentially more severe if terrorists acquired and used weapons of mass destruction.

The United States has long maintained the option of preemptive actions to counter a sufficient threat to our national security. The greater the threat, the greater is the risk of inaction— and the more compelling the case for taking anticipatory action to defend ourselves, even if uncertainty remains as to the time and place of the enemy's attack. *To forestall or prevent such hostile acts by our adversaries, the United States will, if necessary, act preemptively* (emphasis added).[33]

The implications of this new doctrine for the international order were so far reaching that few grasped the changes that lay ahead. For with this doctrine the US announced that it was no longer bound by the two basic principles on which the Westphalian international order had rested: respect for a nation's sovereignty and non-interference in its domestic affairs. On the contrary, the US now claimed a virtually unlimited right to intervene in the internal affairs of other nations, not excluding the right to do so militarily, if it deemed this necessary to *prevent* the development of a future threat to its security. Perhaps, most significant of all, this doctrine buried the United Nations as the future seat of global authority and legitimacy. For the US reserved the right to determine whether developments within a nation could constitute a future threat to its security exclusively for itself. Nowhere either at West Point, or in the National Security Strategy did Bush mention involving any other nation or organisation in the determination of threat. This ruled out the gradual evolution of new international norms, mediated by the UN Security Council, such as was happening in response to the challenges posed by violations of human rights, and the need to protect the environment.

Preparation for War

By the time Bush unveiled his National Security Strategy, his administration had already chosen Iraq to be the first guinea pig. His reference to Iraq in his State of the Union address signalled the beginning of preparations to invade that country. By 5 July 2002 when the Defense Department first leaked details of a plan to invade Iraq to the *New York Times*[34], it was common knowledge not only in Washington but most of the European capitals, that the US was preparing a military invasion.[35] By the end of July, the Air Force had begun to transport men and materials to the Gulf.[36] The strategy that the US and UK actually used when they did invade Iraq on 20 March 2003, of hitting its decision-making centres first in the hope of paralysing the armed forces, was leaked to the *New York Times* as early as 30 July 2002.[37]

Bush informed the rest of the world about his plans for Iraq in a speech to the UN General assembly on 12 September 2002.

> In cells, in camps, terrorists are plotting further destruction and building new bases for their war against civilization. And our greatest fear is that terrorists will find a shortcut to their mad ambitions when an outlaw regime supplies them with the technologies to kill on a massive scale. *In one place and one*

> regime, we find all these dangers in their most lethal and aggressive forms, exactly the kind of aggressive threat the United Nations was born to confront.
> ...As we meet today, it's been almost four years since the last UN inspector set foot in Iraq—four years for the Iraqi regime to plan and to build and to test behind the cloak of secrecy. We know that Saddam Hussein pursued weapons of mass murder even when inspectors were in his country. Are we to assume that he stopped when they left?
> The history, the logic and the facts lead to one conclusion: Saddam Hussein's regime is a grave and gathering danger. To suggest otherwise is to hope against the evidence. To assume this regime's good faith is to bet the lives of millions and the peace of the world in a reckless gamble, and this is a risk we must not take.

This was followed by an elaborate justification for military action against Iraq that was to be repeated ad nauseam over the next six months. Iraq (read Saddam Hussein) was a threat to its neighbours: its own past actions gave ample proof of this. Iraq had built and used weapons of mass destruction not only against Iran but also against its own people, the Iraqi Kurds. The Iraqi regime was a particularly horrible, tyrannical one, that had imprisoned, tortured and killed its own people by the thousands, and committed unspeakably barbarous acts against them. Lastly, Saddam Hussein had systematically nurtured terrorism for use against Iran and Israel, and against Iraqi dissenters abroad. It therefore posed a serious and continuing threat to its neighbours, to its own people, to the rest of the world and to the US.[38]

But Bush also used the occasion to unveil his novel doctrine of preventive attack, and serve the UN notice that the old rules of the Westphalian state system no longer applied. The UN, he warned, faced two choices: it could join the US in framing and enforcing the new rules of international engagement, or it could render itself obsolete.

Delegates to the General Assembly, we have been more than patient. We've tried sanctions. We've tried the carrot of oil for food and the stick of coalition military strikes. But Saddam Hussein has defied all these efforts and continues to develop weapons of mass destruction.

The first time we may be completely certain he has nuclear weapons is when, God forbid, he uses one. We owe it to all our citizens to do everything in our power to *prevent* that day from coming...

My nation will work with the U.N. Security Council to meet our common challenge. If Iraq's regime defies us again, the world must move deliberately, decisively to hold Iraq to account. We will work with the U.N. Security Council for the necessary resolutions.

But the purposes of the United States should not be doubted. The Security Council resolutions will be enforced, the just demands of peace and security will be met or action will be unavoidable and a regime that has lost its legitimacy will also lose its power...

With every step the Iraqi regime takes toward gaining and deploying the most terrible weapons, our own options to confront that regime will narrow. And if an emboldened regime were to supply these weapons to terrorists allies, then the attacks of September 11 would be a prelude to far greater horrors.

If we meet our responsibilities, if we overcome this danger, we can arrive at a very different future. The people of Iraq can shake off their captivity. They can one day join a democratic Afghanistan and a democratic Palestine inspiring reforms throughout the Muslim world....Neither of these outcomes is certain. Both have been set before us. We must choose between a world of fear and a world of progress. *We cannot stand by and do nothing while dangers gather....*

By heritage and by choice, the United States of America will make that stand. And, delegates to the United Nations, you have the power to make that stand, as well (emphasis added).[39]

In an off-the-cuff remark not pasted on the White House website, Bush was even more explicit: "The UN can join us", he told the assembled delegates with a disarming smile, "or it can remain a debating society".

Undermining the United Nations

Although Bush and Blair kept insisting, right till the week before the war, that the Bush administration had not 'yet' decided to invade Iraq, its determination to do so no matter what Saddam Hussein did or did not do, was betrayed by the lengths to which it went to sabotage any initiative that the UN might take to make Iraq abide by the Security Council's resolutions of the previous twelve years and thus make a military invasion more difficult to justify. This tactic was first employed in early July. The Pentagon leaked its war plans to *The New York Times* exactly a day after Kofi Annan, Secretary General of the United Nations, began negotiating with Iraqi foreign minister Naji Sabri, in Vienna for the return of the inspectors to Iraq. The talks collapsed hours after the newspaper hit the stands.[40]

The Iraqis soon realised what the Americans were trying to do. On 2 August 2002, in a move that caught the US and UK by surprise, they invited Hans Blix the head of UNMOVIC and Mohammed el Baradei head of the IAEA, to visit Baghdad as soon as possible to work out the modalities for the return of the inspectors.[41] On 21 September 2002 Kofi Annan gave Iraq some kind of reassurance that paragraph 22 of UNSC Resolution 687 would in fact be honoured, and sanctions lifted as soon as the UN inspectors pronounced Iraq to be free of weapons of mass destruction.[42] This prompted Iraq to accept the return of the inspectors. Another round of talks was scheduled for the end of September, to be held in Vienna, with Hans Blix, the head of UNMOVIC. This was to settle the practical details of the return of the inspectors. On the eve of these talks, the US Air Force launched a bombing raid on Basra, and destroyed a radar system. As the Russian government pointed out, if the purpose was to scupper the Vienna talks, it could hardly have been better timed.

When the Iraqis refused to be provoked and agreed on 1 October to allow the inspectors back into the country, the US State

Department announced immediately that it would 'go into thwart mode'. On the very next day it leaked a draft of the resolution that it was placing before the Security Council. The contents of this draft were virtually a plan for unopposed invasion and therefore designed to be rejected by Iraq. The choice of sites for inspection was not to be made by UNMOVIC alone but by 'any member country', an euphemism for the US and UK. The inspectors too could be chosen by 'any country' and would enjoy unrestricted rights of entry into and exit from Iraq. They would be "accompanied...by sufficient US security forces to protect them". They would have the right to declare exclusion zones, no-fly zones and air transit corridors; allowed to fly and land as many surveillance aircraft of any kind that they wanted, to set up encrypted communication networks, and seize any equipment they chose to.[43]

The US' insistence on the right to appoint inspectors who would work with UNMOVIC, was a particularly sore issue with the Iraqi government which had acutely resented the way in which the CIA had infiltrated its agents into UNSCOM in the 1991–98 period. It also had not forgotten that in 1998, selected inspectors, like the American Richard Spertzel, had deliberately refused to certify that the Presidential sites were free of biological weapons, in order to make sure that the weapons inspectors could never declare Iraq to be free of weapons of mass destruction.[44] To make certain that Saddam could not frustrate their war plans by allowing UNMOVIC to resume weapons inspections under the Security Council's Resolution 1284, the US and the UK instructed Blix not to enter Iraq till a new resolution had been adopted. This resolution itself was intended to be so humiliating that it would leave Iraq little option but to reject it.

The Struggle for Empire

Throughout the six months that separated Bush's UN speech from the invasion of Iraq, his administration kept insisting that UN Resolution 687, and its successors had given the US and other members of the UN all the authority they needed to invade the country and depose Saddam Hussein.[45] So why then did the Bush administration work so hard to obtain the cover of a new UN resolution for its invasion of Iraq? Why did George Bush personally lay out his case for taking military action to oust Saddam Hussein's regime in Iraq?

One explanation, often aired in the US media, when it became clear that it was not going to get the Security Council's endorsement to use 'all necessary means' to disarm Iraq, was that that Bush fell into a 'UN Trap' because of a combination of excessive caution and overconfidence in the State Department. Secretary of State Colin Powell persuaded him that a UN-mandated military action would have fewer adverse repercussions in the Middle East, and would be more acceptable to the world at large. He also assured him that despite their reservations against endorsing an unprovoked invasion of Iraq, France, China and Russia would not use their veto to thwart the US. The State Department was also sure that it would be possible to rope in the nine votes needed to pass a resolution in the Security Council that cleared the way for military action. According to the neo-conservatives who were driving the US' Iraq policy, they erred on all counts.[46]

This explanation of the Bush administration's actions is disingenuous because it ignores the fact that Bush was seeking the endorsement of a security doctrine that had never been invoked before, and ran directly against all accepted norms. Having decided to apply his new security doctrine to Iraq, Bush faced the task of gaining acceptance for it from the world community. It was therefore neither caution nor overconfidence that drove the State Department, but an awareness of the enormity of what the US was asking the world to accept. Colin Powell was acutely aware that the aims of the proposed military action went far beyond those of Operation Desert Fox, which the US and UK had also invoked earlier UN resolutions to justify. 'Desert Fox' had aimed at disciplining Saddam Hussein and not at overthrowing him. Its military purpose had been to degrade Iraq's capacity to produce weapons of mass destruction. Its political goal had been to punish him for not cooperating with, and then throwing out, the weapons inspectors. By definition, therefore, it had left him the option of retaining power by cooperating wholeheartedly with the United Nations Security Council resolutions. Desert Fox did not, therefore, challenge the Westphalian international order.

By contrast the goal of 'regime change' that Bush had espoused found no mention in the resolutions on Iraq; unambiguously violated Article 2 (7) of the UN charter, and therefore constituted a direct assault on the Westphalian order. If the US pursued it unilaterally, it would take the world into uncharted territory in which none of the rules of conduct that had governed international relations during the previous three centuries would remain in force.

The State Department therefore wished to minimise the break with the existing order, and maximise the continuity. The only way to do this was to prove that Iraq was deliberately flouting UN Security Council resolutions that it had itself accepted, and had therefore made it necessary to use force to uphold the authority of the Security Council. From the point of view of the neo-conservatives, the Achilles' heel of this strategy was that it gave those who opposed the invasion of Iraq a chance to propose an alternative. If Iraq agreed to take back the inspectors, cooperated wholeheartedly with them, answered all their questions, allowed them free and unfettered access to all sites, and permitted them to interview whomsoever they chose, and if the inspectors declared themselves satisfied with the cooperation they were receiving, then there would be no need for an invasion or for a change of regime in Iraq.

This strategy therefore backfired. The neo-conservative think tank to which Bush owed so much of his policy, *The Project for the New American Century*, had foreseen this possibility and was therefore stridently opposed to it. In an editorial in the *Weekly Standard*, William Kristol and Robert Kagan jointly warned the administration against falling into what they called 'The UN Trap':

> There is no point in kidding ourselves: the inspection process we are about to embark upon is a trap...it was designed to satisfy those in Europe who oppose military action in Iraq; *and it was negotiated by those within the Bush administration*

who have never made any secret of their opposition to military action in Iraq" (emphasis added).⁴⁷

In the months that followed, the more Iraq cooperated with the UN inspectors under Hans Blix and Mohammed al Baradei, the stronger became the case against military action and the more difficult did it become for the US to push through its invasion plans and still retain a cloak of legitimacy. In the end the US failed and had to fall back on the extremely dubious cover provided by earlier UN resolutions. But the prolonged battle in the UN Security Council that preceded its failure etched out in the sharpest possible way the alternatives the world faced as it struggled to cope with the impact of globalisation upon the Westphalian international order. The first was to return to a Hobbesian world in which might constituted right, and the US was a global policeman, judge and executioner, accountable to no other country or organisation. The second was a world governed increasingly by the charter of the United Nations, in which the authority to sanction the use of force against nation states was vested increasingly in the UN Security Council.

During their struggle to retain a cloak of legitimacy for their invasion of Iraq, the US and the UK left no stone unturned to persuade the world at large that Iraq had concealed weapons of mass destruction and created new facilities for manufacturing them; that it was still bent upon deceiving the weapons inspectors and retaining its destructive capability, and therefore that it was itself leaving the international community with no alternative but to disarm it by force. On the other, they relentlessly pursued the build-up of military forces in the Gulf, the establishment of command headquarters and advance headquarters in Qatar and Kuwait, and finally, from the end of February, well before Hans Blix and Mohammed el Baradei delivered their last reports, in launching sustained air raids on Iraqi airfields, radar and other military installations well beyond the 'no-fly' zones in order to 'soften them up' for the invasion that was to come.

In both the charade at the UN and the buildup to war, there was the closest possible cooperation between the US and the UK. Twelve days after Bush spoke at the UN and invited the world to join the

US in its crusade against Saddam Hussein's regime, the British government released a report, allegedly culled from its intelligence sources and analysis that claimed to prove, beyond reasonable doubt that Iraq had and continued to manufacture WMD.

> Saddam has continued to make progress with his illicit weapons programmes. As a result of the intelligence we judge that Iraq has:

- Continued to produce chemical and biological agents;
- Military plans for the use of chemical and biological weapons including against its own Shia population. *Some of these weapons are deployable within 45 minutes of an order to use them;*
- Command and control arrangements in place to use chemical and biological weapons;
- Developed mobile laboratories or military use, corroborating earlier reports about the mobile production of biological warfare agents;
- Pursued illegal programmes to procure controlled materials of potential use in the production of chemical and biological weapons programmes;
- Tried covertly to acquire technology and materials which could be used in the production of nuclear weapons;
- Sought significant quantities of uranium from Africa, despite having no active civil nuclear power programme that could require it;[48]
- Recalled specialist to work on its nuclear programme;
- Illegally retained up to 20 Al-Hussein missiles with a range of 650 km capable of carrying chemical or biological warheads; started deploying it al-Samoud liquid propellant missile and has used the absence of weapons inspectors to extend its range to at least 200 kms, which is beyond he limit of 150 km imposed by the United Nations;
- Started producing the solid -propellant Ababil-100, and is making efforts to extend its range of at least 200 km...
- Constructed a new engine test stand or the development of missiles capable of reaching the UK Sovereign Base Area in Cyprus

96 • The End of Saddam Hussein

and NATO members (Greece and Turkey), as well as Iraq's Gulf neighbour and Israel;
- Pursued illegal programmes to procure materials for use in its illegal development of long range missiles;
- Learnt lessons from previous weapons inspections and has already begun to conceal sensitive equipment and documentation in advance of the return of the inspectors.

The report went into a great deal of detail, listing chemicals and biological materials producing factories and plans that had previously contained units devoted to producing WMD, and giving aerial photographs that showed that these had been rebuilt after UNSCOM left Iraq.

Less than a fortnight after Blair released the British report, the Bush administration released the CIA's assessment of Iraq's Weapons of Mass Destruction. This report had nothing to add to the British report[49] and reached the same conclusion:

> Iraq *has continued* its weapons of mass destruction (WMD) programme in defiance of UN resolutions and restrictions... Baghdad *has* chemical and biological weapons as well as missiles with ranges in excess of UN restrictions; *if left unchecked, it will probably have a nuclear weapon during this decade.*
> ...Since inspections ended in 1998, Iraq has maintained its chemical weapons effort, energized its missile program and invested more heavily in biological weapons...
> Iraq has largely rebuilt missile and biological weapons facilities damaged during Operation Desert Fox and has expanded its chemical and biological infrastructure under the cover of civilian production.....
> Iraq's aggressive attempts to obtain proscribed high strength aluminum tubes are of significant concern...these tubes could be used in a centrifuge enrichment program. Most intelligence specialists assess this to be the intended use but some believe that these tubes are probably intended or conventional weapons programs.

The distinctive feature of both the reports was their absolute freedom from doubt. Nowhere in the executive summaries of was there even a hint of reservation about the conclusions they had reached. It was almost as if the writers knew that news agencies and nine out of ten newspaper correspondents would not go beyond this section of the paper or would not have the space to print anything more.

But the rest of the world was not so easily convinced. Analysts writing for the print media, and many TV commentators concluded that neither report had much to add to what was already known. For instance, of the 50-page British report, only 16 pages were devoted to the current situation. The rest was a rehash of UNSCOM's findings and time worn accusations against the Saddam regime for its violation of human rights in Iraq. These 16 pages did not contain a single piece of hard information that showed beyond even reasonable doubt that Iraq had revived its WMD programmes. For instance its key paragraph on nuclear weapons reads as follows:

> Intelligence shows that the present Iraqi programme is *almost certainly* seeking an indigenous ability to enrich uranium to the level needed for a nuclear weapon. It indicates that the approach is based on gas centrifuge uranium enrichment, one of the routes Iraq was following for producing fissile material before the Gulf War. But Iraq needs certain key equipment, including gas centrifuge components and components for the production of fissile material before a nuclear bomb could be developed (emphasis added).[50]

The small but crucial reservation, 'almost certainly', finds no echo in the executive summary given above. Had it done so the summary would have read, 'May be trying covertly to acquire.... nuclear weapons'. But it did not.

The US and UK reports failed to sway the doubters on the UN Security Council. They were therefore compelled to strike a compromise with France, Russia and other members. This was reflected in Resolution 1441, passed on 8 November 2002 whose operative part read as follows:

> The Security Council... Acting under Chapter VII of the Charter of the United Nations,
>
> 1. Decides that *Iraq has been and remains in material breach of its obligations* under relevant resolutions, including Resolution 687 (1991), in particular through Iraq's failure to cooperate with United Nations inspectors and the IAEA, and to complete the actions required under paragraphs 8 to 13 of Resolution 687 (1991);
> 2. Decides, while acknowledging paragraph 1 above, *to afford Iraq, by this resolution, a final opportunity to comply with its disarmament obligations under relevant resolutions of the council*; and accordingly decides to set up an enhanced inspection regime with the aim of bringing to full and verified completion the disarmament process established by Resolution 687 (1991) and subsequent resolutions of the council;
> 3. Decides that, in order to begin to comply with its disarmament obligations, in addition to submitting the required biannual declarations, the government of Iraq shall provide to UNMOVIC, the IAEA, and the council, not later than 30 days from the date of this resolution, a currently accurate, full, and complete declaration of all aspects of its programs to develop chemical, biological, and nuclear weapons, ballistic missiles, and other delivery systems such as unmanned aerial vehicles and dispersal systems designed for use on aircraft, including any holdings and precise locations of such weapons, components, sub-components, stocks of agents, and related material and equipment, the locations and work of its research, development and production facilities, as well as all other chemical, biological, and nuclear programs, including any which it claims are for purposes not related to weapon production or material;
> 4. Decides that false statements or omissions in the declarations submitted by Iraq pursuant to this resolution and failure by

Iraq at any time to comply with, and cooperate fully in the implementation of, this resolution shall constitute a further material breach of Iraq's obligations and *will be reported to the council for assessment* in accordance with paragraph 11 and 12 below; ...

11. Directs the executive chairman of UNMOVIC and the director general of the IAEA to report immediately to the council any interference by Iraq with inspection activities, as well as any failure by Iraq to comply with its disarmament obligations, including its obligations regarding inspections under this resolution;
12. *Decides to convene immediately* upon receipt of a report in accordance with paragraphs 4 or 11 above, *in order to consider the situation* and the need for full compliance with all of the relevant council resolutions in order to secure international peace and security;
13. Recalls, in that context, that *the council has repeatedly warned Iraq that it will face serious consequences as a result of its continued violations of its obligations*.[51]

As the absence of any weapons of mass destruction were later to show, this resolution was deeply flawed. It started off with a completely one-sided interpretation of the events that led to the withdrawal of UNSCOM from Iraq in 1998. All of the blame for this was laid unhesitatingly upon Iraq, whereas in reality UNSCOM was cold bloodedly manipulated by the US through a chairman of less than shining integrity, to create a situation in which the economic sanctions against Iraq could be kept in place indefinitely. Second, the resolution started by dismissing Iraq's protestations that it had accounted for all of its weapons of mass destruction out of hand, and proclaiming that Iraq was, and remained, in material breach of its obligations it proclaimed in its first operational clause. Since the US and UK failed to find any weapons of mass destruction even six months after invading and occupying Iraq, this 'finding' turned out to be a figment of the Anglo-Saxon imagination. If the premise of 1441 was false, then it followed that the Security Council had been wrong to place all of the responsibility for restoring normality in the region upon Iraq. What Resolution 1441 demonstrated with brutal clarity was the extent to which justice and objectivity had become the first victims of the US' new national security doctrine and the resulting assault upon the Westphalian international order.

But even this miserable excuse for international adjudication made it clear that no country had the right to take unilateral recourse to war. Paragraphs 1 to 10 incorporated the stiff conditions that the US and UK had demanded in their draft of the resolution, but paragraphs 4 and 12 incorporated the insistence of the majority of the Security Council members that only the Security Council could decide that Iraq was in further material breach of its obligations. No single member or group of members, acting on its own, could make this judgement. Even less could it, or they, take military action and claim to be acting under the umbrella of the Security Council. Paragraph 13 spelt out that it was for the Security Council to decide when Iraq would have to face 'serious consequences', an euphemism for military action, if it failed to meet its obligations.

According to the resolution, Iraq had 30 days to submit a full and detailed account of all of its weapons of mass destruction. UNMOVIC and the IAEA had a further 60 days to certify that Iraq had given a full account, that it was cooperating fully in the verification process, and that the WMD that remained were being destroyed. But the weapons inspection began even before Iraq's 30 days were up. Weapons inspectors began moving into Baghdad on November 18 and the first inspections began on 27 November. By 3 December, inspectors in Baghdad were telling journalists that they were receiving 'full cooperation'[52]. These preliminary indications of Iraqi cooperation put the US in an increasingly difficult position. Iraq would be in 'further material breach' of its obligations only if it failed to get the inspectors' certification of full cooperation. Iraq seemed determined not to give it that opportunity.

It is not therefore wholly surprising that when Iraq presented a 12,000-page document to UNMOVIC on 7 December, both the US and UK took only days to denounce it as incomplete. The document was in Arabic and had to be translated first before its contents could be examined to determine whether Iraq had lied, or was otherwise in material breach of its obligations. Despite that, it took Colin Powell only ten days to denounce it as an attempt to inundate the inspectors with worthless material in order to distract them from the issues on which it was silent. Powell categorically refused to believe Iraq's categorical assertion, when presenting the report, that it was completely free of weapons of mass destruction. He pointed out that the document had not accounted for stocks of chemical and biological weapons and precursor compounds that had remained unaccounted for when UNSCOM pulled out of Iraq in December 1998. He thus seized upon precisely the same weakness in the evidence of Iraq's compliance with Resolution 687, that had been exploited by the Clinton administration and the complaisant Butler, four years earlier, to prolong the economic sanctions. This was that Iraq could not produce incontrovertible proof of the amounts of chemical and biological weapons it claimed to have destroyed unilaterally before the July 1991 deadline for unilateral destruction expired.

A day later, British Foreign Secretary Jack Straw baldly accused Saddam Hussein of lying about his WMD programmes and insisted that Iraq was in 'further material breach' of its obligations.[53] Even as he was doing so, the British government began to charter ships to move heavy armour and weapons to the Gulf.[54] Exactly a day after Straw had set the ball rolling, the US also accused Iraq of being in further material breach of its obligations.

A pattern of cooperation, amounting to collusion, had thus begun to emerge. The US and UK would discuss their strategy in private, then the UK would take the lead in making the case for an invasion, and the US would follow. The reasoning behind this strategy was not difficult to follow—the UK had not so far been a target of terrorism by Al Qaeda, and was therefore not a victim. Blair also spared no effort to convince the world, and his own party, that he was not overtly committed to an invasion of Iraq. Thus Britain's 'findings' had greater prima facie credibility, especially in Europe, whose support the US deemed essential to its plans.

Unfortunately for the desperate duo, events on the ground did not go the way they wanted them to. On 31 December, five weeks after the weapons inspectors began their work, they admitted finding 'zilch'. By this time they had visited the most important of the sites that the US and UK intelligence reports had submitted to them as the most likely places to find Saddam's weapons of mass destruction or production facilities. This was therefore a significant admission. But the inspectors also said that they had received very little guidance from Western intelligence sources. The two remarks cast a great deal of doubt upon the veracity and accuracy of the intelligence reports on whose basis the US and UK had built their case for war.

The US' plans received a further setback when Hans Blix and Mohammed el Baradei presented an interim report on 27 January. Baradei made it clear that his teams had not discovered any evidence of a nuclear weapons development programme and asked for more time to investigate a number of specific allegations, such as Iraq's purchase of aluminium tubes for gas centrifuges and its reported attempt to purchase uranium yellow cake from Niger. Blix reported that that in over 400 site visits, including visits to all the suspect sites named and photographed by British and American intelligence, UNMOVIC and IAEA had not found a single new chemical or biological weapons making facility or actual stockpile of proscribed weapons. On 27 January, the only facility over which some doubt remained was a reconstructed plant at Al Fallujah, that the Iraqis claimed was intended to produce phenols and chlorine. UNMOVIC had not ruled this out but wanted more time to determine whether it could also be used to manufacture chemical weapons. (It later gave that plant too a clean bill of health). The only infringement of the ban against the manufacture of proscribed weapons that UNMOVIC had discovered was a minor one: two missiles that Iraq had developed had actual ranges of 161 and 183 kms, against the limit of 150 kms prescribed by the Security Council.

But Blix also informed the Council that Iraq's 7 December declaration had not answered several of the questions that had been listed in UNSCOM's March 1999 report—the so-called Amorim report—and was therefore incomplete. The bulk of UNMOVIC's doubts centred on the inconsistencies and omissions in Iraq's account of what had happened to stocks of chemical and biological weapons or precursors that were known to have existed in 1991. So long as these existed, the possibility that Iraq was holding on to some WMD could not be completely ruled out. He also said that while the Iraqi authorities had cooperated well in the *process* of weapons inspection, on the *substance* of inspection, which required it to come forward on its own with details of its programmes, and explanations of what had happened to them, it had not been sufficiently forthcoming. He concluded that Iraq seemed not to have come to a genuine acceptance of the need to comply with the UN resolutions. Blix urged Iraq to cooperate in substance with UNMOVIC and the Security Council to remove the doubts that remained.

Britain and the US immediately seized upon his caveats to accuse Iraq of being in further material breach of UN resolutions. The Bush administration had been saying for some time that Resolution 1441 had two components: Iraq had first to make a full declaration of its remaining and reconstituted Weapons of Mass Destruction capability, and second, had to cooperate fully with UNMOVIC in rooting it out and destroying it. Iraq had failed the first test. But other members of the Security Council were not convinced. Iraq had insisted that it did not have any weapons of mass destruction. If this was true, then it could not declare weapons of mass destruction that it did not have. The fact that nothing had been found by UNMOVIC till then left the possibility open that Iraq was indeed telling the truth. Only further painstaking investigation by UNMOVIC, with the full cooperation of Iraq, could resolve this question. The Blix report therefore strengthened the hands of those who wanted weapons inspectors to be given more time to complete their work and Iraq another chance to cooperate fully with them.

Scepticism of the US case for war was deepened by an interview Blix gave to the New York Times on 31 January.[55] 'Mr. Blix', the newspaper reported,

> took issue with what he said were Secretary of State Colin L. Powell's claims that the inspectors had found that Iraqi officials were hiding and moving illicit materials within and outside of Iraq to prevent their discovery. He said that the inspectors had reported no such incidents.

Similarly, he said, he had not seen convincing evidence that Iraq was sending weapons scientists to Syria, Jordan or any other country to prevent them from being interviewed. Nor had he any reason to believe, as President Bush charged in his State of the Union speech, that Iraqi agents were posing as scientists.

He further disputed the Bush administration's allegations that his inspection agency might have been penetrated by Iraqi agents, and that sensitive information might have been leaked to Baghdad, compromising the inspections.

Finally, he said, he had seen no persuasive indications of Iraqi ties to Al Qaeda, which Mr. Bush also mentioned in his speech. "There are other states where there appear to be stronger links," such as Afghanistan, Mr. Blix said, noting that he had no intelligence reports on this issue.[56]

Faced by a rising tide of scepticism about the reliability of their intelligence reports, American and British spokesmen first refused to elaborate further on the information they possessed, other than to say that their information was based upon intelligence inputs, much of it from sources within Iraq who would be imperilled if more precise details were aired in public. But faced with a further weakening of the case for an invasion, the US Secretary of State Colin Powell took the unprecedented step of personally presenting more detailed intelligence information to the Security Council. The new information in his 35-minute presentation on 5 February was:

- Two monitored conversations showing that there was a determined effort to clean out or 'evacuate' sensitive materials on the eve of the IAEA inspectors' visit.
- 2,000 pages of sensitive documents relating to Iraq's nuclear weapons programme were discovered in the home of an Iraqi scientist. This was proof that the regime was hiding sensitive documents in the homes of Iraqi scientist and Baath party members.
- Two photos taken by satellite. The first showed munitions

bunkers with two telltale facilities, one of them a decontamination vehicle, which were 'signature' items that betrayed the presence of chemical weapons. The second showed the same bunkers without the signature items. UN inspectors' vehicles could be seen entering the compund at the bottom of the picture. Powell concluded that the chemical weapons had been moved minutes before the inspectors arrived and hazarded the guess that the Iraqis had been 'tipped off'. He also asserted that the inspectors were under constant surveillance by Iraqi intelligence.
- One day before Powell was to speak the British, again not coincidentally, distributed a paper prepared by its intelligence agencies that described 'in exquisite detail', Iraq's deception activities. Alluding to it Powell called it a 'fine paper'.
- Three more photographs of ballistic missile facilities showing large cargo trucks and a truck mounted crane. Powell concluded that since these sites were known to UNMOVIC, the Iraqis were sanitising them before its visit.
- As evidence that Iraq was preventing access to its scientists Powell claimed that on Saddam's orders Iraqi officials issued a false death certificate to one Iraqi scientist, who went into hiding. A dozen other experts had been placed in house arrest not in their own houses, to prevent their interrogation.
- The first hand account of an engineer involved in the program, which proved that Iraq had mobile biological weapons laboratories mounted on trucks and railway wagons, that could within a matter of months replace all of biological agents that Iraq had produced before the Gulf War. Powell produced evidence from three other such human sources. On the basis of their evidnce the US had concluded that Iraq had at least seven mobile bioweapon production facilities.
- A taped conversation between two officers of the Second Republican Guard, which strongly suggests that they were stocking 'these horrible nerve agents'.
- Covert attempts to purchase high strength aluminum tubes of a tolerance specifications far higher than that used by the

US in its own rocket manufacture. The demand for higher and higher tolerance requirements in successive batches of tubes. The purchase in its last batch of tubes with an anodised coating on its inner and outer surfaces.
- Attempts to purchase a magnet production plant from Russia, India, Slovenia, and Romania, to produce magnet of 20 to 30 grams weight—the size required in a gas centrifuge plant.
- Attempt to buy machines that can balance Gas centrifuge rotors.
- The purchase of 380 SA-2 rocket engines in violation of Resolution 687, as late as December 2002, after the passage of Resolution 1441.
- The construction of a rocket engine test stand capable of testing engines with a range of 1200kms.
- The development of an UAV (unmanned aerial vehicle) capable of flying 500 kms non-stop. This could be used to deliver chemical and biological weapons

In all, Powell asserted that Iraq could have 25,000 litres of Anthrax stored in a dry form that would last years; 550 tons of mustard gas; 30,000 empty munitions and 500 tons of chemical agents to fill them with, and 6,500 chemical bombs left unaccounted from the Iran-Iraq war. At a conservative estimate, he concluded, Iraq had between 100 tons and 500 tons of chemical weapons agents. This was enough to fill 16,000 battlefield rockets. It was not clear whether this included or was in addition to the amounts he had mentioned earlier.

Powell also went to some lengths to establish that Saddam's regime had formed a link with Al Qaeda, and therefore that the transfer of WMD to it was at best only weeks or months away. Noting that Al Qaeda had set up an armed camp under an organisation called the Ansar-ul-Islam in Kurdish territory not controlled by Iraq, Powell asserted that it had been invited to Iraq by an agent of Baghdad who was at the most senior levels of this organisation. In May 2002, its leader, Abu Musab al Zarqawi had visited Baghdad for medical treatment. During his visit no fewer than two dozen extremists had converged on Baghdad to establish a base of operations there. Two Al Qaeda operatives arrested crossing from Iraq into Saudi Arabia were believed to be part of this new cell. Powell then went on to detail acusatons that Iraq had reached an understanding with Osama bin Laden as far back as the early 1990s when the latter was still in Sudan. Osama would spare Iraq in exchange for unspecified help from it. An Iraqi diplomat in Pakistan had been the liaison between Al Qaeda and Baghdad between the late 1990s and 2001.

Powell's speech had a powerful impact upon the listeners, the media and, above all, on American public opinion. Opinion polls showed a significant decline in opposition to a war on Iraq in the US. The very next day, in a formal statement to the press at the White House, Bush said,

> Saddam Hussein was required to fully cooperate in the disarmament of his regime; he has not done so. Saddam Hussein was given a final chance; he is throwing that chance away. Saddam Hussein can now be expected to begin another round of empty concessions, transparently false denials. No doubt, he will play a last-minute game of deception. The game is over.

It did not take long however, for the shaky base of some at least of Powell's conclusions to surface. In his statement to the Security Council on 14 February, Mohammed el Baradei stated that the 2,000 pages of documents found at the scientists home referred to "activities or sites already known to the IAEA and appear(ed) to be the personal files of the scientist in whose home they were found...Nothing contained in the document alters the conclusion previously drawn by the IAEA concerning the extent of Iraq's laser enrichment program".

Blix also punctured another of Powell's assertions. Warning the Council about the limitations of intelligence and its susceptibility to misinterpretation he said,

> The presentation of intelligence information by the US Secretary of State suggested that Iraq had prepared for

inspections by cleaning up sites and removing evidence of proscribed weapons programmes. I would like to comment only on one case, which we are familiar with, namely, the trucks identified by analysts as being for chemical decontamination at a munitions depot. This was a declared site, and it was certainly one of the sites Iraq would have expected us to inspect. We have noted that the two satellite images of the site were taken several weeks apart. The reported movement of munitions at the site could just as easily have been a routine activity as a movement of proscribed munitions in anticipation of imminent inspection. Our reservation on this point does not detract from our appreciation of the briefing.

Other holes appeared soon afterwards in the case against Iraq. Most of these related to the deliberate abuse of intelligence by the British and American governments to hustle their own legislatures into approving of the war on Iraq. Within a day of Powell's speech, the British intelligence report that detailed Iraq's evasion of the inspectors to which he had referred to with so much admiration turned out to be a crude fabrication out of published material and a student's Ph.D thesis of the late 1990s.[57] The document had been cobbled together in the Communications Department of the Prime Minister's office. It was thus anything but an intelligence report on current Iraqi evasion strategies.

A far worse scandal erupted over the British allegation, also picked up by Washington, that Iraq had been trying to buy 500 tons of uranium yellow cake, enough to extract 100 bombs' worth of fissile uranium, from Niger. It had been referred to tangentially in Blair's dossier against Saddam Hussein of 24 September. Although Powell had not referred to it at the UN he had apparently used it in briefings of the Senate Foreign Relations Committee to still doubts about the need to launch an invasion of Iraq, in the run to the passage of a joint congressional resolution authorising the President to declare war on Iraq.[58] Bush finally incorporated it into his state of the union speech for 2003. On 7 March, Mohammed el Baradei told the

Security Council that the documents concerning the deal were fakes. One of the correspondents, the Niger Minister for foreign affairs Allele Habibou had been out of office since 1989. The uranium yellow cake produced by the Niger company was also so completely pre-sold to France, Japan and Spain, that it was virtually impossible to siphon off such a large quantity. Investigation by journalists showed that the forgery may have originated in a British programme or spreading disinformation called the Information Operations (I/Ops). When the British report on Iraq's WMD came out IAEA had repeatedly asked the British government for copies of the concerned letters, but had been refused. The Americans had however obtained them and eventually IAEA obtained them from the Iraq Nuclear Verification Office in the Bush administration.[59]

Seymour Hersh, who first broke the story, left open the possibility that the US had been duped. But a subsequent news report in the *New York Times* strongly suggested that the US had known that the documents were fakes at least since February 2002, but had used the supposed information to persuade Congress to declare war on Iraq nonetheless.[60]

In the three weeks that elapsed between 27 January and the second report of the inspectors under Resolution 1441 on 14 February Iraq made increasingly desperate and, in retrospect, pitiable efforts to meet some of Blix's criticisms of its attitude to UNMOVIC. Sometime in January, facing criticism of its declaration, Iraq had invited a delegation from South Africa to learn from it how it had gone about its destruction of WMD. During a visit to Baghdad on 8–9 February, Blix and el Baradei ran into its members. During their meetings with Iraqi oficials, Iraq ageed to remove all constraints on the use of surveillance aircraft for weapons inspection and monitoring. On 13 February, the day that Blix was to address the Council, Iraq announced domestic legislation banning research and manufacture of all proscribed weapons. Finally, Iraq began to actively persuade it scientists to agree to interviews by UNMOVIC inspectors, in the absence of tape recorders, and Iraqi officials. These measures made Blix give a far more upbeat report to the Security Council on February 14. But Colin Powell dismissed all of these acts saying "These are all tricks being played on us (the Council)". But by then the US and UK were beginning to look more and more isolated. Opinion both within the Security Council and around the world continued ti harden against war and in favour of continuing the inspection regime.[61]

The case for war received one final round of buffeting when Blix and el Baradei submitted their (as it turned out) final reports to the UN Security Council on 7 March.

El Baradei's report refuted categoricaly the US assertion that high strength aluminum tubes Iraq was importing were for uranium enrichment:

> Extensive field investigation and document analysis have failed to uncover any evidence that Iraq intended to use these 81mm tubes for any project other than the reverse engineering of rockets.
> The Iraqi decision-making process with regard to the design of these rockets was well documented. Iraq has provided copies of design documents, procurement records, minutes of committee meetings and supporting data and samples. A thorough analysis of this information, together with information gathered from interviews with Iraqi personnel, has allowed the IAEA to develop a coherent picture of attempted purchases and intended usage of the 81 mm aluminum tubes, as well as the rationale behind the changes in the tolerances.
> Drawing on this information, the IAEA has learned that the original tolerances for the 81mm tubes were set prior to 1987, and were based on physical measurements taken from a small number of imported rockets in Iraq's possession. Initial attempts to reverse engineer the rockets met with little success. Tolerances were adjusted during the following years as part of ongoing efforts to revitalize the project and improve operational efficiency. The project languished for long periods during this time and became the subject of several committees, which resulted in specification and tolerance changes on each occasion.

The IAEA also concluded that all the magnets that Iraq had imported had been put to non-nuclear uses. These magnets were of varieties that could not be used in a gas centrifuge.

Blix's final report also greatly weakened the case for war by pointing out that Iraq's cooperation, while belated, had, in recent weeks become 'proactive'. Blix therefore said that the completion of weapons inspections would not take years, or weeks, but months. He thus made as strong a case for the continuation of weapons inspections and therefore against a military invasion as it was possible for an 'apolitical' international civil servant to make.[62]

In the UN, by this time, the case for war was in tatters. The US and UK stuck to the position they had taken after Blix first expressed his dissatisfaction with the Iraqi declaration of 7 December[63] that Iraq was in further material breach of Resolution 1441 and therefore had to face 'serious consequences'. But each step that Iraq took to respond to Blix's criticism and cooperate more actively—allowing unfettered aerial surveillance and unmonitored interviews with its scientists, and destroying its Al Samoud-II missiles, reinforced the belief of the remaining members of the Council including France, Russia Germany and China, that since the threat of a military invasion a had proved sufficient to make Iraq co-operate fully with UNMOVIC, it made absolutely no sense to abandon the inspection route and invade the country so long as Blix and el Baradei felt sufficiently satisfied with Iraq's cooperation to urge the continuation of inspections.

The differences came out in the open when immediately after Blix presented his 7 March report, in a move that had been carefully premeditated, to be made irrespective of what Blix had to say, British Foreign Minister Jack Straw announced a ten-day ultimatum to Saddam Hussein. Straw asked the Council to tell Iraq that it would face the threat of an invasion "unless, on or before 17 March 2003, the council concludes that Iraq has demonstrated full, unconditional, immediate and active cooperation in accordance with its disarmament obligations".[64] This was no more than an offer of a fig leaf to France, Germany, Russia and China, to hide a decision to defer to the US' demand, for a resolution on these lines would have required only one veto to fail and automatically trigger an attack on Iraq. The French Foreign Minister, Dominique Villepin, however, saw through the ruse immediately and rejected the proposal. Chile then proposed a time-bound disarmament plan but this was rejected by the US. Straw persisted by presenting Iraq with a six-point charter of demands, but the French and Russian vetoed that too. As the ten days clicked away, France made one more effort, proposing a 30-day extension of the deadline for Iraq to comply fully with the UN resolutions, but this too was rejected by the US. The US announced that it would persist with introducing the second resolution and would 'override' a French or Russian veto so long as it got nine positive votes. But in the end all it had for certain was the support of Bulgaria. The remaining members of the Security Council let the US know that they would either vote against such a resolution or abstain. In the end, the US, UK and Spain found that they did not have even the nine positive votes they needed to claim a moral victory at the UN.

Bush and Blair were able to maintain their high moral tone only by denigrating the capacities of the UN inspectors. Faced with the IAEA's categorical assertion that Iraq not only did not have a nuclear weapons programme but was not, as of March 2003, trying to establish one, Powell retorted in his reply that this was the same organisation that, in 1991, had come within a hair's breadth of declaring that Iraq had no nuclear weapons program, until a defector provided information that showed that Iraq had been as little as two years away from a nuclear device. So far as chemical and biological weapons were concerned, Powell, Straw and other spokespersons began to insist that if Iraq did not actively cooperate with UNMOVIC, the latter could burrow around in Iraq for years and find nothing. In saying this they conveniently forgot the achievements of UNSCOM, which had faced even more determined obstruction from the Iraqi government, but succeeded in eliminating, even by their own biased estimates of the time, at least 90 per cent of all of Iraq's WMD, and all of its WMD manufacturing facilities.[65]

The 7 March meeting of the Security Council therefore stripped the US and UK of all remaining legal cover for their proposed invasion of Iraq. But by that time the US had decided that it was facing a new adversary in its quest for world dominance—the United Nations. In the days that followed Bush's references to the UN became more and more unfriendly. US spokesmen let it be known that they were prepared to ignore French, Russian and Chinese vetoes, and would consider any nine votes in favour of a second resolution declaring Iraq to be in further material breach, an endorsement by the UN of their invasion plans. But in the end the three sponsors of the resolution, Britain, Spain and the US, were unable to get anywhere close to the nine votes they needed in their favour. Thus was the struggle to legitimise the invasion of Iraq finally lost. When the UK and US invaded Iraq on May 20, they did so in a straightforward exercise of brute power with no international sanction whatsoever. Thus did the 355 year-old Westphalian international order come to an end.

Notes

1. Unicef website; "Iraq: Country in Crisis". The UNICEF's figures on rise in child mortality in Iraq have been heavily criticised by the US and UK governments. Both claim that Iraq is using doctored figures as part of its propaganda war against the sanctions and that UNICEF became a party to the deception. The UNICEF figures were based upon a sample survey of 40,000 households selected randomly, 24,000 in the South and Centre and 16,000 in the North. UNICEF experts were associated with every phase of the preparation and sampling process and subsequent analysis. The attacks on it show that when Governments start telling lies anyone who tries to tell the truth becomes a liar.
2. Told by World Food Programme officials to BBC, CNN and other media at the start of the Iraq war, March 2003.
3. Roula Khalaf, Edward Alden and Ander Postelnicu, "Iraq says UN weapons inspectors can return". *The Financial Times* 16 September 2002. Iraq announced that it would allow the Inspectors to return one week after Kofi Annan, who had been holding talks with Iraqi representatives since July, said that sanctions would be lifted once UNMOVIC completed its task.
4. Bill Keller. "The Sunshine Warrior" *The New York Times* 22 September 2002.
5. Daniel Benjamin "Saddam Hussein and Al Qaeda are not allies". *The New York Times* 30 September 2002.

6. There were terrorists with international agendas—such as the anarchists at the end of the nineteenth century, the Baader-Meinhof in Germany and the Brigato Rosso in Italy, but they remained marginal to politics and in the end changed nothing.
7. By contrast, terrorist attacks by various far right groups within the US, such as the bombing of the Oklahoma Federal Building in 1995, fall into the conventional category of terrorism.
8. US State Department. "Patterns of Global Terrorism, 1993 and subsequent years".
9. Such as an attempt to bring down ten American airliners in the Far East on the same day, which was discovered in 1994.
10. In video tapes obtained by the US government from Eastern Afghanistan, and subsequently aired on CNN, Osama bin Laden was seen discussing the success of the attack, and admitting that he had not expected the world trade towers to collapse.
11. Bill Keller "The Sunshine Warrior" op.cit.
12. Ibid.
13. "Defence Planning Guidance". A policy statement on America's mission in the post-Cold war world. See Carnegie Endowment for Peace website: "Crisis in Iraq".
14. Ibid. In an article in the *Wall Street Journal*, Wolfowitz criticised Clinton bitterly for leaving the Kurds and Shias in the lurch and called it Clinton's Bay of Pigs. He unambiguously, albeit implicitly advocated an invasion of Iraq.
15. Jason Leopold. "Rumsfeld and Wolfowitz's war on Iraq began before 1998—now its official". Posted on the internet website *Online opinion* http://www.onlineopinion.com,au/2003/Felsos/Leopold.htm. 25 February 2003. Leopold is a former bureau chief of the Dow Jones Wire Services.
16. Ibid.
17. ibid.
18. Bruce Murphy "Neoconservative clout seen in US Iraq policy Milwaukee Journal Sentinel." 5 April 2003.
19. Bruce Murphy "Neo Conservative Clout seen in US Iraq policy". *The Milwaukee Journal Sentinel*. 5 April 2003. The $10 million figure is cited by Israeli parliamentarian Uri Avnery in "The Night After". *Counterpunch*. 10 April 2003.
20. Thomas Donnelly (Principal author), Donald Kagan and Gary Schmidt (Project co-chairmen): "Rebuilding America's Defenses: Strategy, Forces and Resources for a New Century". *A Report of the Project for the New American Century*. September 2000. Introduction.

21. Uri Avneri op. cit. Perle is a central character in the neo-con movement and in the destruction of Iraq. Until early 2003, he was the chairman of the Defense Policy Board of the Defense Department. He is also a director of the *Jerusalem Post*, now owned by extreme right-wing Zionists. In the past he was an aide to Senator Henry Jackson, who led the fight against the Soviet Union on behalf of the Jews who wanted to leave. He is a leading member of the influential right-wing American Enterprise Institute. Lately he was obliged to resign from his Defense Department position, when it became known that a private corporation had promised to pay him almost a million dollars for the benefit of his influence in the administration. "The Night after." *Counterpunch*, 10 April 2003.
22. Keller op. cit.
23. Ibid.
24. Dana Milbank and Claudia Deane "Hussein Link to 9/11 Lingers in Many Minds". *The Washington Post* 5 September 2003.
25. Laurie Milroie *The War Against America: Saddam Hussein and the World Trade Center Attacks—A study of Revenge*. Regan Books(HarperCollins) 2002. The most significant feature of this book is that the copyright is owned by the American Enterprise Institute, the parent think tank of the neo-conservatives.
26. Keller op. cit.
27. A training camp for terrorists was indeed found after the invasion of Iraq, but it turned out to be a camp for Palestinians and revealed no links whatever with Al Qaeda.
28. See Mohammed El Baradei's report to the UN Security Council, 7 March 2003.
29. Schmitt "Why Iraq?" *The Weekly Standard*, late 2001.
30. The senators were Trent Lott, Joseph Lieberman, John McCain, Jesse Helms, Richard Shelby, Sam Brownback, Henry Hyde, Harold Ford Jr. and Benjamin Gilman.
31. Both the letters can be sen at the New American Century Website, http://www.newamericancentury.org/congress-120601.htm
32. Grotius, the father of international law, wrote in 1625 that war was justified only by injury received. This definition of a just war was itself taken from the works of Christian thinkers like St.Augustine, and Thomas Aquinas.
33. George W. Bush: State of the Union address, 29 January 2002.
34. The text of the Doctrine may be found at http://www.whitehouse.gov/nsc/nss.html
35. *The New York Times*, 6 July 2002. A Pentagon official revealed was preparing 'a major air campaign and land invasion' to 'topple President Saddam Hussein'.

36. For instance, Robert Kagan "Nation building: America will Have to Stay in Iraq". *The International Herald Tribune*, July 22, 2002. Kagan made it clear that an invasion was in the offing and asked if the Bush administration had a workable plan for a post Saddam Iraq.
37. Keller op. cit.
38. David E. Sanger and Thom Shanker. "US weighs cutting off Iraq leaders in first strike". *New York Times*, and *IHT*, 30 July 2002.
39. The text of what Bush had to say was as follows:

> Twelve years ago, Iraq invaded Kuwait without provocation. And the regime's forces were poised to continue their march to seize other countries and their resources. Had Saddam Hussein been appeased instead of stopped, he would have endangered the peace and stability of the world. Yet this aggression was stopped by the might of coalition forces and the will of the United Nations.
> To suspend hostilities, to spare himself, Iraq's dictator accepted a series of commitments. The terms were clear to him and to all, and he agreed to prove he is complying with every one of those obligations. He has proven instead only his contempt for the United Nations and for all his pledges. By breaking every pledge, by his deceptions and by his cruelties, Saddam Hussein has made the case against himself. In 1991, Security Council Resolution 688 demanded that the Iraqi regime cease at once the repression of its own people, including the systematic repression of minorities, which the council said threatened international peace and security in the region. This demand goes ignored.
> Last year, the U.N. Commission on Human Rights found that Iraq continues to commit extremely grave violations of human rights and that the regime's repression is all-pervasive.
> Tens of thousands of political opponents and ordinary citizens have been subjected to arbitrary arrest and imprisonment, summary execution and torture by beating and burning, electric shock, starvation, mutilation and rape.
> Wives are tortured in front of their husbands; children in the presence of their parents; and all of these horrors concealed from the world by the apparatus of a totalitarian state.
> In 1991, the U.N. Security Council, through Resolutions 686 and 687, demanded that Iraq return all prisoners from Kuwait and other lands. Iraq's regime agreed. It broke this promise.
> Last year, the Secretary General's high-level coordinator for this

issue reported that Kuwaiti, Saudi, Indian, Syrian, Lebanese, Iranian, Egyptian, Bahraini and Armeni nationals remain unaccounted for; more than 600 people. One American pilot is among them.

In 1991, the U.N. Security Council through Resolution 687 demanded that Iraq renounce all involvement with terrorism and permit no terrorist organizations to operate in Iraq.

Iraq's regime agreed that broke this promise.

In violation of Security Council Resolution 1373, Iraq continues to shelter and support terrorist organizations that direct violence against Iran, Israel and Western governments. Iraqi dissidents abroad are targeted for murder.

In 1993, Iraq attempted to assassinate the Amir of Kuwait and a former American president. Iraq's government openly praised the attacks of September 11. And Al Qaeda terrorists escaped from Afghanistan and are known to be in Iraq.

In 1991, the Iraqi regime agreed destroy and stop developing all weapons of mass destruction and long range missiles and to prove to the world it has done so by complying with rigorous inspections. Iraq has broken every aspect of this fundamental pledge.

From 1991 to 1995, the Iraqi regime said it had no biological weapons. After a senior official in its weapons program defected and exposed this lie, the regime admitted to producing tens of thousands of liters of anthrax and other deadly biological agents for use with scud warheads, aerial bombs and aircraft spray tanks.

U.N. inspectors believe Iraq has produced two to four times the amount of biological agents it declared and has failed to account for more than three metric tons of material that could be used to produce biological weapons. Right now, Iraq is expanding and improving facilities that were used for the production of biological weapons.

United Nations' inspections also reviewed that Iraq like maintains stockpiles of VX, mustard and other chemical agents, and that the regime is rebuilding and expanding facilities capable of producing chemical weapons.

And in 1995, after four years of deception, Iraq finally admitted it had a crash nuclear weapons program prior to the Gulf War.

We know now, were it not for that war, the regime in Iraq would likely have possessed a nuclear weapon no later than 1993.

Today, Iraq continues to withhold important information about its nuclear program, weapons design, procurement logs, experiment data, and accounting of nuclear materials and documentation of foreign assistance. Iraq employs capable nuclear scientists and technicians. It retains physical infrastructure needed to build a nuclear weapon.

Iraq has made several attempts to buy high-strength aluminum tubes used to enrich uranium for a nuclear weapon. Should Iraq acquire fissile material, it would be able to build a nuclear weapon within a year.

And Iraq's state-controlled media has reported numerous meetings between Saddam Hussein and his nuclear scientists, leaving little doubt about his continued appetite for these weapons.

Iraq also possesses a force of SCUD type missiles with ranges beyond the 150 kilometers permitted by the U.N. Work at testing and production facilities shows that Iraq is building more long range missiles that can inflict mass death throughout the region.

In 1990, after Iraq's invasion of Kuwait, the world imposed economic sanctions on Iraq. Those sanctions were maintained after the war to compel the regime's compliance with Security Council Resolutions. In time, Iraq was allowed to use oil revenues to buy food. Saddam Hussein has subverted this program, working around the sanctions to buy missile technology and military materials. He blames the suffering of Iraq's people on the United Nations, even as he uses his oil wealth to build lavish palaces for himself and to buy arms for his country.

By refusing to comply with his own agreements, he bears full guilt for the hunger and misery of innocent Iraqi citizens. In 1991, Iraq promised U.N. inspectors immediate and unrestricted access to verify Iraq's commitment to rid itself of weapons of mass destruction and long range missiles. Iraq broke this promise, spending seven years deceiving, evading and harassing U.N. inspectors before ceasing cooperation entirely.

Just months after the 1991 cease-fire, the Security Council twice renewed its demand that the Iraqi regime cooperate fully with inspectors, condemning Iraq's serious violations of its obligations. The Security Council again renewed that demand in 1994, and twice more in 1996, deploring Iraq's clear violations of its obligations. The Security Council renewed its demand three more times in 1997, citing flagrant violations, and three more times in 1998, calling Iraq's behavior totally unacceptable. And in 1999, the demand was renewed yet again.

As we meet today, it's been almost four years since the last U.N. inspector set foot in Iraq—four years for the Iraqi regime to plan and to build and to test behind the cloak of secrecy. We know that Saddam Hussein pursued weapons of mass murder even when inspectors were in his country. Are we to assume that he stopped when they left?"

These charges remained utterly unchanged in the face of mounting evidence against them, till the very end. The evangelist in Bush was impervious to empirical refutation.

40. President George W. Bush. Address to the UN General Assembly. 12 September 2002.
41. Ewen McAskill. "UN and Iraq fail in weapons talks". *The Guardian* 6 July 2002.
42. Duncan Campbell and Patrick Wintour. "Iraq invites UN weapons inspectors for talks to Baghdad". *The Guardian* 3 August 2002.
43. Roula Khalaf, op. cit.
44. George Monbiot "Inspection as Invasion". *The Guardian* 8 October 2002. *The Financial Times* called the contents of the US draft 'intentionally provocative'. This was quoted with approval by William Kristol and Robert Kagan in an editorial in the *Weekly Standard*, on November 18, 2002. *The Washington Post* also reported that, in a meeting with Powell which was attended by National Security Adviser Condoleeza Rice, and Paul Wolfowitz, Blix, while strongly favouring clauses that gave the inspectors unfettered access to all sites, had 'expressed discomfort with' others declaring new military exclusion zones, giving members of the Security Council the right to attach their own people to accompany the inspectors, and 'spiriting people out of the country in order to question them'. Karen De Young and Colum Lynch "Push for New terms on Iraq gains at the UN". *The Washington Post* 5 October 2002.
45. Scott Ritter. *War on Iraq: What the Bush Team Doesn't Want you to Know*. New York: Context Books, 2002. Quoted in Chapter 10.
46. This claim did not break wholly new ground. The Clinton administration had made exactly the same claim when, along with the UK, it pounded Iraq from the air for four days in December 1998.
47. It is no secret that the neo-conservative think tank to which Bush owed so much of his policy, the Project for the New American Century, was stridently opposed to it. In an editorial in *The Weekly Standard*, William Kristol and Robert Kagan jointly warned the administration against falling into what they called 'The UN Trap'.

"There is no point in kidding ourselves: the inspection process we are about to embark upon is a trap...it was designd to satisfy those in Europe who oppose military action in Iraq; *and it was negotiated by those within the Bush administration who have never made any secret of their opposition to military action in Iraq*" (emphasis added). The Weekly Standard, 18 November 2002.

48. The Weekly Standard, 18 November 2002
49. This was the alleged attempt to purchase 500 tons of Uranium yellow cake from Niger, an allegation that was later shown to not only false but a crude forgery. See Seymour Hersh: Who Lied to Whom? The New Yorker. 31 March 2003.
50. Both reports were almost certainly based upon the same pool of shared information.
51. British report on Iraq's Weapons of Mass destruction, op. cit. 25
52. The remaining operative clauses of the resolution were as follows:

> 5. Decides that Iraq shall provide UNMOVIC and the IAEA immediate, unimpeded, unconditional, and unrestricted access to any and all, including underground, areas, facilities, buildings, equipment, records, and means of transport which they wish to inspect, as well as immediate, unimpeded, unrestricted, and private access to all officials and other persons whom UNMOVIC or the IAEA wish to interview in the mode or location of UNMOVIC's or the IAEA's choice pursuant to any aspect of their mandates; further decides that UNMOVIC and the IAEA may at their discretion conduct interviews inside or outside of Iraq, may facilitate the travel of those interviewed and family members outside of Iraq, and that, at the sole discretion of UNMOVIC and the IAEA, such interviews may occur without the presence of observers from the Iraqi government; and instructs UNMOVIC and requests the IAEA to resume inspections no later than 45 days following adoption of this resolution and to update the council 60 days thereafter;
> 6. Endorses the 8 October 2002 letter from the executive chairman of UNMOVIC and the director general of the IAEA to General Al-Saadi of the government of Iraq, which is annexed hereto, and decides that the contents of the letter shall be binding upon Iraq;
> 7. Decides further that, in view of the prolonged interruption by Iraq of the presence of UNMOVIC and the IAEA and in order for them to accomplish the tasks set forth in this resolution and

all previous relevant resolutions and notwithstanding prior understandings, the council hereby establishes the following revised or additional authorities, which shall be binding upon Iraq, to facilitate their work in Iraq:

_UNMOVIC and the IAEA shall determine the composition of their inspection teams and ensure that these teams are composed of the most qualified and experienced experts available;

_All UNMOVIC and IAEA personnel shall enjoy the privileges and immunities provided in the Convention on Privileges and Immunities of the United Nations and the Agreement on the Privileges and Immunities of the IAEA;

_UNMOVIC and the IAEA shall have unrestricted rights of entry into and out of Iraq, the right to free, unrestricted, and immediate movement to and from inspection sites, and the right to inspect any sites and buildings, including immediate, unimpeded, unconditional, and unrestricted access to presidential sites equal to that at other sites, notwithstanding the provisions of resolution 1154 (1998);

_UNMOVIC and the IAEA shall have the right to be provided by Iraq the names of all personnel currently and formerly associated with Iraq's chemical, biological, nuclear, and ballistic missile programs and the associated research, development, and production facilities;

_Security of UNMOVIC and IAEA facilities shall be ensured by sufficient U.N. security guards:

_UNMOVIC and the IAEA shall have the right to declare for the purposes of freezing a site to be inspected, exclusion zones, including surrounding areas and transit corridors, in which Iraq will suspend ground and aerial movement so that nothing is changed in or taken out of a site being inspected;

_UNMOVIC and the IAEA shall have the free and unrestricted use and landing of fixed and rotary winged aircraft, including manned and unmanned reconnaissance vehicles:

_UNMOVIC and the IAEA shall have the right at their sole discretion verifiably to remove, destroy, or render harmless all prohibited weapons, subsystems, components, records, materials, and other related items, and the right to impound or close any facilities or equipment for the production thereof; and

_UNMOVIC and the IAEA shall have the right to free import and use of equipment or materials for inspections and to seize and export any equipment, materials, or documents taken during inspections, without search of UNMOVIC or IAEA personnel or official or personal baggage;

8. Decides further that Iraq shall not take or threaten hostile acts directed against any representative or personnel of the United Nations or of any member state taking action to uphold any council resolution;

9. Requests the secretary-general immediately to notify Iraq of this resolution, which is binding on Iraq; demands that Iraq confirm within seven days of that notification its intention to comply fully with this resolution; and demands further that Iraq cooperate immediately, unconditionally, and actively with UNMOVIC and the IAEA;

10. Requests all member states to give full support to UNMOVIC and the IAEA in the discharge of their mandates, including by providing any information related to prohibited programs or other aspects of their mandates; including on Iraqi attempts since 1998 to acquire prohibited items, and by recommending sites to be inspected, persons to be interviewed, conditions of such interviews, and data to be collected, the results of which shall be reported to the council by UNMOVIC and the IAEA;

53. This and the following chronology is taken from *The Guardian*. The judgements they contain are also those of its correspondents.
54. Ibid.
55. *The Guardian*.
56. The editorial opinion in *The Guardian* on 28 January summed up the feelings of hose who were opposed to war:
'John Negroponte, the US ambassador to the UN, claimed immediately after hearing the reports that Iraq was running an "active programme of denial and deception". He demanded that the council urgently consider its "responsibilities" in the face of Iraq's "clear violations". But this sounded like canned condemnation, preemptively prescripted. It was echoed, shamefully, by Jack Straw; and by the White House which, putting a notably mendacious spin on the UN assessments, flatly asserted that Iraq had been proven to be in non-compliance with last autumn's resolution 1441 and that this constituted grounds for war.
This will not be how most of the rest of the world views Mr Blix's and Mr El Baradei's scrupulously fair and balanced findings. Britain's

UN envoy, Jeremy Greenstock, was much closer to the mark when he referred to "a catalogue of unresolved questions" that the Iraqi government must answer'.
57. Judith Miller and Julia Preston "Blix says he saw nothing to prompt a war". *The New York Times* 31 January 2003.
58. "Downing Street admits blunder on Iraq" Dossier. *The Guardian* 7 February 2003.
59. Seymour Hersh. "Who lied to whom? Why the administration endorsed a forgery about Iraq's nuclear program". *The New Yorker* 31 March 2003.
60. Ibid.
61. Nicholas D. Kristoff "Missing in Action: The Truth". *The New York Times* 6 May 2003.
62. Julian Borger in Washington and Ewen MacAskill "A case for war? Yes, say US and Britain. No, say the majority" *The Guardian* 15 February 2003. 'The US and Britain's drive to gain international backing for a war with Iraq was in deep trouble last night in the face of unexpectedly upbeat reports by United Nations weapons inspectors.
American and British diplomats had hoped to circulate draft language as early as today for a new UN resolution authorising an invasion. But after yesterday's heated security council showdown, in which the overwhelming majority made clear their opposition to war, that strategy is in jeopardy…'.
63. Timothy L. Obrien "Bitter Split Deepen at UN. Arms inspectors give ammunition to both sides". *International Herald Tribune* 8–9 March 2003. Contrary to the impression created by many news reports of his address, Blix did not assume in his report that there were weapons of mass destruction in Iraq that were still to be found.
64. "On 8 January, Blix said that the Iraqi declaration was 'incomplete". *The Guardian* 9 January, 2003.
65. Julian Borger and Gary Younge (in New York) and Patrick Wintour "Showdown as Britain sets 17 March deadline on Iraq". *The Guardian* 8 March 2003.
65. In an interview given to BBC on April 22, Blix took strong objection to the way in which the US and UK had sought to denigrate the work of the inspectors. See Sally Bolton and agencies "Blix attacks US war intelligence".*The Guardian.* 22 April 2003.
'The chief UN weapons inspector, Hans Blix, has claimed that the US tried to discredit his team and used "shaky" intelligence to make the case for war in Iraq…'.

4

Manufacturing Consent

America was forced to invade Iraq without the sanction, legal or moral, of the international community. The latter had been missing from the very beginning: Opinion polls carried out regularly across Europe and the USA showed that the vast majority of the people were against the war. Even in the US, a *CBS–New York Times* poll conducted in October 2002 revealed that by a 2-to-1 margin Americans wanted to give UN weapons inspectors more time to do their work before military action is taken. A majority, 56 per cent, said that one country should not be able to attack another country unless it is attacked first.[1] The opposition was even stronger in the countries that had backed the US openly, notably Spain, Britain and Italy, than in those that had opposed it or steered clear of involvement. In all three countries 70 to 85 per cent expressed their opposition to the war consistently almost till the end.[2] They showed their opposition to the war in mass rallies across the globe that had no precedent. In the first of them, on 16 February 2003 an estimated 30 million people demonstrated against the impending invasion in over 60 cities.

Behind the mass protests was a feeling that no amount of American and British government propaganda was able to eradicate: that this would be an unjust war. The sentiment was summed up by Ignacio Ramonet in *Le Monde Diplomatiue* (April 2003). In a cover page piece entitled 'Illegal Aggression', he wrote: "Sans trop se faire d'illusions, chacun attend du pays le plus puissant de la Terre qu'il soit aussi une puissance éthique, champion du respect du droit et modèle de soumission à la loi. Ou du moins qu'il ne tourne pas ostensiblement le dos aux grands principes de la morale politique. (Everyone expects the worlds mightiest power to be an ethical power, a champion of respect for Law and a model of submission to Law. At the very least (one expects) it not to turn its back ostentatiously on the grand principles of political morality)". Two months earlier, on 15 January 2003, more than 500 eminent international jurists and judges had sent an appeal to the UN Security Council not to countenance an invasion of Iraq, claiming that it would go against every principle of international law.[3]

The US and UK were aware from the start that a large part of the world would regard the doctrine of 'preemptive', (in reality *preventive*) as an attempt to legitimise the unjustified exercise of power. From the very early days of their preparations for invading Iraq, therefore both governments launched a high pressure campaign to 'manufacture consent'. The elements of this campaign were not much different from similar campaigns run in the past. It consisted first of presenting a lie, or at least a statement whose veracity had still to be established, as a self-evident and well established truth and repeating it ad nauseam, without a single reservation or condition, till a punch-drunk public which did not have access to an alternative stream of information, came to believe that it was the truth. Second, it was to frighten the public with threats of imminent danger till it went into a war-mongering frenzy in which it would justify any military action. The third, based upon the successful completion of the first two, was to claim a moral, almost divine, sanction to take military action. What they contemplated doing had to be done. It was the duty of civilised people to do in order to protect civilisation and human rights. God was rather obviously on their side.[4] This was the main reason why both countries embarked upon a highly *public* campaign to justify the invasion of Iraq, that used speeches by the president and the Vice-President, calculated leaks to the press, and off the reord briefings by spokespersons.

From October 2002, if not earlier, both prepared, in effect, for war on two fronts. The first was the 'real' war, for which troops, armour, ships, aircraft, munitions and supplies had to be built up relentlessly to Kuwait and Qatar. The second was the virtual war, for the hearts and minds of Americans, Europeans and then, as a bonus, the rest of the world. This duality persisted not only through the war, but for months afterwards till the pretence of morality died a natural death at the hands of an international media infuriated at the way in which its trust had been abused.

The lie that they repeated over and over again was that Saddam Hussein's Iraq had deceived the weapons inspectors thereby violating its own commitments to the UN Security Council, and was busy adding to his stocks of weapons of mass destruction, some of which could be deployed in as little as 45 minutes! It would be tedious to list the number of times that Bush, Blair, Powell, and innumerable White House, Downing Street and State Department spokespersons repeated this accusation as a known and incontrovertible fact. Suffice it to say that the most spectacular triumph of this relentless propaganda barrage occurred when 15 members of the Security Council voted for a resolution whose preamble stated that Iraq was in material breach of UN resolutions. No country, not even Ba'athist Syria, questioned this statement. It was as if the long and sordid history of how the US sabotaged the inspection process in 1998, and pressurised or enlisted Butler into preventing sanctions from being lifted, had simply been wiped clean.

The main threat Bush used to drive the American public into supporting an invasion of Iraq was that Saddam would pass these weapons on to the Al Qaeda. This was built up on the back of an extremely effective propaganda campaign to suggest that Iraq had been behind the 9/11 terrorist attacks. Indeed Bush and Powell asserted without a shadow of reservation that senior Al Qaeda operatives were known to be in Baghdad, and an Al Qaeda camp had been established in Northern Iraq. Thus the transfer of WMD and technology could take place within days. Iraq therefore had to be neutralised immediately, if the US was to be rendered safe from an even more deadly terrorist attack than 9/11. Even waiting for another six months to let Blix's weapons inspectors complete their job carried to great a risk. So effective was this propaganda that despite no evidence of Saddam–Al Qaeda links ever being discovered, as late as the beginning of September 2003, almost five months after the war ended, 69 per cent of Americans surveyed in a *Washington Post* poll still thought it likely that Iraq was involved in the 9/11 attacks.[5] However, for the decision makers, whether in the British parliament, or the US Congress, Bush and Blair reserved some choice morsels. The first was Blair's claim that Saddam had WMD ready for use. The second was that he had retained an active nuclear weapons programme—witness his attempt to purchase uranium yellow cake from Niger. The first proved crucial in winning for Blair the support of the British parliament. The second was equally pivotal in persuading the two houses of the US Congress to vote for a resolution authorising war on Iraq. Both allegations turned out to be false. But what is more important, reporters like Seymour Hersh, Nicholas Kristoff and Andrew Gilligan of the BBC unearthed information after the war was over that the two governments knew that they were false even when they decided to use them.[6]

The Struggle to Retain Hegemony

Why were the two countries prepared to go so far to persuade the public of the moral rectitude of the attack upon Iraq? The answer is that they were contemplating unleashing an unprovoked war, and an unprovoked war was, in the deepest, most Christian meaning of the term, an unjust war. It therefore contained the potential for destroying the US' hegemony of the world. Without a general acceptance of its hegemony, the US could not go about reshaping the international order to suit its needs and ambitions in the post-Westphalian, 'globalised' world.

The word 'hegemony' did not figure even once in the millions of words that were spoken and written before and during the Iraq war. Yet an awareness of its importance, and of the fact that it requires the existence of a moral dimension that confers legitimacy upon the exercise of power, permeated virtually every thing that the Bush and Blair administrations said or did in the run up to the Iraq war. Both governments were acutely aware that they had to obtain at least the world's acquiescence, if not support, in the invasion of Iraq. The case they made did not have to stand up in a court of law. All it had to do was make people entertain the possibility that it was well founded.

As mentioned before, the moral case for invasion was based on four separate accusations, Saddam's penchant for war and unpredictability; his past use of proscribed weapons of mass destruction, especially on his own people, his total disregard for the human rights of his subjects, and his links with Al Qaeda.

A close look at these accusations shows that they contained exaggerations and distortions and in one case deliberate suppression of at least a part of the truth. Iraq's attacks upon Iran and Kuwait did indeed demonstrate a penchant for using force to settle international disputes. But they did not either directly or indirectly create a case for *pre-emptive* military action of the kind envisaged by the Bush doctrine. These were acts of war, by one recognised state on another, of the kind that the world was familiar with and for which the instruments of deterrence had been devised. Bush and Blair needed to make Saddam into a special kind of head of state—one on whom deterrence would not work. To do this they demonised him even more than they had already. His use of poison gas against the Kurds in 1988 was the strongest of several cards in their pack. In all there are believed to have been some 40 such attacks[7], but the worst by far was at Halabja in March 1988, which killed at least 5,000 Kurds. This became the strongest single argument against continuing with a policy of containment, and in favour of invasion.

"Only after the first wave of air and artillery bombardments had driven the inhabitants to underground shelters did the Iraqi helicopters return to unleash their lethal brew of mustard gas and nerve agents", wrote an anonymous writer, in an information sheet produced for the US Department of State.[8]

And in his radio address to the nation on 16 March, just before he set off for the Azores, Bush reminded his listeners that it was the

15th "bitter anniversary" of Mr. Hussein's chemical weapons attack on the Iraqi Kurdish village of Halabja. The attack, Mr. Bush said,

> Provided a glimpse of the crimes Saddam Hussein is willing to commit, and the kind of threat he now presents to the entire world....We know from human rights groups that dissidents in Iraq are tortured, imprisoned and sometimes just disappear. Their hands, feet and tongues are cut off, their eyes are gouged out, and female relatives are raped in their presence.[9]

But all the while that the Bush and Blair administrations were making use of this argument, the US was in possession of a report prepared by the Defense Intelligence Agency which had pointed out, as far back as 1991, that the bodies of the dead Kurds showed that they had been killed by a blood agent, in this case a cyanide-based gas. Cyanide gas was used by the Iranians and not by the Iraqis, who were using mustard gas. Based on this the DIA had concluded unambiguously that at Halabja the Kurds had been killed by the Iranian army. This was revealed in an article in *The New York Times*, Stephen Pelletiere, who was the senior CIA analyst on Iraq during the Iran–Iraq war and, in 1991, headed an army investigation on how Iraq would fight a war against the US. Pelletiere pointed out that Halabja had seen a battle between the Iranians and the Iraqis, having been captured first by the former. Both sides had used gas in the combat, but since the victims they examined had been killed by cyanide gas, it was virtually certain that they had died in the Iranian attack. He concluded:

> I am not trying to rehabilitate the character of Saddam Hussein. He has much to answer for in the area of human rights abuses. But accusing him of gassing his own people at Halabja as an act of genocide is not correct, because as far as the information we have goes, all of the cases where gas was used involved battles. These were tragedies of war. There may be justifications for invading Iraq, but Halabja is not one of them.[10]

George W. Bush's second accusation, that Iraq was forming links with Al Qaeda, and could pass on its weapons of mass destruction to it at any moment, was even weaker. Bush and Colin Powell assured America and the world that they had hard evidence of such links, despite the fact that the CIA was anything but convinced that such a link existed. The CIA had in fact examined this possibility on several occasions in the nineties and found no such link.[11] It remained convinced of the absence of such links as late as September 2002, when British and American troops had already begun to arrive in Kuwait and Qatar.[12] The aftermath of the war showed that the CIA's scepticism had been fully justified. The lone guerrilla training camp the US troops found turned out to be devoted exclusively to training Palestinians for their 'war' against Israel. Powell, Rumsfeld, and Bush had built up their case on the basis of dubious snippets of 'intelligence' supplied by Iraqi exiles and defectors, notably Ahmed Chalawi's Iraqi National Congress, which the CIA had rejected as being unreliable or unverifiable.[13]

Only the third accusation, that Iraq had played hide and seek with the UN weapons inspectors for 12 years; that several stockpiles of chemical weapons and chemical and biological weapons had not been accounted for when UNSCOM left Iraq in 1998, and that Saddam Hussein had had four unpoliced years in which to add to Iraq's weapons of mass destruction, contained enough truth to 'add something to the power of the dominant group' and thereby sustain the US' claim to hegemony.

That was why, as the date for the invasion of Iraq drew closer, and no weapons of mass destruction were unearthed by UNMOVIC's inspectors, the US engaged in an increasingly vigorous effort to sustain the belief that Saddam Hussein did have such weapons; that UNMOVIC's failure to unearth them only highlighted the limitations of the inspection process when the country being inspected did not wish to co-operate, and therefore that only an invasion of the country and a change of regime would truly lift the threat that Iraq posed to its neighbours and the rest of the world.

As December turned into January and then into February and UNMOVIC failed to discover any weapons of mass destruction in

Iraq, the US found it more and more difficult to maintain its claim to hegemony in the face of a rising tide of scepticism. Its response was to ignore the absence of corroboration and insist more and more emphatically that it *knew* that the weapons actually existed because of its incomparably superior sources of intelligence. But as scepticism deepened and fed into the growing anti-war movement, both governments began to look for alternative hegemonic justifications for the war they had already decided to wage.

Days after Powell's address to the UN Security Council, Bush shifted the emphasis in his speeches from Iraq's possession of WMD, which he continued to assert with undiminished certitude, to its links with Al Qaeda. In a radio address to the American people on 8 February he said:

> One of the greatest dangers we face is that weapons of mass destruction might be passed to terrorists who would not hesitate to use those weapons. Saddam Hussein has longstanding, direct and continuing ties to terrorist networks. Senior members of Iraqi intelligence and al Qaeda have met at least eight times since the early 1990s. Iraq has sent bomb-making and document forgery experts to work with al Qaeda. Iraq has also provided al Qaeda with chemical and biological weapons training. And an al Qaeda operative was sent to Iraq several times in the late 1990s for help in acquiring poisons and gases.
> We also know that Iraq is harboring a terrorist network headed by a senior al Qaeda terrorist planner. This network runs a poison and explosive training camp in northeast Iraq, and many of its leaders are known to be in Baghdad.

With no 9/11 to fall back upon, Blair took a different tack. On 15 February, as between 750,000 and 1,000,000 Britons braved piercingly cold winds to register their protest against a war on Iraq in the largest peacetime rally the country had ever seen[14], he told the Labour Party's spring conference in Glasgow that "ridding the world of Saddam would be an act of humanity. It is leaving him there that is inhumane'.

Blair went on to build this 'moral' case for a war by detailing the privations, repression and torture endured by the Iraqi people. "...But these victims will never be seen. They will never feature on our TV screens or inspire millions to take to the streets. But they will exist nonetheless".[15]

Blair's justification for waging war disclosed the full extent to which the international law that had governed the Westphalian State system had already collapsed. On behalf of the 'civilised world', Blair had laid claim to prosecuting, judging and executing anyone, or any regime, that did not meet 'its' standards of conduct, standards of which the US and UK were the prime custodians. If Bush was a modern day *conquistador* then Blair had become his pet Jesuit priest.

In the five weeks that preceded the start of the war it was Blair's alternative justification that came to dominate the hegemonic discourse. Saddam Hussein had imprisoned, tortured and killed hundreds of thousand of Iraqis. It was Saddam and not the US that was to blame for the sufferings of the people during the 12 years of economic sanctions. Iraq was not, therefore, being invaded but 'liberated'. Tyranny would be replaced by freedom and democracy. The sanctions would end the moment he was ousted. The people would therefore welcome the American and British troops. The Iraqi army would not fight, but surrender in droves. British and American aircraft flew repeatedly over Iraqi lines not just exhorting the soldiers to surrender but advising them of how they should go about doing so.

When, to their consternation, British and American troops met determined resistance and found no cheering crowds awaiting them, the Iraqi fighters became 'irregulars', 'Ba'ath party fanatics', 'Saddam loyalists' *'fidayeen'*, and after Bush officially declared the war to be over, simply 'terrorists'. They were never 'resistance groups', or 'guerrillas', still less 'nationalists'. Indeed the one word that was never used during the entire Iraq drama was 'nationalism'. Instead it was implied that 'positive' nationalism, of the kind that had gone into the making of the modern nation state, was a preserve of the west. Nationalism in the 'Third World' was a destructive force, built upon atavistic loyalties, and needed to be discouraged. In Iraq, moreover, a country that consisted of three disparate ethnic groups, two of which were held in servitude by the third, to speak of there being such a thing as Iraqi nationalism would be patently absurd.

When Saddam Hussein's government collapsed and the entire administration melted away, US and UK spokesmen hastened to claim that Iraqis were revelling in their newly restored freedoms. A statement by Richard Boucher, spokesman for the State Department, typified the claims that the two governments were making. "The flowering of Iraqi politics on such a rather quick basis is really something to behold," Boucher told reporters at the daily State Department briefing 23 April. "You also have this phenomenon of hundreds and hundreds of thousands of Iraqi pilgrims now making a pilgrimage they haven't been able to make for 20 years. And all that becomes possible because of the new situation that's been created by the coalition forces—the new atmosphere of freedom that we've been able to create that leads to the emergence of politicking in Iraq, which is a good thing, as well as the ability of Iraqis to celebrate their religious liberty for the first time in two decades."[16]

So great was the anxiety of the 'coalition' to depict invasion as liberation that its spokesmen claimed the outbreak of looting that occurred in Baghdad on 10 April to be a release of pent-up anger against the hated dictator, now made possible by his fall. This Nelsonian neglect reached its apogee when the American forces stood by and allowed the National Archaeological Museum to be ransacked and its priceless treasures to be destroyed in an insensate, but also calculated burst of rage on 11 April, two days after the Saddam regime fell. American field commanders refused frantic pleas by museum staff to post at least one tank in front of the museum to deter looters, claiming that they had no orders to do so. They did this despite the fact that less than three months earlier US archaeologists had met officials from the Pentagon to urge that Iraq's treasures be safeguarded and to put the Baghdad museum on a military database.[17] They felt no such qualms, however, about protecting the oil ministry.

The media and the manufacture of consent

Given the crucial importance, for the 'coalition', of being able to claim some legitimacy for what most of the world considered to be an unjust war[18], the 'spin' that official spokesmen put on events was only to be expected. What was distinctly new, and disturbing, was the role assigned to and, with only few exceptions, tamely accepted by the international media. This was to act as legitimisers of the Anglo-American invasion. By accepting this role the media unwittingly became instruments in the destruction of the Iraqi state and the Westphalian order.

This was not an entirely new development. Some degree of partisanship was only to be expected from war corespondents who lived and travelled with troops and saw them being killed. Indeed the institution of the war correspondent can be traced back at least to the Crimean war. But after the Cold War ended and in a proliferation of small wars, the US began to chip away at the foundations of the Westphalian order, journalists were thrust into a new role—as the legitimisers of military intervention. The Anglo-Saxon media, especially in the US, willingly stepped into this new role. It did this by making a small, seemingly innoccuous change in its reporting practices. This was to deny the 'opponent'—in this case the victims of coercive action—a voice that the world could hear. Such an 'omission' was, and remains to a large extent, unthinkable in domestic reporting. A reporter who writes a story that damages an individual or a company without giving the affected person or institution an opportunity to present his or her side of the story, would be risking his career. But in reporting international relations, this 'omission' has rapidly become the rule rather than the exception.

The transformation first became apparent in the coverage of Iraq before, during and after the first Gulf War. During the six months between Iraq's invasion of Kuwait and the start of the war, no Western newspaper or TV channel gave space to any senior member of the Iraqi government to explain why *it* felt justified in invading Kuwait. When the Iraqis passed an official transcript of the records of April Glaspie's last meeting with Saddam Hussein to the *New York Times*, the *Times* published it, but without comment. When the Bush (Sr.) administration began to call Saddam Hussein the Butcher of Baghdad, and accused him of having gassed the Kurds in Northern Iraq, specifically in Halabja, major TV networks in the Anglo-Saxon world and the wire services carried these accusations without once distancing themselves from the assertions with phrases like 'according to the State Department spokesman' or using tired, but useful words like 'alleged'.[19] When Bush continued to demonise Saddam Hussein as 'another Adolf Hitler' and to invoke the biblical term 'evil' to describe his regime, TV channels and wire service reports made no disclaimers. Still less did they consider it necessary to get Baghdad's response to these epithets. The cumulative impact of this barrage on TV viewers, and on readers of all but the most serious and independent columnists in a handful of newspapers, was to convince them that Iraq was ruled by a tyrannical, bloodthirsty, irrational and power-hungry despot who needed to be stopped from gobbling up other Middle Eastern countries at any cost. That this description of Saddam was not entirely wrong only made his demonisation easier.

When the war began, the media treated it "like a video game all the family could play. There was a demon to fight, hi-tech weapons to fight him with, it was all over quickly and 'we won'. The bonus was the miraculously small number of casualties".[20]

Journalists hugged this belief to their breasts because it freed journalists from their humanitarian 'dilemma'.[21] The dilemma was none other than the obligation to report what the war was doing to the other side.

The spin masters in the allied military command were quick to seize upon this sudden liberation of the journalists' conscience. They nursed it with carefully edited videoclips of bombs falling precisely upon bridges, factories and munitions dumps. Faith in the 'smartness' of the new generation of weapons came close to becoming a religion. The military never told the journalists that only 7 per cent of the munitions they used in the war were 'smart'. And only long after the war was over did the US authorities reveal that 70 per cent of the 88,500 tonnes of bombs they dropped on Iraq missed their targets. Many of these fell on civilians. But that, again was seldom reported.[22]

The first Gulf War also saw the start of the news management that flowered into the system of 'embedding' journalists with invading forces practised in Iraq in 2003. The device used then was 'The Pool'. A British invention used in the Second World War, the Pool allowed only selected journalists to visit the front, and then under military escort. They then shared their reports with their colleagues. Those who attempted to strike out on their own were often blackballed or denied military 'cooperation'. This meant being denied transport, a stratagem that effectively stopped them from seeing any more of the 'action'. The pool system ensured that journalists saw only what the military intended them to see. Thus when columns of retreating Iraqi soldiers were strafed and bombed from the back as they were fleeing, in what carrier based navy pilots later described as a 'duck or 'turkey' shoot, or when the US army used bulldozers and snow ploughs mounted upon tanks to bury Iraqis dead or alive in 70 miles of trenches, there were no journalists around to report the massacres.[23]

What was even more disturbing than the media's willingness to put itself knowingly in a position where it could report only one side of the story, was its unwillingness to believe anything that might give the lie to the official version that they were uncritically feeding to their readers and viewers.

A revealing example of this profound bias was the treatment it gave to the US bombing of the Al Amiriya bunker, in which 300 to 400 women and children were burnt to death.[24] When the Iraqis voiced an angry protest and aired TV footage showing that it was only an air raid shelter, US military spokesmen insisted that it was a military facility and that the bombs had zeroed in on communications that had been emanating from it. This was swallowed without a murmur, and the Iraqi protest dismissed as propaganda by not only the tabloid press in the UK but also by most of the respectable news media. *The Sun* reported, "Saddam Hussein tried to trick the world yesterday by claiming that hundreds of women and children died in a bomb attack on an 'air raid shelter'. He (note the personalisation) cunningly arranged TV scenes designed to shock and appal".[25]

The major networks edited their tapes allegedly to spare their viewers distress, but also left open the possibility that Saddam may indeed have been using the bunker as a command post. Only after the war was over and the unedited tapes of CNN and WTN became available to the *Columbia Journalism Review* was it finally established that this had indeed been an air raid shelter.[26]

The exchange between BBC newscaster Peter Sissons and the BBC's correspondent in Baghdad, Jeremy Bowen on the *Nine O'Clock News* the same night graphically demonstrates the willingness with which the media hd already adopted the role of the legitimiser. After prefacing a report from Baghdad with the American statement that the bunker had been a military instalation, Sissons had the following exchange with Bowen:

Sissons: A few moments ago I spoke with BBC's Jeremy Bowen in Baghdad and asked him whether he could be *absolutely sure* that there had been no military communications equipment in the shelter, which the allies believe was there.
Bowen: Well, Peter, we looked very hard for it... I'm pretty confident, as confident as I can be, that I've seen all the main rooms...
Sissons: Is it conceivable that it could have been in military use and was converted recently to civilian use?
Bowen: Well, it would seem a strange sort of thing to ....
Sissons: Let me put it another way, Jeremy. Is it possible to say with *certainty* that it was never a military facility? [27]

The media legitimised the invasion of Iraq in 2003 in much the same way as it had the Gulf War: before the invasion it denied Iraq a voice that the world could hear; during the invasion the majority of the international media again tamely accepted the constraints of the pool system, now renamed 'embedding of journalists'; after the war it studiously downplayed any news that could cast doubt on the official explanation for what was happening, or not happening, in Iraq.

Bush was able to build an unshakable belief in the world that Iraq had hidden weapons of mass destruction and hoodwinked the UN weapons inspectors only because the media, without exception repeated these assertions without once questioning them. Not one newspaper or TV network sent a correspondent to Baghdad to report what the Iraqis had to say. Iraqi reactions were sought but only perfunctorily. Reports that devoted several hundred words to the accusations would only add phrases like 'the government of Iraq denied these allegations'. What it said beyond that denial—its explanation for what was being reported—was neither solicited nor published. The story narrated in Chapter 3 of this book was therefore never told to the public, in whole or in part.

During the seven months that elapsed between Bush's characterisation of Iraq as a part of the 'axis of evil' and his speech at the United Nations inviting the world body to join him on a crusade against Saddam Hussein, Iraq was relentlessly pounded with two accusations. The first was that it had hidden weapons of mass destruction from the UN weapons inspectors and built more after 'throwing them out' of Iraq in December 1998, and that it harboured aggressive designs and was therefore a threat to its neighbours and the rest of the world. Every single newspaper and TV channel repeated these accusations ad nauseam, but none considered it necessary to air, or publish Iraq's side of the story. Even extremely responsible newspapers like *The Guardian*, and *The Independent*, which were unswervingly opposed to the war, ran frequent stories datelined Baghdad, but did not consider it necessary to carry an interview with an Iraqi official that presented the Iraqi side of the story to their readers.

Any correspondent who had been asked by his newspaper or network to assess how serious a threat Iraq posed to its neighbours, to Europe and the US, would have learned within hours that the economic sanctions had starved Iraq close to death: that more than half of its people lived off food distributed by the World Food Program and other UN and international agencies under the oil for food program[28]; that its per capita income had declined from $ 4000 to $ 150[29]; that the infant mortality rate had climbed from 50 per 1,000 in 1990 to 125 per 1,000 in 1998[30]; that its infrastructure had been so badly shattered that two thirds of its people did not have safe drinking water while a third did not have safe sanitation; that its armed forces had not been able to purchase any modern tanks, field guns or aircraft in or over a decade, and that attrition had reduced it to a third of its original size. He or she might have wondered whether a country in such dire straits had the capacity to even think of attacking its neighbours, and would have wondered whether even Saddam was capable of losing a quarter of a million persons in the 1991 war and learning no lessons from it.

These were questions that needed to be asked, of the Iraqi authorities, of Bush and his advisers, of the ordinary people of Iraq and of its professors and analysts. In a domestic issue, journalists would have raised these doubts as a matter of course, if for no other reason then to make their 'story' more interesting. But when it came to Iraq, these questions and doubts were never raised because no one thought it necessary to entertain any scepticism about the 'coalition's' claims. The golden rule of responsible journalism, the obligation to check a story with those whom it harms, was discarded as casually as a worn out pair of shoes.

As a result, Iraq and its people were deprived of a voice with which to address the world, when they needed it most. During nine long months of mounting tension, as they wondered whether the US and UK would unleash a war upon their tired and starved nation, and who would live and who would die, if they did, they waited in silent impotence.

The pronounced bias that had developed in the visual media in particular was revealed by a study of media coverage in five countries commissioned by the *Frankfurter Allgemeine Zeitung*. This study showed that dissenting voices on Iraq were given only 2 per cent of the air time on BBC. It was somewhat higher on ABC in the USA, but the improvement was only relative, for ABC aired dissent during only 7 per cent of its air time.[31] BBC's senior management actually cautioned its staff in a confidential memorandum dated february 6, to 'be careful' about voicing dissent. The network's head of news justified this on the grounds that this was partly because "there was a degree of political consensus within Westminster, with the Conservatives supporting the government's policy on the war and the liberal democrats, while opposed to the war, supporting the UK forces".[32] The BBC did not believe that either Iraq or the 700,000 to a million protesters, who marched through London on 15 February 2003, deserved a voice.

Perhaps the most brazen demonstration of Iraq's insignificance in a matter that meant life or death to its people was the way CNN and BBC aired the debates in the UN Security Council over the reports of UNMOVIC and IAEA. Both would transmit, in full, the speeches of Blix and Baradei, and the comments of the US, the UK, France, Russia, and China. They would then transmit the remarks of one non-permanent member. Then, over silent footage of the remaining members' speeches, they would bring in a succession of 'experts', from previous American administrations, from think tanks and former military officrs, who would air their understanding of what the Blix and Baradei reports *actually meant,* while the foreign ministers of half a dozen countries went on speaking in the background unheard. *Among those who were thus reduced, literally, to performing puppets, was the Permanent Representative of Iraq, whose country's fate was being decided.*

When the US and UK failed to get sufficient support for a second resolution in the Security Council authorising them to declare war on Iraq, and decided to invade the country without it, relations between the hegemonic powers and the media entered a new phase. For the first time since the end of the Cold War, the US found its claim to the moral leadership of the 'civilised' world being challenged directly by countries that it could not dismiss as being 'rogue states' or atavistic dictatorships. The challenge was thrown by from France and Germany and it was, moreover, a moral challenge. Both were Christian countries, both were highly indusrialised, both were democracies, and both considered that an invasion of Iraq would be unjust, in the sense given to the concept by St. Augustine and Thomas Aquinas, and consecrated as international law by Grotius.

Behind the disagreement at the UN on whether to extend the mandate of the UN inspector or declare Iraq in material breach of past resolutions and invade it, lay two totally opposed views of how the post-Cold War, global order should be built and managed. France, Germany and the majority of the members of the Council endorsed the concerns that the US had expressed, and shared its view that as the world grew more and more intermeshed and interdependent, national sovereignty could no longer remain wholly unfettered. But restrictions of the sovereignty guaranteed to member nations, in the UN charter, they maintained, had to come through consensus. This would modify the tenets of the Westphalian international order and not destroy it. The challenge split not only the Security Council but the Atlantic alliance and NATO. It was nothing less than a challenge to the US' claim to hegemony.

The violently xenophobic reaction of American leaders showed that they were perfectly aware of the seriousness of this development. On the ground, France's challenge changed very little. The US and UK troops were deployed in full strength on Iraq's borders and poised to go in; both had made it clear over and over again that they would go into Iraq with or without a second Security Council resolution; both had received legal sanction for the invasion from their own attorneys-general, who had decided with all the weiht of their Juridical office that UN Resolution 1441 did provide them with a legal case for invading Iraq. And France's opposition did not make any difference to the military equation between Iraq's starveling army and the hi-tech soldiers of the 'coalition of the willing'. So why could the US not play down the disagreement and treat it as an honest difference of opinion in a democratic forum? The answer is that France and Germany's challenge shattered the illusion that the US was acting not only in its own but the world's interest, which was necessary to convert mere military and economic *dominance* into *hegemony*[33].

Once the United States found its hegemony to be challenged, enlisting the media assumed a new, unprecedented, importance. For it became the sole avenue, the indispensable tool, for recapturing it. The story of what the US was going to do, why it was doing it, and all the good things that would come out of it *had to be told, and had to be told in the right way*. It did not take long for this to be translated into policy. On 27 January 2003, CNN reporters received the following instructions:

> All reporters preparing packages must submit the scripts for approval... Packages may not be edited till the scripts are approved... all Packages originating outside Washington, LA or New York, including all international bureaus must come to the ROW in Atlanta for approval.

The ROW was the Row of Script editors in Atlanta who decided precisely *how* a story would be played when it went on the air.

> A script is not *approved* for air unless it is properly marked approved by an *authorised* manager....when a script is updated it must be re-approved preferably by the original approving authority.[34] (emphasis added)

The purpose of the script approval system was fairly obvious: it was not to keep pornography out of CNN's telecasts or ensure that they did not become too violent. It was not to screen out the ramblings of a reporter who might have suddenly gone insane. It was to ensure that 'objectivity' was maintained at all times. Who decided whether a 'package' was objective? Not the reporter who was on the spot, and had lived with a problem for days or even weeks, but a 'manager' in Atlanta. The criteria by which scripts got approved or sent back for editing were never spelt out.[35]

CNN was perhaps the least of the offenders in the US market. Its concept of 'objectivity' may not have coincided with those of European journalists such as Robert Fisk, but it was at least its own. Its script editors and managers may, like the BBC, have been under instructions to be 'careful' about how they presented the news, but it did not give the news a slant at the behest of bosses who had other interests to serve. This was not true of other TV networks in the US. Speaking of the actual coverage of the war a few weeks later Greg Dyke, Director of the BBC observed, "many US wrapped themselves in the American flag and swapped impartiality for patriotism".[36]

While CNN's reporters tried to maintain some objectivity, this was wholly abandoned by another international media giant Rupert Murdoch. His American TV channel, Fox News abandoned all pretensions of objectivity during the war and reaped a handsome dividend. Its ratings shot ahead of those of the more balanced CNN for the first time in its existence. Fox achieved this by beating the drum of patriotism and paranoia: its telecasts appeared with an American flag in the corner and interlarded with terrorism alert updates virtually tailor-made, as Noam Chomsky was to observe, to keep the American 'herd' panic stricken.[37]

Fox's blatant partisanship provoked criticism from both the heads of BBC and CNN.[38] But Murdoch, it turned out, had other fish to fry. In the months before the war Fox News, along with CBS and NBC had mounted enormous pressure on the US Federal Communications Commission to lift or relax bans that prevented foreign news companies from buying into American ones, and prevented a TV network from owning another network, Radio station or newspaper in the same market. Each of these companies stood to gain billions from a relaxation of the FCC's embargo. Murdoch was also trying to get the government not to reject its $ 4.1 billion bid to buy a controlling share in the US satellite TV operator, DirecTV. This made him more than a shade keen to ingratiate himself with the White House.[39] Thus did the economic imperatives of globalisation, to break down national barriers to the creation of a single market, fuse with the drive to destroy the system of laws and conventions built over three centuries to safeguard the Westphalian state system.

Once the US and UK had decided to go invade Iraq without an explicit UN mandate, it became necessary to portray the war itself in a way that enabled them to hold the moral high ground. This led to the most important, but not necessarily the most healthy media innovation of our times, the system of 'embedding' journalists with the military formations. Born out of the 'pool' system it marked a huge step forward in the management of news that, according to the BBC's director of news, Richard Sambrook, 'changed the face of war reporting forever', and not necessarily for the better.[40] The US government could not have stated its purpose in offering the incomparable facilities of 'embedment' to journalists more explicitly than it did:

> Media coverage of any future operation will, to a large extent, shape public perception of the national security environment now and in the years ahead. This holds true for the US public; the public in allied countries whose opinion can affect the

durability of our coalition; and publics in other countries where we conduct operations, whose perceptions of us can affect the cost and duration of our involvement. ... *we need to tell them the factual story—good or bad—before others seed the media with disinformation and distortions, as they most certainly will continue to do.* Our people need to tell our story...(emphasis added).[41]

Notwithstanding the pious intention to allow journalists to report 'the factual story-good or bad', the Pentagon in practice took no chances with the stories that actually got out. The key feature of embedment was that in exchange for the privilege of obtaining visuals and sound bytes of guns firing, buildings being blown up, and aircraft rocketing ground targets with all the accompanying din of battle, embedded journalists had to sign an agreement to submit their copy and footage to the army authorities for clearance before they sent it to their parent organisations for dissemination.

While the principle of exerting control over what the public was allowed to know, was not new, the language used to justify 'embedment' revealed the change of the context in which the control had to be established. Its purpose was to 'shape public perception of the national security environment'. This was a tacit admission that people were not already persuaded that Iraq presented a threat to the US' security and that the persuasion had to continue. This had hardly been necessary when the US entered the Second World War, when it sent its troops to Korea, and later to Vietnam. However disastrous the last intervention turned out to be, doubts about the need for it arose only years after the troops had already gone in, when Americans began to perceive the quagmire in which they were trapped. This time, by contrast, the media had not simply to report a war, but to help the government to persuade the American people that it was both just and necessary. And it was not only the American public but the public in allied and 'target' countries, who needed to be persuaded. In short, the purpose of embedment was to ensure that the media persuaded its readers and viewers that what was good for the US was good for the whole world, *including the country that was being invaded*! There could have been no clearer exposition of the hegemonistic purpose that underlay the exercise.

In view of what happened during the war, the most disturbing feature of the 'guidelines' was its implicit separation of the media into 'the good guys', i.e. the embedded journalists and the 'others'—the 'bad guys'—who would definitely try to 'seed the media with distortions and disinformation'. Who could these 'others' be? They could hardly be Iraq's information minister whose claims, in his daily briefings, of the number of American tanks, armoured personnel carriers, and helicopters destroyed became the subject of black humour as the war progressed. The only 'others' were the non-embedded journalists—the so-called 'independents' and the crews of the Arab TV networks, Abu Dhabi TV and Qatar-based *Al Jazeerah*—who stayed in Basra and Baghdad and were at the receiving end of the missiles, bombs, artillery shells, cluster bombs, and rockets—and therefore could not help seeing and reporting things in a different way.

It is significant that despite the experience of the pool system in Iraq and Kosovo in the past, the vast majority of American newspapers welcomed the system of embedding journalist with the front line forces.[42] It would make the coverage of the war more dramatic while reducing the risk to the journalists. But embedding had innate disadvantages. If a journalist went in uniform with a military formation he was forced to stay with it. Having come with such a force, anyone who tried to strike out on his own to get an Iraqi view of what was happening, risked being taken for a soldier and shot. As a result the price of being embedded was to get only one side of the story, which was what the US and UK governments wanted.

Prolonged contact with the armed forces impaired the objectivity of the embedded journalists. This was reflected by their adoption of the language and rationalisations of the armed forces. Thus the coalition forces had come to 'liberate' not 'occupy' it. The resistance they were encountering was from Ba'ath party 'fanatics', from *fidayeen* and irregulars, never from people outraged by the violation of their country. Iraqis were often referred to as the enemy and the coalition forces as 'we'. The change of language led Richard

Sambrook, head of news at BBC, to apologise to his viewers for the loss of impartiality.

Again, as in the 1991 Gulf War, the embedded journalists never saw and were never showed Iraqi casualties. Their reporting was therefore reinforced once more the impression that this war was inflicting very little pain on the Iraqis. That made it all the easier for the reporters to continue subscribing to the myth that Iraq was being liberated.

Fully aware of the drawbacks, the more independent-minded networks and newspapers sent in independent journalists in addition to the embedded ones. About 20 embedded journalists also left their military unit and struck out on their own when the war came to its closing stages and the US troops entered Baghdad.[43] But the independents were outnumbered by many magnitudes by the embedded journalists. In all somewhere between 500 and 700 journalists went in as embedded journalists, including 128 from Britain. The independents, by contrast, were only a few score.

Not content with having ensured that journalists would not see what the invading forces did not want them to see, the US authorities decided to stage appropriate pieces of theatre for them to see and report home. Two such dramas were 'the saving of Private Jessica Lynch' and 'the toppling of Saddam's statue'.

The Saving of Private Lynch

The story of Private Jessica Lynch's rescue could not have come at a more opportune moment. After the euphoria of the war's first few days, the Allied military campaign appeared to have stalled. In place of 'shock and awe', the media had begun to carry stories of Iraqi women and children being gunned down at checkpoints and US prisoners of war being paraded in front of cameras by their captors. The American public needed a morale booster. The saga of Jessica Lynch's capture, and heroic rescue, was exactly what they needed. It is a story of brutal Iraqi captors, gloating over the capture of a young and beautiful girl, and torturing her after they had killed, probably in captivity, her heroic comrades in arms and if a heroic midnight rescue by the US marines using all the awesome power of

American technology to effect a bloodless rescue. Each and every component of this story was crafted to reinforce the impression of America's moral superiority; her God-given right to assume the championship of civilisation against the barbarian, her awesome technology and her consequent invincibility. Offering resistance to such an elemental force was not only futile, but also morally wrong. Thus did the US seek to attach moral legitimacy to brute military power. This is the story the US military authorities gave out at the time. It was also the first piece of good news in days for the US Central Command in Qatar, which might explain why officials called a news conference at 4.30 AM to announce to a sleepy press corps that a POW had been recovered.

> Jessica's ordeal began on 23 March, day four of the war, when 15 members of the 507th (her unit) took a wrong turn near the southern city of Nasiriyah. The unit was attacked by members of the Saddam Fedayeen, which had been mounting the fiercest Iraqi resistance against American troops.
> Details of the ambush emerging from the war zone are confused and often contradictory, although it is thought at least two of Jessica's colleagues were killed in the initial exchanges. Five were taken captive and shown on Iraqi television, while another eight were listed as Missing in Action, among them Jessica.
> 'She was fighting them to the death. She did not want to be taken alive,' said one US military official in Iraq, who described a scene in which the 19-year-old recruit fired her weapon until she ran out of ammunition, 'killing several enemy soldiers'. Eight days later US special forces stormed the hospital, capturing the "dramatic" events on a night vision camera. They were said to have come under fire from inside and outside the building, but they made it to Lynch and whisked her away by helicopter.

Jessica owed her rescue to a selfless Iraqi lawyer, whose real name, for obvious reasons, the US authorities withheld.

'Mohammed' described how he had first noticed security guards outside the door of a hospital wing, then asked a doctor friend what was going on.

> The doctor took him to another part of the hospital from where they could see Jessica lying in bed, bandaged and covered in blankets. Standing over her was a Fidayeen commander, who was slapping the American prisoner. 'My heart was cut,' he said.
> When the lawyer returned the following day, Jessica was in the room alone and he took the chance to go and speak to her. 'I said "good morning". She thought I was a doctor. I said "Don't worry". She smiled.' That brief exchange set off the chain of events that led to the soldier's dramatic rescue.

According to Mohammed's account, which has yet to be verified by independent sources, he went in search of some US military personnel, walking six miles out of Nasiriyah before finally meeting up with US Marines who had been trying to secure a road on the eastern side of the city.

"This was very dangerous for me as the American soldiers were shooting everything," he said, putting his hands in the air to show how he approached the US soldiers. 'What do you want?' one Marine asked. He told them about the American prisoner at the hospital, about some discarded US military uniforms and the presence of the Fedayeen.

Twice over the next two days, according to Mohammed's version of events, he revisited the hospital at the request of the Marines, counting the number of Iraqi militia who were guarding what had essentially become a military base, taking note of the hospital's layout and tracing possible rescue routes for US troops. 'I drew them a map. I drew five maps,' he told reporters.

Mohammed, his wife and six-year-old daughter left their family home in Nasiriyah last Tuesday night, just hours before the US Navy Special Operations Forces (known as Seals) stormed the city's hospital. It was the first time a US prisoner of war had been recovered from enemy hands since the Second World War.

The now famous video footage, which has been replayed repeatedly on American TV over the past three days, shows four men stretchering Jessica down the hospital steps to the waiting helicopter. "There was not a firefight inside of the building, but there were firefights outside, both getting in and getting out," said a spokesman for Central Command. "But these guys are pros. Any hairy moments that came up they dealt with very quickly."

It was hardly surprising that the US media, which had been gorging on the startling but confused reporting of its 'embedded' reporters, seized on a story which combined human interest with a clear narrative spine.

But missing from this tableau of selfless Iraqi co-operation and American military efficiency were the less palatable details of the Nasiriyah rescue mission. During the raid, the Navy Seals seized a member of the Fedayeen militia who led them to 11 bodies, two in the hospital ward and nine in a freshly dug grave. It is now believed that nine of the bodies were those of Private Lynch's colleagues from the 507th Company. The remains have been shipped back to the US for forensic tests.[44]

When footage of the rescue was released, General Vincent Brooks, US spokesman in Doha, said: "Some brave souls put their lives on the line to make this happen, loyal to a creed that they know that they'll never leave a fallen comrade." Back home in Palestine, West Virginia Jessica became the toast of her town. A Film was planned around her bravery and her rescue.

Only after the war ended did the true story of her capture and rescue come out. Here is the unvarnished account of one of the journalists who visited the hospital at Nasiriyah:

> All Hollywood could ever hope to have in a movie was there in this extraordinary feat of rescue—except, perhaps, the truth. So say three Nasiriya doctors, two nurses, one hospital administrator and local residents interviewed separately last week in a Toronto Star investigation.
>
> The medical team that cared for Lynch at the hospital formerly known as Saddam Hospital is only now beginning to appreciate

how grand a myth was built around the four hours the US raiding party spent with them early on April Fool's Day. And they are disappointed.

For Dr. Harith Houssona, 24, who came to consider Lynch a friend after nurturing her through the worst of her injuries, the ironies are almost beyond tabulation.

"The most important thing to know is that the Iraqi soldiers and commanders had left the hospital almost two days earlier," Houssona said. "The night they left, a few of the senior medical staff tried to give Jessica back. We carefully moved her out of intensive care and into an ambulance and began to drive to the Americans, who were just one kilometer away. But when the ambulance got within 300 meters, they began to shoot. There wasn't even a chance to tell them 'We have Jessica. Take her.'"

One night later, the raid unfolded. Hassam Hamoud, 35, a waiter at Nasiriya's al-Diwan Restaurant, describes the preamble, when he was approached outside his home near the hospital by US Special Forces troops accompanied by an Arabic translator from Qatar.

"They asked me if any troops were still in the hospital and I said 'No, they're all gone.' Then they asked about Uday Hussein, and again, I said 'No,'" Hamoud said. "The translator seemed satisfied with my answers, but the soldiers were very nervous."

At midnight, the sound of helicopters circling the hospital's upper floors sent staff scurrying for the x-ray department— the only part of the hospital with no outside windows. The power was cut, followed by small explosions as the raiding teams blasted through locked doors.

A few minutes later, they heard a man's voice shout, "Go! Go! Go!" in English. Seconds later, the door burst open and a red laser light cut through the darkness, trained on the forehead of the chief resident.

"We were pretty frightened. There were about 40 medical staff together in the x-ray department," said Dr. Anmar Uday,

24. "Everyone expected the Americans to come that day because the city had fallen. But we didn't expect them to blast through the doors like a Hollywood movie."
Dr. Mudhafer Raazk, 27, observed dryly that two cameramen and a still photographer, also in uniform, accompanied the US teams into the hospital. Maybe this was a movie after all.
Separately, the Iraqi doctors describe how the tension fell away rapidly once the Americans realized no threat existed on the premises. A US medic was led to Lynch's room as others secured the rest of the three-wing hospital. Several staff and patients were placed in plastic handcuffs, including, according to Houssona, one Iraqi civilian who was already immobilized with abdominal wounds from an earlier explosion.
One group of soldiers returned to the x-ray room to ask about the bodies of missing US soldiers and was led to a graveyard opposite the hospital's south wall. All were dead on arrival, the doctors say.
"The whole thing lasted about four hours," Raazk said. "When they left, they turned to us and said `Thank you.' That was it."
The Iraqi medical staff fanned out to assess the damage. In all, 12 doors were broken, a sterilized operating theatre contaminated, and the specialized traction bed in which Lynch had been placed was trashed.
"That was a special bed, the only one like it in the hospital, but we gave it to Jessica because she was developing a bed sore," Houssona said.
What bothers Raazk most is not what was said about Lynch's rescue, so much as what wasn't said about her time in hospital.
"We all became friends with her, we liked her so much," Houssona said. "Especially because we all speak a little English, we were able to assure her the whole time that there was no danger, that she would go home soon..."
A few days after her release, Lynch's father told reporters none of the wounds were battle-related. The Iraqi doctors are

more specific. Houssona said the injuries were blunt in nature, possible stemming from a fall from her vehicle.

"She was in pretty bad shape. There was blunt trauma, resulting in compound fractures of the left femur (upper leg) and the right humerus (upper arm). And also a deep laceration on her head," Houssona said. "She took two pints of blood and we stabilized her. The cut required stitches to close. But the leg and arm injuries were more serious."

Nasiriya's medical team was going all out at this point, due to the enormous influx of casualties from throughout the region. The hospital lists 400 dead and 2,000 wounded in the span of two weeks before and during Lynch's eight-day stay.

"Almost all were civilians, but I don't just blame the Americans," Raazk said. "Many of those casualties were the fault of the fedayeen, who had been using people as shields and in some cases just shooting people who wouldn't fight alongside them. It was horrible."

But they all made a point of giving Lynch the best of everything, he added. Despite a scarcity of food, extra juice and cookie were scavenged for their American guest.

They also assigned to Lynch the hospital's most nurturing nurse, Khalida Shinah. At 43, Shinah has three daughters close to Lynch's age. She immediately embraced her foreign patient as one of her own.

"It was so scary for her," Shinah said through a translator. "Not only was she badly hurt, but she was in a strange country. I felt more like a mother than a nurse. I told her again and again, Allah would watch over her. And many nights I sang her to sleep."

In the first few days, Houssona said the doctors were somewhat nervous as to whether Iraqi intelligence agents would show any interest in Lynch. But when the road between Nasiriya and Baghdad fell to the US-led coalition, they knew the danger had passed.

"At first, Jessica was very frightened. Everybody was poking their head in the room to see her and she said `Do they want to hurt me?' I told her, 'Of course not. They're just curious. They've never seen anyone like you before.'

"But after a few days, she began to relax. And she really bonded with Khalida. She told me, `I'm going to take her back to America with me."

Three days before the US raid, Lynch had regained enough strength that the team was ready to proceed with orthopedic surgery on her left leg. The procedure involved cutting through muscle to install a platinum plate to both ends of the compound fracture. "We only had three platinum plates left in our supply and at least 100 Iraqis were in need," Raazk said. "But we gave one to Jessica."

A second surgery, and a second platinum plate, was scheduled for Lynch's fractured arm. But US forces removed her before it took place, Razak said.

Three days after the raid, the doctors had a visit from one of their US military counterparts. He came, they say, to thank them for the superb surgery.

"He was an older doctor with gray hair and he wore a military uniform," Raazk said.

"I told him he was very welcome, that it was our pleasure. And then I told him: `You do realize you could have just knocked on the door and we would have wheeled Jessica down to you, don't you?'

…What troubles the staff in Nasiriya most are reports that Lynch was abused while in their case. All vehemently deny it.

Told of the allegation through an interpreter, nurse Shinah wells up with tears. Gathering herself, she responds quietly: "This is a lie. But why ask me? Why don't you ask Jessica what kind of treatment she received?"

But that is easier said than done. At the Pentagon last week, US Army spokesman Lt.-Col. Ryan Yantis said the door to Lynch remains closed as she continues her recovery at Washington's Walter Reed Army Medical Center.

"Until such time as she wants to talk—and that's going to be no time soon, and it may be never at all—the press is simply going to have to wait."[45]

What the American military was up to was revealed by a BBC correspondent, who followed the story further a few days later.

The American strategy was to ensure the right television footage by using embedded reporters and images from their own cameras, editing the film themselves. The Pentagon had been influenced by Hollywood producers of reality TV and action movies, notably the man behind Black Hawk Down, Jerry Bruckheimer. Bruckheimer advised the Pentagon on the primetime television series "Profiles from the Front Line", that followed US forces in Afghanistan in 2001. That approached was taken on and developed on the field of battle in Iraq.[46]

The fall of Saddam's statue

On 9 April 2003, the war had been going on for three weeks. American forces were in Baghdad and were meeting little resistance. The only question that remained in peoples' minds was to what extent Saddam Hussein would resort to scorched earth tactics in Baghdad, mining roads and blowing up bridges to kill as many Americans as possible, before the inevitable end. Then suddenly the electrifying news flashed across the world that the war was over. The people of Baghdad had risen at last against the hated dictator, and themselves ended his regime. The symbol of their revolt was their pulling down of Saddam's statue in Firdous square, at the heart of the city. According to the commentary carried by BBC and CNN the crowds had come to the square, tried to pull down Saddam's statue and when this proved difficult, had asked a US marine vehicle standing nearby to help them do so. They had then attached a cable to the statue, and the vehicle had obligingly pulled it down. The crowd had then attacked the head and body, broken it up and carried bits away.

The video footage of this event was flashed on the television screens all over the world every few minutes till it became the icon of the war and perhaps the most frequently viewed teleclip in the world after the image of two aircraft hitting the World Trade Towers on 9/11 and bringing them down.

Manufacturing Consent • 155

The images exerted a powerful influence on peoples' minds. Most people around the world believed the commentary. Even Iraqis did so, for the remnants of the army stopped fighting, at least in Baghdad, and government employees simply did not turn up for work the next day. Even the correspondent of the sober and anti-war *The Guardian* felt obliged to endorse the view that people were at last coming out and expressing their joy at being liberated.

> The minders were distracted; a chemist motioned to come inside. "This is the price of freedom, between you and me," he said. "This son of a bitch destroyed us. Ariel Sharon—all the dictators in the world—become angels beside him."
> It was not an entirely unexpected confession. The last days of the war had brought increasing moments of candour from Iraqis, trained over the years to suppress all critical thoughts of the regime...After unburdening himself of his hatred for Saddam, the chemist begged me not to reveal his name, or his shop's location."I wish the coalition forces would come here," he said. "I would guide them to all the Iraqi positions. But if the coalition forces stay longer in Iraq, I think it is going to be a disaster."[47]

The television footage of the fall of Saddam's statue made media history. Both BBC and CNN used close shots the entire time, so that the crowd filled the screen. Shots of this crowd were interspersed between others showing the statue being slowly pulled down and falling over. The American Mechanised Vehicle that did the pulling was not shown, only referred to in passing as a vehicle that had been in the vicinity. A handful of people were shown tugging Saddam's head away. One was making a V for victory sign while another kicked the head. These shots were, in turn interspersed with others showing huge numbers of Shias, who had flowed out of Saddam city, beating their breasts with clubbed fists in a traditional Shia religious ritual that had been banned during Saddam's reign. The three sets of shots created an impression of a huge crowd demonstrating agains the dictator as some of its members pulled

Saddam's statue down. The commentary invited viewers to witness the rebellion and the celebrations that were breaking out. Rumsfeld called it 'breathtaking'; the British army described it as 'historic'; the BBC contented itself with calling it 'amazing'. But even at the time it was happening some correspondents who were eyewitnesses were expressing doubts. "The crowds seemed to know what was expected of them" commented *The Guardian* in the same report.[48] One television commentator even observed that the crowd was small.

In fact the crowd was small. And the entire event was staged by the US military authorities. Photographs taken from the adjoining Palestine Hotel where nearly all the independent journalists in Baghdad were staying show, upon close examination, that

- There had been no crowd in Firdous square around the statue when a number of tanks, a US mechanised vehicle, and several Humvees descended upon it.
- Three, possibly four, tanks took up positions around the square, facing outwards. Interspersed between them were American soldiers also facing outwards. They were clearly there to guard whatever was going on in the square and whoever was doing it.
- In the square there are only a handful of people, estimated at 150 to 200 including a large number of US soldiers. The Iraqis do not number more than a hundred. They are joined by the mechanised vehicle.
- The handful of Iraqis throws a rope over the statue for the MV to pull down. After some false starts, a US marine puts an old Iraqi flag from before the Gulf War over Saddam's face. The MV then pulls down the statue.[49]

An account given by Neville Watson, a clergyman from Australia and a peace activist, who was less than 300 yards away, in a video-conferenced interview with Alan Sutherland of the Information Clearing House, an internet newspaper, tallies closely with the above reconstruction.

ALan Sutherland: Reverend Watson, welcome to Insight.....So tell me, what are we to make of the scenes of Iraqi jubilation on the streets that we've been seeing here?

Neville Watson: *Well, there certainly was some jubilation, but I certainly wouldn't go along with that presented by television. The one that I've seen a lot of since I've been back is the toppling of the statue of Saddam and I can hardly believe it was the same one that I saw, because it happened at only about 300m from where I was and it was a very small crowd. The rest of the square was almost empty, and when we inquired as to where the crowd came from, it was from Saddam City. In other words, it was a rent-a-crowd.*[50]

Who were the members of this crowd? And who organised them? The mainline media—even *The Guardian*—did not doubt that the crowd had collected spontaneously to celebrate liberation. Al Jazeerah TV reported that many among them were Kurds settled in Baghdad. However, it was Watson who was closes to the mark. Two photographs, among the thousands taken during the war gave the gam away. The first, taken on 6 April showed Ahmad Chalabi, the head of the Iraqi National Congress, arriving in Nasiriyah with 700 of his "free Iraqi Forces" aboard four C-17 aircraft. Immediately behind him was an aide with a round face, receding hairline, arched eyebrows and a stylishly shaped beard and mustache. The second, taken on 9 April shows the same man raising his hand towards the camera in a V for Victory sign. This picture was taken at Firdous square at the toppling of Saddam's statue and aired all over the world. How in the middle of the war did a close associate of Chalabi travel from Nasiriyah to Baghdad? And why did he do so? The answer is obvious: the Americans brought him to rent the crowd that toppled Saddam's statue.[51]

Good Journalists and Bad Journalists

Perhaps the worst long-term damage that the embedding system did was to create the belief in the minds of soldiers feeling the stress of battle that those who were not with them were against them. This led to independent journalists being shut out from contact with the soldiers and, more detrimentally, of entire areas under US or UK control. Not surprisingly, in view of their challenge to US hegemony, the prime sufferers were correspondents from the European countries that had opposed the invasion. This led the European Broadcasters Union to accuse the Military Field Information Centre in southern Iraq of having created a caste system among war correspondents. One among several examples was its refusal to feed French footage out of its equipment to France-2 in Paris. According to Tony Naets, the EBU's head of news, "They have created a caste system with embedded journalists—usually from countries in the so-called coalition who can associate with the troops—and the truly independent broadcaster who is prevented from coming anywhere near the news".[52]

This feeling almost certainly underlies the repeated attacks that journalists came under from US forces in Iraq. In all, 17 journalists lost their lives[53] in the three-week war. The majority of them were killed not by the Iraqis but by the US military. This made the death rate among journalists, despite their non-combatant status, about 20 times higher than among the American and British armies.[54] The casualties began with three reporters and camera crew of the British television network ITN. It climaxed with an American tank firing a shell deliberately into the Palestine hotel, an attack with two missiles on the offices of Al Jazeerah, and another on Abu Dhabi TV, in two separate buildings. The Palestine Hotel was where all the independent journalists in Baghdad were staying. By the last days of the war, it had become one of the best known buildings in the world because it was the location from which BBC and other independent channels were sending their telecasts. Two cameramen of Reuters were killed at the hotel. Al Jazeerah lost its chief reporter, Tarek Ayoub, who had just taken over the Baghdad office and was in the middle of a broadcast when he died. Of the 15 officially declared dead at the end of April, three had been killed by the Iraqis; five died in genuine accidents and seven were killed by Americans.[55]

While the death of the ITN crew might have been a tragic accident, the attacks on the Palestine Hotel and the offices of the to Arab TV channels bore all the marks of premeditation. The US central command immediately justified the attack on the hotel by claiming hat the tank had come under sniper fire (to which it is utterly invulnerable anyway). But every journalist who was in the hotel at the time, including Robert Fisk, angrily denied this and asserted that the entire area had been free of any firing at the time of the attack. Television footage shot by France 3 and submitted to US Defense Secretary Rumsfeld by the Secretary-General of Reporters Sans Frontieres, Robert Menard, showed that that the area was very quiet and that the tank crew had taken their time, waiting for a couple of minutes and adjusting their gun sights before opening fire. "This evidence does not match the US version of an attack in self defence and we can only conclude that the US army deliberately and without waning, targeted journalists", Menard told *The Guardian*.[56]

The US called the attack on the Palestine Hotel 'unfortunate'[57] and apologised profoundly to Al Jazeerah for the death of Ayoub, but Al Jazeerah insisted that it was not a mistake. It had supplied its Global Positioning system co-ordinates to the US authorities before the war began.[58] This was also not the first but the third time that Al Jazeerah had been targeted by 'Allied' forces within a year. The second time had been when a hotel in Basra where only the Al Jazeerah crew was staying received a direct hit from a bomb. But the first and most significant attack took place on its offices in Kabul. It totally destroyed the building and all of Al Jazeera's equipment, but miraculously occurred when no one was there. Like the 7 April attacks in Baghdad, this too occurred within hours of a missile hitting the BBC office and blowing its correspondent out of his chair. Philip Knightley's account of the BBC's subsequent investigations helps to explain why the 'non-embedded' media came under fire a year later in Iraq:

> The media should have seen it coming. Last year the BBC sent one of its top reporters, Nik Gowing, to Washington to try to find out how it was that its correspondent, William Reeve, who had just re-opened the Corporation's studio in Kabul and was giving a live TV interview for BBC World, was blown out of his seat by an American smart missile. Four hours later, a few blocks away, the office and residential compound of the Arab TV network Al-Jazeera was hit by two more American missiles.

The BBC, Al-Jazeera, and the US Committee to Protect Journalists thought it prudent to find out from the Pentagon what steps they could take to protect their correspondents *if war came to Iraq*. (emphasis added). Rear Admiral Craig Quigley was frank. He said the Pentagon was indifferent to media activity in territory controlled by the enemy, and that the Al-Jazeera compound in Kabul was considered a legitimate target because it had 'repeatedly been the location of significant al-Qaeda activity'. It turned out that this activity was interviews with Taliban officials, something Al-Jazeera had thought to be normal journalism.

All three organisations concluded that the Pentagon was determined to deter western correspondents from reporting any war from the 'enemy' side; would view such journalism in Iraq as activity of 'military significance', and might well bomb the area.

This view was reinforced in the early days of the war in Iraq, when the Pentagon wrote officially to Al-Jazeera asking it to remove its correspondents from Baghdad. Downing Street made the same request to the BBC. In the US a Pentagon official called media bosses to a meeting in Washington to tell them how foolhardy and dangerous it was to have correspondents in the Iraqi capital. But no one realised it might also be dangerous to work outside the system the Pentagon had devised for allowing war correspondents to cover the war: embedding. In total, 600 correspondents, including about 150 from foreign media, and even one from the music network MTV, accepted the Pentagon's offer to be embedded with military units.[59]

On 18 August 2003, US soldiers killed yet another Reuters cameraman, Lebanese-born, award-winning Mazen Dana, while he was filming the arrival of a convoy of military vehicles at the notorious Abu Ghraib prison. By then the war had been over for four months. The US army authorities claimed that the troops had mistaken Dana's video camera for a rocket propelled grenade launcher, but other journalists who had been with him, including his sound recorder, accused the soldiers of behaving in a "crazy" and negligent fashion. They claimed the Americans had spotted the Reuters crew outside the jail half an hour before Mazen Dana was killed and must have realised he was not a guerrilla carrying a rocket-propelled grenade launcher.[60]

Despite the accumulation of circumstantial evidence, it is still difficult to conclude that anyone in the US armed forces actually directed its armoured formations or air force units to target journalists and their offices. But the unfortunate side effect of 'embedment' was that it almost certainly removed the inhibitions in the combat forces that had protected journalists in the past. From the US' point of view, however, embedment served at least its immediate purpose. For more than a month, the embedded journalists saturated the air waves with stories and footage that confirmed the view that technology had reduced modern warfare to a bloodless video game. During thousands of minutes of air time devoted to the war, the major networks did not show a single dead Iraqi soldier, and most definitely no dead Iraqi civilian. They also did not show a single dead American or Briton[61] lest (God forbid) his or her mother or father, or wife, husband and children, might be watching. As a result when, after finding no WMD both Bush and Blair claimed that it did not matter because Saddam Hussein had been ousted and who could deny that the world (and of course Iraq) was a better place without him, people forgot the lies they had been told; forgot the more than 300 dead American and Britons, and 20,000-plus dead Iraqis, and swallowed the newly minted justification hook, line and sinker.

Notes

1. Associated Press. "Poll: Bush should wait on Iraq" 7 October 2002.
2. The opinion polls were tracked religiously by the Economist in various issues in late 2002 and 2003. Only in Britain, and the US did the opposition weaken and turn into a lukewarm support for 'our boys in uniform' when it became apparent that war was only days away.
3. Appeal by eminent jurists on International Law concerning the recourse to the use of force against Iraq.- Universite Libre de Bruxelles. *Le Monde Diplomatique* April 2003.

4. See Noam Chomsky. *Media Control–The Spectacular Achievements of Propaganda*. Second edition. New York: Seven Stories Press, 2002.
5. Dana Milbank and Claudia Deane. "Hussein Link to 9/11 Lingers in Many Minds". *Washington Post* 5 September 2003.
6. Seymour Hersh "Who lied to whom? Why the administration endorsed a forgery about Iraq's nuclear program". *The New Yorker* 31 March 2003; Nicholas D. Kristoff: "Missing in Action: The Truth" *The New York Times* 6 May 2003.
7. US Department of State : International Information Programs: "The Lessons of Halabja: An Ominous Warning".
8. Ibid.
9. Elisabeth Bumiller "US names Iraqis who would face war crimes trial". *New York Times* 16 March 2003.
10. Stephen C. Pelletiere "A War Crime or an Act of War". *The New York Times* 31 January 2003.
11. Daniel Benjamin "Saddam Hussein and Al Qaeda are notallies". *The New York Times*, 30 September 2002.
12. Dana Priest "US eases stance on Iraqi link to Al Qaeda". *The Washington Post*. 11 September, 2002.
13. Julian Borger op. cit. *The Guardian* 29 May 2003 Borger identified the 'Office of Special Plans' in the US Department of Defence as the conduit through which the unreliable evidence was funnelled directly into US policy making. This was confirmed by Dafna Linzer, "Bush, Blair Face Heat on Iraq Weapons". Associated Press 1 June 2003. See also Seymour Hersh and Nicholas Kristoff. op. cit. See Chapter 14 footnotes.
14. Brian Appleyard "Blair demands overthrow of Saddam as millions march-Streets of London Paved With Protest". *The Sunday Times* 16 February 2003.
15. Tony Allen-Mills, David Cracknell and Sarah Baxter. "The Other Man Under Siege". *The Sunday Times* 16 February 2003.
16. US Department of State International Information Programs "US Sees Political, Religious Freedom Growing Quickly in Iraq State Dept. spokesman discusses Iraq, France" by Jane Morse. Washington File Staff Writer. 23 April 2003.
17. Robert Fisk "A Civilisation Torn to Pieces". *The Independent* 13 April 2003.
18. This sentiment was summed up succinctly by Ignacio Ramonet, writing in *Le Monde Diplomatiue* (April 2003). In a cover page piece entitled 'Illegal Aggression', he wrote:
    Sans trop se faire d'illusions, chacun attend du pays le plus puissant de la Terre qu'il soit aussi une puissance éthique, champion du

respect du droit et modèle de soumission à la loi. Ou du moins qu'il ne tourne pas ostensiblement le dos aux grands principes de la morale politique.

Roughly translated, this reads: "Everyone expects the worlds mightiest power to be an ethical power, a champion of respect for Law and a model of submission to Law. At the very least (one expects) it not to turn its back ostentatiously on the grand principles of political morality. On 15 January 2003, more than 500 eminent international jurists and judges sent an appeal to the UN Security Council not to countenance an invasion of Iraq, claiming that it would go against every principle of International Law. (Appel de juristes de droit international concernant le recours à la force contre l'Irak-Univesite Libre de Bruxelles)".
19. There were notable exceptions, like John Pilger of *The Guardian* and Robert Fisk of *The Independent*, but these were few and far between and their voices were drowned in the tidal wave of skilfully orchestrated condemnation.
20. John Pilger. *Hidden Agendas*. London: Vintage Press, 1998. p. 44.
21. This perceptive comment was made by Greg Philo and Greg Mc Laughlin, in a review of the reporting of the war quoted by Pilger. op. cit. p. 45.
22. Pilger op. cit. p. 48
23. Ibid.
24. Maggie O'Kane of *The Guardian* who stayed in Baghdad throughout the first Gulf War and visited the bunker, conferred that there had been 400 persons, mostly women and children, in it. "The most pitiful sight I have ever seen." *The Guardian* 14 February 2003.
25. Pilger op cit.
26. Ibid. p.46
27. Ibid. p. 47
28. Associated Press "Chronic poverty in Iraq may worsen". 9 June 2003
29. Mona Megalli and Peg Mackey "US says donors must come to the aid of Iraq". Reuters, 21 June 2003.
30. UNICEF and Government of Iraq ministry of Health: Child and Maternal mortality Survey 1999. Preliminary report.
31. David Miller "Taking sides". *The Guardian* 22 April 2003.
32. Ibid.
33. For a discussion of the difference, see Giovanni Arrighi. *The Long Twentieth Century*. New York: Verso, 1994. Chapter 1.

34. The document was titled "Reminder of script approval policy". Quoted by Robert Fisk "How the News will be censored in this war". *The Independent* 25, February 2003.
35. Fisk gave an example of the purpose that script approval was intended to serve. "Just where this awful system leads is evident from an intriguing exchange last year between CNN's reporter in the occupied West Bank town of Ramallah, and Eason Jordan, one of CNN's top honchos in Atlanta.
The journalist's first complaint was about a story by the reporter Michael Holmes on the Red Crescent ambulance drivers who are repeatedly shot at by Israeli troops. "We risked our lives and went out with ambulance drivers... for a whole day. We have also witnessed ambulances from our window being shot at by Israeli soldiers... The story received approval from Mike Shoulder. The story ran twice and then Rick Davis (a CNN executive) killed it. The reason was we did not have an Israeli army response, even though we stated in our story that Israel believes that Palestinians are smuggling weapons and wanted people in the ambulances."
The Israelis refused to give CNN an interview, only a written statement. This statement was then written into the CNN script. But again it was rejected by Davis in Atlanta. Only when, after three days, the Israeli army gave CNN an interview did Holmes's story run–but then with the dishonest inclusion of a line that said the ambulances were shot in "crossfire" (ie that Palestinians also shot at their own ambulances).
The reporter's complaint was all too obvious. "Since when do we hold a story hostage to the whims of governments and armies? We were told by Rick that if we do not get an Israeli on-camera we would not air the package. This means that governments and armies are indirectly censoring us and we are playing directly into their own hands."op.cit. 25/2/03.
36. Dominic Timms "Dyke attacks 'unquestioning US media". *The Guardian* 24 April 2003.
37. Jason Deans. "Fox challenges CNN's US ratings dominance". *The Guardian* 27 March 2003.
38. Dominic Timms op. cit. *The Guardian* 24 April 2003.
Noam Chomsky makes this observation in *Media Control: The Spectacular Achievements of propaganda*. New York: Seven Stories Press, 2002.
39. Annie Lawson. "US broadcaster's war stance under scrutiny". *The Guardian* 14 April 2003. Jeffrey Chester, Executive Director of the

Center for Digital Democracy, accused Fox and the other TV cnetworks of having a 'serious conflict of interest' when it came to reporting the policies of the Bush administration."It is likely that decisions about how to cover the war in Iraq—especially on television—may be tempered by a concern not to lienate the White House". He wrote.

40. Ciar Byrne "War reporting 'changed forever', says BBC". *The Guardian* 31 March 2003.
41. Memorandum containing guidelines for 'guidance, policies, and procedures on embedding news media during possible future operations/deployments in the CENTCOM AOR. Issued by the US secretary of Defense. February 03.
42. Robert Fisk "How the news will be censored in this war". *The Independent* 25 February 2003.
43. Jason Deans "Journalists quit embedded roles". *The Guardian* 11 April 2003. The BBC was so dissatisfied with the restraints placed upon its reporters by he very fact of embedment, that it detached them from the troops the moment they reached Baghdad.
44. Lawrence Donegan "How Private Jessica became America's icon". *Observer* 6 April 2003.
45. Mitch Potter: "The real saving of Private Lynch" *Toronto Star* 4 May 2003.
46. John Kampfner "Saving Private Lynch story Flawed". BBC's news programme "Correspondent". May 15 2003.
47. "The Toppling of Saddam: An end to thirty years of brutal rule". *The Guardian* 10 April 2003.
48. Ibid.
49. The photos were taken by a Reuters cameraman. These and the description given above are available at http://www.informationclearinghouse.info/article2842htm.
50. "The Toppling Of Saddam Statue: An Eyewitness Report". SBS TV Australia: 17 April 2003.http://www.informationclearinghouse.info/article3024htm.
51. http://www.informationclearinghouse.info/article2842htm
52. Ciar Byrne "Independents 'frozen out' by armed forces". *The Guardian* 3 April 2003.
53. Phillip Knightley "Turning the tanks on the reporters". *The Guardian* 15 June 2003. At the time of writing, two of them were still listed as 'missing'.
54. The total number of soldiers killed was less than 200 out of 200,000. But 17 out of less than 800 journalists were killed—more than one in

fifty. If one calculates the ration of independent journalist it would be many times higher still.
55. Ciar Byrne "US soldiers were main danger to journalists, says Simpson". *The Guardian*, 27 June 2003.
56. Ciar Byrne "Press Watchdog accuses US army over Baghdad deaths". *The Guardian* 9 April 2003.
57. Claire Cozens "US: Press deaths 'unfortunate". *The Guardian* 8 April 2003.
58. Claire Cozens "Al Jazeerah claims military cover up". *The Guardian* 8 April, 2003.
59. Phillip Knightley op. cit.
60. Jamie Wilson "US troops 'crazy' in killing of cameraman". *The Guardian*, 19 August 2003.
61. The only exceptions were the Arab news channels, whom Bush and Powell immediately, with a total lack of irony, accused of committing a war crime.

5

The Unravelling of Consent

In the end, all the strenuous efforts the US and UK made to maintain the consent for the invasion of Iraq that they had so single-mindedly manufactured came to naught. Six months after the war ended, both Bush and Blair found themselves battling for their very survival against a rising tide of scepticism and suspicion. For by then, each and every one of the accusations they had made against Saddam Hussein to justify his forcible eviction had turned out to be unfounded. Had the occupation forces discovered any evidence whatever that Saddam had been trying to rebuild his proscribed weapons factories; and had there been the faintest sign of an Al Qaeda–Saddam link, all of the Machiavellian tactics that the US used over six long years to demonise Saddam, put Iraq in the dock, dismiss the reservations of its own NATO allies, and launch an invasion of a broken down, destitute nation, would have been forgiven.

But in the end, there were no weapons of mass destruction. And as it became clearer day by day, that it was the self-styled champions of western civilisation that had lied and cheated their countries into war, and poor, brutal and primitive Iraq that had been telling the truth all along, the consent manufactured through the endless repetition of lies, the endless representation of suspicion as gospel truth and the endless vilification of a single man and his administration, gradually broke down. With it went the moral superiority that America needed to convert its unchallengeable military dominance into global hegemony.

Weapons of mass destruction

On 27 May 2003, 48 days after the fall of Baghdad, the US Secretary of Defense Donald Rumsfeld, the man most responsible for the war on Iraq, admitted that the US inspectors had not found any weapons of mass destruction and might never find them because *they may have been destroyed before the war*.[1] Rumsfeld, who had till then stoutly maintained that it was only a mater of time before the missing WMD turned up, changed his tune when he received a report from the CIA and Defence Intelligence Agency that although two mobile laboratories found in northern Iraq represented the "strongest evidence to date that Iraq was hiding a biological warfare programme, no traces of biological agents had been found. Nor was there any indication that the trucks had been used for that purpose". The two mobile laboratories had been the US's final chance of vindicating its decision to wage an unprovoked war on Iraq. Rumsfeld's admission came after six weeks of an increasingly frantic but fruitless struggle to find some evidence of the existence of weapons of mass destruction in Iraq. This had involved more than 1,000 American biologists, chemists, nuclear operators and computer and document experts, and several mobile laboratories assembled in the 75th Exploitation Task Force. This task force (derisively labelled the USMOVIC[2]) had scoured every possible potential weapons site and come up with absolutely nothing. Indeed its laboratories had barely been used.[3]

As site after site proved to have nothing, the US army made lists of new sites to be examined. By the end of May, nearly all of the 19 highest priority sites that the US had listed had been examined. This had followed 731 site inspections at 411 sites, and hundreds of tests of samples by UNMOVIC, which had also turned up no chemical and biological weapons or precursors. The inspectors were going through a second list of 68 sites and a third list of 600 lower priority sites had still to be explored.[4]

Shortly after the war ended, when questions first began to be asked about the missing weapons of mass destruction, Rumsfeld, had predicted that the questioning of Iraqi scientists would lead to the discovery of biological and chemical weapons. But this too turned out to be a dead end. One Iraqi scientist did claim that the regime had been manufacturing chemical and biological weapons but had destroyed them four days before the war. He also claimed that a good deal of chemical and biological agents had been buried in the earth and led US inspectors on a merry chase inspecting pieces of ground where he claimed to have seen the materials buried.[5] But the most intensive investigation failed to uncover any evidence to substantiate his statements. Without a single exception, Iraqi scientists, from the weapons chief Gen. Amir al Saadi and biological warfare programme heads like Dr. Rihab Taha and Dr. Huda Ammash, to ordinary laboratory workers had told the US and UK forces to whom they surrendered that while Iraq had had weapons of mass destruction in 1991, these had been destroyed years earlier and not on the eve of the war.[6]

On 27 May, Rumsfeld finally admitted the possibility that interrogating the scientists too might not lead to the discovery of any weapons of mass destruction.

"It's hard to find things in a country that's determined not to have you find them," Mr. Rumsfeld told a meeting of foreign affairs experts. "It's also possible that they decided to destroy them prior to the conflict."

Rumsfeld's admission let the genie out of the bottle. Within days, intelligence agencies on both sides of the Atlantic disclosed that their reports had been deliberately distorted by their political master to create the impression that Iraq definitely had weapons of mass destruction, and create thereby a case for an invasion of the country.

The first rumblings of discontent had surfaced on 7 February 2003, when Whitehall officials protested that the intelligence material being provided by MI 6 and other agencies was being used selectively by Downing Street to make a case for invasion. This had been provoked by the disclosure the previous day, that a British 'intelligence' report handed to the Americans a few days earlier and cited with approval by Colin Powell in his speech to the Security Council two days earlier, had been cobbled together from bits and pieces of published material including a 1999 Ph. D dissertation by an American student, Dr. Al Marashi. Other parts had been lifted from a book published in 1999 titled *Saddam's Secrets* by one Tim Trevan. The entire paper had been concocted in the same Coalition Information Center in the Prime Minister's office which had disseminated the story about Iraq's purchases of uranium yellow cake from Niger. Downing Street was in such haste to keep up with the Bush administration in the making of a case for invasion that it was not dissuaded from using Al Marashi's piece, even though it had been published in the *Middle East Review of International Affairs*, which is published in Israel. This disclosure prompted several MPs including Glenda Jackson, a Labour former minister, to protest that the government was misleading parliament and the public. "And of course to mislead is a parliamentary euphemism for lying," Ms. Jackson told Radio 4's Today programme.[7]

Downing Street's decision to hand over a document of such dubious ancestry to the US State Department showed that this was no 'blunder'. If anything, a competition seemed to have developed between the two governments, and more specifically between officials in Downing Street and their counterparts in the White House and US Defense Department, to see who could produce newer and more convincing justifications for invading Iraq.

Rumsfeld's admission unleashed another attempt by the British intelligence agencies to protect their tarnished reputations. Through unsourced leaks in the media they made it known that MI6 and GCHQ, Britain's eavesdropping centre, had opposed the misuse of their intelligence inputs to push the case for war, as long back as in autumn 2002. A key example was the assertion of the British report on Iraq's weapons of mass destruction, that became the epicentre of the attack on Tony Blair's credibility in June 2003, and led to the suicide of British scientist, David Kelly. The body of the report was guarded in its conclusions: "intelligence indicates that the Iraqi military are able to deploy chemical or biological weapons within 45 minutes of an order to do so". This was converted by Prime Minister Tony

Blair in the foreword to the 24 September report into "discloses that [Saddam's] *military planning allows* for some of the WMD [weapons of mass destruction] to be ready within 45 minutes of an order to use them". The Prime Minister's office had changed an estimate of capability into evidence of concrete military planning for the use of weapons of mass destruction. The assessment presupposed that Saddam's forces had drums of chemical or biological weapons close to missile batteries.[8] If that was so then the Iraqi military would be able to deploy WMD within 45 minutes. *Blair, however projected as a British intelligence finding what was only a precondition for a conclusion in the original assessment.*

Even the original intelligence estimate had an extremely shaky foundation. In a BBC Radio 4 programme on 29 May 2003. Adam Ingram, the armed forces minister, conceded that "That was said on the basis of security service information—a single source, it wasn't corroborated." But this was only half an admission. Sources in British intelligence told *The Guardian* that even that the number of sources was not the real issue: "What mattered was the reliability of the source".[9]

Rumsfeld's admission triggered a similar burst of anger in Washington, in senior former members of the CIA and the Military's Defence Intelligence Agency. Patrick Lang, a former head of worldwide human intelligence gathering for the Defense Intelligence Agency, which coordinates military intelligence believed that the DIA was "exploited and abused and bypassed in the process of making the case for war in Iraq based on the presence of WMD," He said the CIA had "no guts at all" to resist the deliberate skewing of intelligence by a Pentagon that was now dominating US foreign policy.

Vince Cannistraro, a former chief of Central Intelligence Agency counter-terrorist operations, said serving intelligence officers blamed the Pentagon for playing up "fraudulent" intelligence, "a lot of it sourced from the Iraqi National Congress of Ahmad Chalabi."

"There are current intelligence officials who believe it is a scandal," he said, who believed that the administration, before going to war, had a "moral obligation to use the best information available, not just information that fits your preconceived ideas."[10]

The top Marine Corps officer in Iraq, Lt. Gen. James Conway, said on Friday, 29 May 2003 that US intelligence was "simply wrong" in leading military commanders to fear troops were likely to be attacked with chemical weapons in the March invasion of Iraq that ousted Saddam.[11]

Perhaps the most direct and damaging attack came from Ray McGovern, a former CIA analyst with 25 years experience, who heads an organisation of former intelligence officials that had written both to President Bush and Kofi Annan protesting against the abuse of intelligence to start a war against Iraq. In a news analysis programme on BBC World Service TV news, on 3 June 2003, McGovern accused the Bush administration of lying to Congress to hustle it into passing the war powers resolution on 11 October 2002. The brazen doctoring of intelligence inputs to force the country to arrive at a predetermined conclusion was done by a group of persons at the Department of Defense whom he derisively referred to as 'the cabal'. The key piece of evidence that persuaded both houses of Congress was the administration's assertion that Iraq had sought to purchase Uranium yellow cake from Niger, a story that turned out to be a complete fabrication. In the interview, McGovern confirmed, by implication, that the government already knew that the supporting documents were crude forgeries when it presented this evidence to the two houses of Congress.[12] He also asserted that the so-called evidence that Colin Powell had presented to the UN Security Council on 5 February 2003 had not been put together by the CIA but in the National Security Council. It was later found to have been concocted very largely in the office of the Vice President Dick Cheney. So poor was the material that Powell was asked to read out that he threw a good deal of it out at the last minute in disgust.

Rumsfeld's admission and the subsequent outburst from the intelligence agencies forced a lame defence of the Iraq war out of Bush. On a visit to St Petersburg when Rumsfeld's admission hit the headlines, Bush tried to fend off criticism by insisting that WMD had been found in Iraq, but went on to add that it was time to stop worrying about what had already been done and start looking ahead: "We've discovered a weapons system—biological labs that

Iraq denied she had and labs that were prohibited under the U.N. resolutions."[13]

Thus did 38,000 litres of botulinum toxin, 25,000 litres of anthrax, 500 tons of sarin, mustard and VX nerve agents boil down to two disused vans that, as it turned out later, had never been close to a biological weapons programme.

Bush did his best instead to turn public attention away from the past to the future: "My opinion is that we must work together to improve the lives of the Iraqi citizens, that we must cooperate closely to make sure that the Iraqi infrastructure is in place so that Iraqi citizens can live decently."[14]

But by then the damage had been done. Congressmen had become deeply uneasy about the possibility that they might have been knowingly duped by the administration. The Democrats in particular had sensed an issue that could bring George Bush down in 2004. Legislators from both parties joined together to ask for an investigation into the possible abuse of intelligence information about Iraq's alleged weapons of mass destruction programme. Henry Waxman, a Democrat senator from California wrote a 40-page letter to President Bush making the same charges and demanding the same explanations as McGovern.[15]

The damage that Blair and Bush sustained was incalculable. The stubborn absence of WMD in Iraq left them with no option but to keep insisting that despite all the evidence to the contrary, these did exist in Iraq. But as month followed month and no WMD were unearthed, their credibility evaporated. For Blair matters came to a head when David Kelly, a British weapons specialist who worked in the Defence department and had been a weapons inspector in Iraq, committed suicide on 7 July. Kelly had earlier met two correspondents from the BBC, Andrew Gilligan and Susan Watts, and given them information that led Gilligan to conclude that the government had knowingly exaggerated the significance of intelligence reports on Iraq's WMD to make a case for war. In the inquiry that followed his death, it soon became apparent that the Defence department had identified Kelly as the source of the leaks, and that a decision had been taken either there or in the Prime Minister's Office, to expose him to parliament and the public. The stress of having to face a parliamentary inquiry, of being hounded by the press, and the prospect of facing much more of the same in the future led the shy, introverted scientist to take his own life. Kelly's death proved a turning point.

By mid-July, opinion polls showed that Blair's popularity had sunk to an unprecedented depth. This prompted the Conservatives, who had stood staunchly by the Prime Minister during the build up to the war, to turn upon him. In a rowdy House of Commons session on 16 July the Conservative leader, Ian Duncan Smith, told Mr. Blair, "You are rapidly becoming a stranger to the truth ...You have created a culture of deceit and spin at the heart of government". Other MPs bellowed disapproval, waved their papers in the air and accused him of having "duped" them into going to war.[16] By mid-August, Blair's credibility had sunk even further to the lowest point in his six years in office. An opinion poll showed that two out of three Britons believed that Blair had deceived Briton about Iraqi weapons of mass destruction.[17]

In contrast to Blair, Bush suffered little immediate damage within the US. The quick end of the war had pushed his popularity ratings sky high. But by 10 July it, too, had begun to fall precipitously. A *Washington Post*–CBS poll released on 11 July showed that while his approval rating was still 59 per cent, it had fallen by nine per cent in three weeks. Ominously for him, the poll found a dramatic reversal in public tolerance of continuing casualties, with a majority saying for the first time that the losses were unacceptable when weighed against the goals of the war.[18]

As the controversy raged through June and July, 1400 weapons inspectors and supporting staff, belonging to now renamed Iraq Survey Group scoured all the remaining pre-selected sites and found nothing. The first intimation that a quiet burial was in the offing came at the end of August, a senior member of the team admitted to the *Los Angeles Times* that the Group did not expect to find anything. "We were prisoners of our own beliefs," he told *The LA Times*. "We said Saddam Hussein was a master of denial and deception. Then when we couldn't find anything, we said that proved it, instead of questioning our own assumptions".[19] On 2 October 2003, David Kay, the chief of the Iraq Survey Group, the team of 1200 weapons inspectors that the US and UK assembled to find Iraq's Weapons of Mass Destruction submitted an 'interim' to the intelligence committees of both houses of the US Congress, that the Group had not found any weapons and probably there were no weapons to be found.

Bush's second key accusation, that Iraq had built links with Al Qaeda, also died a natural death when the occupation forces failed to find any evidence of such links. But scepticism about the Bush administration's honesty deepened when reporters unearthed the fact that even wile Bush had been instilling fear in the American public in speech after speech that Iraq was on the point of handing over its weapons of mass destruction to Al Qaeda, he had all along been in possession of a National Intelligence estimate that had concluded that there was no credible evidence of any link between Saddam and Al Qaeda.[20]

By the end of August, it was clear that the invasion of Iraq had been unjustified. Iraq had no proscribed weapons and was not building any. Its armed forces were so starved of conventional weaponry, and so low in moral that it had chosen not to fight the invaders. It had made no plans to invade any neighbouring country, and had no connections with Al Qaeda. Bush and Blair had made a cruel and monumental blunder, but in a media-driven age where appearances were more important than reality, neither could even begin to admit that they could have made a mistake. Media pressure, of precisely the same kind that had disrupted the US-Iraq relationship after 1988, therefore forced them to go scurrying in search of an alternative justification for what they had done. There was only one left: the defence of human rights and the propagation of democracy. Democracy brought freedom, freedom brought hope, and hope was the antithesis to terror. It was the duty of the 'civilised' West to bestow these blessings upon the unenlightened people of the 'Third World'. If they appeared to resist, it was only out of ignorance, or because they were held in thrall by savage despots. Thus was the 'White Man's Burden' reborn.

As was his wont, Blair was the first to see the need to deploy this weapon of last resort. Faced with three quarters of a million peace marchers in London on February 15, at the Labour Party's spring conference in Glasgow, he built an elaborate moral justification for an invasion by harping upon the repressive and inhuman nature of Saddam's regime:

"If the result of peace is Saddam staying in power and retaining weapons of mass destruction then I tell you there are consequences paid in blood for that decision too. These victims will never be seen. They will never feature on our TV screens to inspire millions to take to the streets. But they exist nonetheless".

Innocents would die in a war, he admitted, but hundreds of Iraqi children were already dying from preventable diseases in what should be a wealthy country. "Ridding the world of Saddam Hussein", he concluded, "would be an act of humanity. It is leaving him in power that is inhumane. That is why I do not shrink from military action, should that indeed be necessary."[21]

Blair thus carried forward to its logical conclusion the argument that had turned the defence of human rights into the most potent weapon of offense against the nation state in the years after the Cold War.

The obvious question that his advocacy raised was, who would be the judge of when the assault on human rights became sufficiently severe to merit armed intervention by other states? Blair answered this in July 2003, during an address to the joint session of the US Congress: The war on Iraq, he said, had been necessary in order to spread "our shared values: not just American values, or British values, but universal values, throughout the world."

These shared values, which justified the invasion of not only Iraq but also Afghanistan in 2001 were, of course, democracy and freedom. "There is this myth that these countries don't want freedom, and that Saddam or the Taliban are popular, but then it becomes apparent that they were not at all popular after they fall", a British official who gave a preview of Blair's speech to the *New York Times,* concluded.[22]

This became the mantra of both the White House and Downing street in the months that followed. In a television programme, "Meet the Press" in March 2003, Vice President Dick Cheney told the anchor, Tim Russert, that there was no possibility of the American and British troops not being greeted as liberators in Iraq. The Vice

President said he knew this because he and the President had met with "various groups and individuals, people who have devoted their lives from the outside to trying to change things inside Iraq. The read we get on the people of Iraq is there is no question but what they want to get rid of Saddam Hussein and they will welcome as liberators the United States when we come to do that."[23] The 'people who have devoted their lives from the outside' were none other than the Iraqi National Congress, which provided most of the intelligence to both MI6 in London and the 'Office of Special Plans' in the Pentagon, which turned out to be so monumentally false.

In September 2003, a by-now beleaguered Bush elaborated this further:

> In Iraq, we are helping the long-suffering people of that country to build a decent and democratic society at the center of the Middle East. Together we are transforming a place of torture chambers and mass graves into a nation of laws and free institutions. This undertaking is difficult and costly—yet worthy of our country, and critical to our security.
> The Middle East will either become a place of progress and peace, or it will be an exporter of violence and terror that takes more lives in America and in other free nations. The triumph of democracy and tolerance in Iraq, in Afghanistan and beyond would be a grave setback for international terrorism…
> Our enemies understand this. They know that a free Iraq will be free of them—free of assassins, and torturers, and secret police. They know that as democracy rises in Iraq, all of their hateful ambitions will fall like the statues of the former dictator. And that is why, five months after we liberated Iraq, a collection of killers is desperately trying to undermine Iraq's progress and throw the country into chaos.[24]

Liberation became the watchword for the 'Allies' action in Iraq. So fully were the invading troops brainwashed into believing this that when they met with real resistance in Basra, Nasiriyah, Najf and along the road to Baghdad, they were genuinely nonplussed. The language of the coalition's briefings and press releases was tailored to suit this message. Thus, the Americans and British were not there as *invaders* but as *allies* of the Iraqis against Saddam Hussein. They were not there to *occupy* Iraq but to *liberate* it. Those who opposed them were by definition not entirely rational. For instance, in the British and American parlance, the attackers were never freedom fighters or guerrillas. Americans never faced 'resistance', much less a guerrilla war. It was not till Gen. John Abizaid took over command of the US forces in Iraq that an American commander dared to admit that the US was facing a classic guerrilla campaign in Iraq.[25]

Above all, there were no nationalists in Iraq. That word was, literally never used by either the 'coalition' authorities or the media. Instead they were remnants loyal to the old regime (later shortened to 'Saddam Loyalists'), Ba'ath party fanatics, *fidayeen,* foreign Islamist elements or simply criminals, in short all people driven by hate, ideology or greed.

Had the coalition forces been genuinely welcomed; had life returned rapidly to normal; had the US announced a timetable for the drawing up of a constitution and for elections that would allow the Iraqis to choose their constitution makers; and had the attacks on the Americans and those who were co-operating with them died down—this final attempt to manufacture consent might have succeeded. But none of these things happened. Instead even the civil administration that had survived 14 years of sanctions and incessant bombing raids, collapsed within hours of the fall of Baghdad and Iraq descended into chaos.

During Saddam's reign, inspite of 12 years of sanctions, Iraqis had power, an abundant supply of gasoline, and thanks in part to the UN's oil for food programme, enough to eat. Their streets were safe, their salaries and incomes were assured, and their currency, although depreciated, was stable. Schools and colleges were open, and girls attended them as freely as boys. There was not a hint of Islamic fundamentalism and the state, for all its oppressiveness, was unflinchingly secular. In short, although Saddam's folly and the UN sanctions dragged Iraq down from First World affluence to Third

World poverty, Iraq was still a functioning state. Above all, the system of financial circulation which is the lifeblood of a market economy was intact. People received their salaries and spent them. This created demand and income for others. The marketplace, in short, flourished.

All this change within days of the Americans' arrival. For months afterwards, the queues for gasoline, even in Baghdad were often three miles long, and the waiting period 8 hours to 24 hours. Power supply was intermittent, more off than on. Between 4 June and 19 June delivery to Baghdad actually fell from 1300 MW to 800.[26] The police simply vanished. As a result, within days all the 158 government buildings in Baghdad had been looted bare, as were all the hospitals and thousands of private homes. The looting and destruction of the Baghdad Archaeological museum, which drew world-wide attention, rivalled what the Taliban did to Bamiyan. As for public safety, in the last week of May there were 70 murders in Baghdad—ten a day![27]

The most striking change was the insecurity that women had begun to feel in Iraqi cities. Kidnapping, rape and, for some, execution by their own relatives for having been raped in so-called 'honour killing', became their fate. "Under Saddam we could drive, we could walk down the street until two in the morning," a young designer told Lauren Sandler of *The New York Times*. "Who would have thought the Americans could have made it worse for women? This is liberation?"[28]

A first-hand account of the feelings of 'Mohamad' (fictional name), an Iraqi army deserter who welcomed the Americans and was plying a taxi in Baghdad at the time of this interview, provides a flavour of what life had become in post-war Baghdad.

> No electricity means no traffic lights, so drivers do whatever they please. The few police back on the streets have no authority to enforce traffic regulations and no weapons to stop the carjackers. Entire sections of the city have been taken over by gangsters. And on top of it all, there are the US soldiers who block off streets with their tanks and cause huge traffic jams, or set up check points throughout the city and harass the drivers.

Mohamad took us to visit his neighborhood off Abu Nuwas Street in Baghdad, a bustling area full of shops just before the war. Now most of the stores are closed because of the lack of electricity and fear of thieves. The men, jobless, sit around in the café playing cards and dominoes. The women hide in their homes, afraid to go outside. The children play in streets full of garbage and raw sewage. "Is this liberation?" Mohamad asks as he looks around his devastated neighborhood.

Everyone complains bitterly about the lack of electricity. During the Gulf War, the electrical grid suffered even greater damage, they claim, but after one month it was up and running. The same is true for the phone system. And that was under Saddam Hussein. "How come in four months, the US, the most highly advanced country in the world, can't get the electricity or the phones back on?" Mohamad and his friends want to know. The heat is so oppressive, reaching 120 degrees some days, that without air-conditioning or fans, Mohamad can't sleep at night. He drags his mattress out on the roof to try to catch a breeze, but you can tell from the bags under his eyes that he's exhausted. With no refrigeration, his food goes bad. Without electricity to pump the water, water is in short supply. And without electricity to pump gas at the gas station, he either has to wait on mile-long lines for gas or buy it in jerry cans on the black market for five times the price.

A bachelor, Mohamad doesn't have a family to support, but he helps out many families in the neighborhood. He gives money to the widow down the street who since the war, no longer gets her pension. He helps the disabled war veterans who have lost their veterans benefits. He helps his diabetic neighbor find treatment now that the hospitals have been looted. He helps the beggars on the street. You can tell immediately that this warrior is a sweet, gentle man who is loved and respected by his community.

But Mohamad's patience is wearing thin. His daily life, and the life of his friends, has become far more difficult than it was under Saddam Hussein. And he sees no relief in sight.

He feels betrayed by George Bush's unfulfilled promises and humiliated by the young American soldiers who bark orders at him in English. He has contempt for Paul Bremer and the new governing council hand-selected by the Americans—many of whom are exiles who know nothing about the reality of present-day Iraq.

Mohamad is no Baathist, but if things don't get better quickly, the open arms with which he initially welcomed the Americans might well turn to fire arms. "I'm trained to fight. That's what I've spent my life doing," he said quietly. "Believe me, I'm not anxious to fight again. I'll give the Americans another few months to turn things around—to provide basic services, to put people back to work, to bring about some order. But if things around here don't get better soon, what choice do I have?"[29]

The turmoil was not an inevitable product of war and regime change, but a product of American shortsightedness and inexperience. The collapse occurred because the Americans did not know how to run a city, much less an occupied country. In a BBC interview, Benjamin Barber, author of *Jihad vs. McWorld,* said in London on or about 15 June 2003, that Washington believed that it had only to clear away the dictatorial regime of Saddam for democracy to take spontaneous root. A similar, ideologically-driven belief had propelled the use of 'shock therapy' to transform socialist into market economies. But Washington had learned no lessons from that catastrophe.

Nor, living as it did in a in a never-ending present, did the Bush administration run a check with history. The neo-conservatives in the Pentagon who backseat drove the invasion were fond of citing MaCarthur's transformation of Japan into a democracy. What they forgot was that Emperor Hirohito legitimised the American occupation for the Japanese people. In return the Americans left the Japanese state structure largely intact and worked through it to transform the country.

Nor did they learn from their own country's experience in Germany, where from Chancellor Adenauer downwards, the allies re-employed a large proportion of the administration of the Third

Reich, not excluding fair numbers from the Nazi party. In Iraq, by contrast, the Americans made every mistake it was possible to make. Instead of reassuring people that their jobs were safe; that they should come as usual to work, and collect new identity papers in due course, even before they arrived in Baghdad, they issued a list of nine top members of the Saddam regime whom they intended to try for war crimes. They also let it be known that they intended to purge the administration completely of all Ba'ath party members, and that a list of around 2,000 officials had been prepared for this purpose.[30] The twin threats were enough to dismantle the entire administration of the country overnight, for in a country where the Ba'ath party had for 35 years been the only avenue to power, this spelt the end of the bureaucracy. The police were similarly warned that they too would be purged. That was the end of the police. Reconstituting a new police and administration proved difficult and time consuming. Till the end of May, the US authorities were running Baghdad with a mere 8,000 policemen. Not surprisingly, chaos prevailed.

As for the army, it too was disbanded wholesale. After two months of silence the L. Paul Bremer government announced that soldiers should collect $50 as severance pay and apply for re-induction. But when they turned up for their severance pay, there was no money. Protests were met with bullets and death. All in all, overnight there were 10 million unemployed Iraqis.[31]

By in effect disbanding the bureaucracy and the army, the Americans disrupted the cash flow in the economy. Since they also did not peg the value of the dinar no one knew whether to accept dinars, and if so, what they were worth. The value of the dinar crashed and overnight the few savings that Iraqis had managed to hold on to evaporated.

There was also almost nothing to buy. Even if the US had intended to make Iraqis pay eventually for the damage the 'coalition' had inflicted on their country, to maintain the flow of purchasing power in the economy, it should have announced a $10 billion loan to the country to meet essential needs till the oil revenues reappeared. This would have been a drop in the bucket compared to the Marshall Plan, and a short-term loan, not a grant.

To the rest of the world, this catalogue of errors was inexplicable. The US has the largest number of universities in the world. Their teaching faculties are cherry-picked from the entire English-speaking world. Their libraries are the best stocked, and the most user-friendly. They churn out the largest number of Ph.Ds, and win the lion's share of the Nobel prizes every year. The departments of commerce, state and defence, not to mention others, and the Congress, have an awesome number of specialised aides on their staffs. Yet, when it came to decision-making, this awe-inspiring concentration of talent and knowledge had produced decisions that were not even worthy of a Third World government.

Only in September did an explanation for this apparent paradox emerge. It turned out that in 2002, the administration had set up a 'Future of Iraq' project, and entrusted it to a plethora of working groups, drawn from 17 governmental agencies and departments. David L. Phillips, an adviser to the Democratic Principles Working Group of the project revealed that many of the problems that the occupation encountered had been anticipated but the advice of the working groups had been ignored. The mistakes stemmed from "poor judgment by civilians at the Pentagon who counted too much on the advice of one exile—Ahmad Chalabi of the Iraqi National Congress—and ignored the views of other, more reliable Iraqi leaders." Chalabi had claimed that there was no need to discriminate between 'good and bad Ba'athists' or to give the Iraqi army a key role in stabilising the country after the end of hostilities. Instead, he advocated the most stringent cleansing action against both organs of the state, claiming that the gap would immediately be filled by members of the vast underground network of the Iraq National Congress.

Chalabi insisted that the entire Iraqi Army 'be immediately disbanded'. The Pentagon agreed, in the end leading many Iraqi soldiers who might otherwise have been willing to work with the coalition to take up arms against it. Chalabi's promised network didn't materialize, and the resulting power vacuum contributed to looting, sabotage and attacks against American forces. The working group also emphasised the need to gain the co-operation with Iraq's existing technocracy to ensure the uninterrupted flow of water and electricity. Though civil servants and professionals for the most part were required to be Ba'ath party members, the working group maintained that not all Ba'athists were war criminals. The group proposed so-called lustration laws to identify and remove officials who had committed atrocities. But the Iraqi National Congress was adamant that all former Ba'ath party members were inherently complicit in war crimes. The coalition provisional authority sided with Chalabi, decided that the Ba'ath party would be banned and dismissed many party members from their jobs.

Perhaps the most damaging revelation by Phillips concerned the transition to Iraqi rule. "Most important, the working group insisted that *all Iraqis* needed a voice in the transition to a stable, democratic Iraq (emphasis added). Participants agreed that exiles alone could not speak for all Iraqis, and endorsed discussions with leaders inside and outside the country as the basis for constituting a legitimate and broadly representative transitional structure. But Chalabi would have none of it".

Before an Opposition conference held in London in December 2002, Chalabi lobbied the United States to appoint a government in exile, dominated by his partisans, to be installed in Baghdad at the moment of liberation, but, concerned about legitimacy, the Bush administration ultimately rejected this proposal. But Chalabi's advocacy had achieved the negative half of its objective. The Bremer administration decide that it was too dangerous to let the Iraqis choose their own representatives either to the governing council or to a constituent assembly. Instead it opted for the fig leaf of a nominated governing council which would have the power only to advise the American administration in Iraq. This decision, which satisfied no one, probably sealed the fate of the US in Iraq, and made sure that the resistance which had till then been disorganised and sporadic, would become institutionalised.[32]

The increasingly frequent and invariably invidious comparisons that ordinary Iraqis began to make with Saddam's regime sapped most of the legitimacy that the 'coalition' had hoped to gain in Iraq from having overthrown an oppressive and brutal dictatorship. But in the rest of the world, the unmistakable evidence of a rising resistance movement in the country sapped whatever legitimacy the occupiers had hoped to gain from their appeal to human rights.

The signs that Iraqis were not exactly welcoming the Americans came in the first weeks of the occupation. The coalition authorities had declared a general amnesty and given the people till 15 June to surrender their arms. But almost no one complied. As the deadline passed, the US army conceded that during the amnesty Iraqis had handed in only 123 pistols, 76 semi-automatic rifles, 435 automatic rifles, 46 machine guns, 11 anti-aircraft weapons and 381 grenades and bombs—a drop in Iraq's ocean of weaponry.[33]

Attacks on US soldiers were not long in coming. Between 1 May and 27 September 2003, 169 American soldiers lost their lives in Iraq. This was 31 more than the 138 they lost in combat till 30 April. The rate of attrition of about 400 per year had begun to seriously trouble the American public, especially since there seemed to be no end in sight to the American military occupation of Iraq. The initial statements of the US military authorities that the resistance was coming from 'pockets', or 'remnants' of the old regime, implying that only a mopping up was left to be done, had given way on 16 July to an admission that the US faced a classical guerrilla campaign. By September it was apparent that this campaign was becoming increasingly organised militarily and focussed politically. Throughout the period of occupation there have been between 15 and 25 attacks a day on American forces in Iraq[34]. The list of targets had grown to include any person, organisation or country that collaborated with the occupying powers to keep Iraq enslaved. Thus it had widened from Iraqi policemen and civilians who were cooperating with the 'coalition' authorities, to the United Nations and countries deemed to be collaborating with the Americans. That was the message sent by the bombing of the Jordanian embassy on 7 August of the UN on 19 August and of Najaf on 29 July and the assassination of Akila el-Hashimi, a woman member of Iraq's 25-member "governing council"—in reality advisers to the American government in Iraq.

By the end of September, the quagmire into which Bush and Blair had led the US and UK, was apparent to most of the world and their popularity in their own counties had just about vanished. Blair had lost the trust, of most of the Labour Party, and many had actively begun to consider the best candidate to replace him. A poll of more than 300 party members between 25 and 27 September found that more than 40 per cent wanted Tony Blair to stand down before the next election and nearly 60 per cent believed he was wrong to sanction war on Iraq. More than 80 per cent believed he exaggerated the case for war either deliberately (37 per cent) or unintentionally (44 per cent). Less than 20 per cent believe there was no exaggeration.[35] Bush's approval rating had, in the meantime, fallen to 50 per cent, and an USA Today/CNN/Gallup survey showed that Democrat aspirant Gen. Wesley Clarke was 3 per cent ahead of Bush in the opinion polls for the next Presidential election.[36]

America's loss of its hegemony

Six months after the second Gulf War, Iraq is destitute and some way down the road to disintegration. As the never more than tepid consent for the war unravels, both the administrations that decided to wage the war are under attack. But these are not the only losers. A third casualty could be American hegemony in the post-Cold War, globalised world. The US has tried to recapture some moral legitimacy for its action by claiming that it ousted a tyrant and 'liberated' the Iraqis from bondage. However, as the US occupation of Iraq gets prolonged, a new Iraqi government proves elusive, and the guerrilla war grows more intense, the US is forfeiting the moral ascendancy that is the true foundation of global hegemony.

The term hegemony has been used in a variety of ways. Here it refers to "the power of a state to exercise the functions of leadership and governance over a system of sovereign states. (during) some kind of transformative action, which change(s) the mode of operation of the system in a fundamental way".[37]

'Hegemonic power' is something more than simple 'dominance'. It is "the power associated with dominance *expanded by the exercise of intellectual and moral leadership* (emphasis added)... Whereas dominance rests primarily on coercion, hegemony is the *additional* power that accrues to a dominant group by virtue of its capacity to place all issues around which conflict rages on a 'universal' plane.

Hegemony exists when this claim is at least partly true and therefore generally accepted. A situation in which the claim of the dominant group to represent the general interest is increasingly questioned and eventually rejected is defined as a failure of hegemony".[38]

The US' *dominance* of the world is unchallengeable. It accounts for around 30 per cent of world GDP and 40 per cent of world trade. Its technological lead over other industrialised countries is considerable and growing larger all the time. Its military power is unmatched: not only does it account for almost 40 per cent of global arms spending—which is more than the combined defence budgets of the next 15 countries—but also because of the unique marriage it has achieved of computer age technology with the weapons of war and strategies of battle. Until the attack upon Iraq, Its claim to *hegemonic power* in the era of global capitalism was equally beyond challenge. The US already enjoyed the hegemony of the "American century". It had played a crucial role in defeating Germany and Fascism in Second World War.

It had made generous use of Marshall Plan aid to put Germany and much of Europe back on its feet. It had protected Western Europe from the threat (perhaps more imagined than real) of a Soviet invasion during the immediate post-World War years, and it had led the capitalist world during the Cold War. It had taken the lead in creating the United Nations, creating and then dismantling the Bretton Woods financial system, and in removing trade barriers under GATT. In the early 1990s, it finally completed the architecture of the Bretton Woods system by taking the lead in creating the World Trade Organisation. It had also taken the lead in forming the string of alliances, such as NATO, CENTO and SEATO, which created the post-war international order. It was therefore the one country that could play the transformative role of the hegemonic power during capitalism's fifth cycle of expansion.

In 1982 it led the shift from trade liberalisation by consensus to consensus peppered with large doses of coercion, that took shape in the Uruguay round of GATT and was institutionalised in the World Trade Organisation. After the Cold War, the US again took the lead, this time in restricting the sovereignty of nation states. It did so by using a succession of hegemonistic justifications, most notably the protection of human rights and the propagation or defence of democracy. Four out of the nine American, NATO, or UN interventions in other sovereign countries that preceded 9/11 were justified by the need to protect human rights, a purpose that commands near universal support in the world in theory if not always in practice. Two others, the no-fly zone in Iraq and Operation Desert Fox used UN resolutions as a fig leaf, although in a highly questionable manner.

The invasion of Iraq, by contrast was an exercise of *dominance*, pure and simple. What the rising chorus of disagreement and disbelief revealed was the US' loss of *hegemony*. The most unambiguous evidence of this was the continuation of the rift between the permanent members of the Security Council, and in particular between 'Old Europe' and the US, after the war was over. This became apparent during the debate in the Security Council over a US proposal to lift economic sanctions on Iraq.

Bush made this proposal on 17 April, only days after the war on Iraq ended. It was immediately opposed by Russia and France, on the grounds that the sanctions had been imposed by the UN and could therefore only be lifted by it. They therefore proposed that UNMOVIC be asked to return to Iraq, complete its inspections, and certify to the UN Security Council that Iraq was free of WMD. Only then could the sanctions be lifted. Lifting them without UN certification, solely on the US' assurance that since it had ousted Saddam Hussein the need for the sanctions had vanished, would further weaken the authority of an already badly bruised Security Council. Their stand was endorsed by the current President of the Council, the Permanent Representative of Mexico, who said that the lifting of sanctions would be governed 'strictly' by the conditions laid down in the two UNSC resolutions that had imposed them.[39]

The US opposed this tooth and nail and made it clear that it would veto any such resolution. It did not mind the IAEA returning to Iraq, but refused to allow UNMOVIC in because of Blix's criticism of its misuse of intelligence information. In the end the US got its way. On 22 May 2003, the Security Council voted 15-0 to do so, phase out the UN food for oil programme under which Iraqis had lived a hand-to-mouth existence for 12 years, and hand over the control of Iraqi oil to the US and the UK. It was a triumph for the US because on the surface at least the Security Council appeared to be retrospectively conferring legitimacy to its invasion of Iraq. Its Permanent Representative to the UN described the resolution as a 'momentous' event for the Iraqis that had become possible only because Iraq had been 'liberated'.

But in reality, it was an exercise of raw power by the US in which other members, notably France and Russia, reluctantly acquiesced. They did so because this was the only way left for the world community to alleviate the distress of the Iraqis and restore civil society. All that Russia and France gained from the exercise was a slightly higher status for the UN observers in Baghdad, and a vague promise from the US and UK to give it a greater role in the rebuilding of Iraq.[40] The rift among the permanent members of the council remained as wide as ever.

Both America's dominance and its loss of hegemony were highlighted once more by the G-8 summit in Evian in June. Since it was being chaired by President Jacques Chirac, there was some speculation about whether Bush would attend it personally. When the White House announced that he would, it was taken as a signal that the world leaders were in the mood to leave the past behind and make a new start in tackling the problems of the future. Chirac strove to reinforce this by turning the G-8's attention to the issues of poverty alleviation and development in the developing countries. To do this he invited the heads of government of China, India and Brazil, and several African states.

But Bush was not prepared to be mollified. He came to the summit, stayed for a few photo opportunities and left early. He snubbed Chirac by announcing that the US would devote $15 billion over 5 years to fighting AIDS before he arrived at Evian. This not only denied Chirac a 'breakthrough agreement' that could mark the success of the summit, but also put France's trebling of its contribution to $180 million in the shade. At the same time, he blocked progress towards supplying generic life-saving drugs to the poorest developing countries and France's attempt to get an agreement to stop dumping farm produce in Africa. He thus showed that he did not mind paying taxpayers' money to fight AIDS so long as it went into ensuring that the pockets of the drug cartels would not be hurt.

In exchange he obtained a declaration from the G-8 putting Iran and North Korea on notice that it would not stand by and allow them to acquire nuclear weapons. However, the interpretations given of this by Paris and Washington, once again highlighted the challenge to American hegemony. Washington read the leaders' declaration as implicitly authorising the use of force against countries that violated international nonproliferation norms, but Mr Chirac called this a "very bold" interpretation. "There never was any talk of using force whatsoever. We have to have a dialogue with Iran," he said.[41]

As *The Guardian* commented, "Leaders of the globe's richest nations met and talked about saving the world, but it was the agenda of the mightiest country, the United States, that prevailed. The final communique could have been written in Washington by a small team in the White House rather than in the Alpine foothills by the eight nations at Evian".[42]

More evidence of America's loss of hegemony came from a Pew survey of 21 nations released on 3 June 2003. It showed a deepening skepticism toward the US.

> The survey found that the war has widened the rift between Americans and Western Europeans, further inflamed the Muslim world, softened support for the war on terrorism, and significantly weakened global public support for the pillars of the post-World War II era—the U.N. and the North Atlantic alliance. Majorities in five out of seven NATO countries surveyed favoured a more independent relationship with the US on diplomatic and security affairs. Fully three quarters in France (76%) and solid majorities in Turkey (62%) Spain (62%), Italy (61 %) and Germany (57%), believe Western Europe should take a more independent role than it has in the past.[43]

All through the ensuing months, fresh evidence of the US' loss of hegemony continued to accumulate. By the end of June, 64 American soldiers had lost their lives in Iraq and the Bush administration could no longer hide from itself that it was caught in a quagmire. It could neither control Iraq on its own nor leave the country precipitately. But it could not find a single taker for its view that having fought the war it had the right to rule Iraq till a peace of its making had been imposed upon that country. In July 2003, India, whom the Bush administration had backed upon to send a division of troops (20,000), finally pleaded that it could not do so. Pakistan, which had also half-committed itself to providing three brigades also pleaded inability to do so. Although the UN had retrospectively legitimised the US' military occupation of Iraq and had taken a watchdog's role in its reconstruction, for the first time in the history of peacekeeping operations, no Third World country offered its troops for the 'stabilisation' of Iraq. The fissure between the US and 'Old Europe' reinforced by Russia and China, remained as wide as ever.

India and Pakistan had said that they might reconsider their decision if there was a second UN resolution. In August, the US decided to go for a second resolution, offering to increase the role of the UN substantially. But it baulked at meeting France, Germany and Russia's demand that it hand over control of Iraq to the UN. As a result, more than two months after the US had agreed to secure a second resolution from the UN, the issue remained deadlocked. By then it had become evident that the writ of the US had ceased to run. In future it would have to be imposed by force.

Notes

1. Julian Borger. "Pentagon cools on finding weapons". *The Guardian* 29 May 2003.
2. Nicholas Watt, Owen Bowcroft, and Richard Norton-Taylor. "Weapons teams scour Iraq". *The Guardian* 12 April 2003.
3. Brian Whitaker and Rory McCarthy. "As the hunt for weapons grows bigger the hope of success gets smaller". *The Guardian* 30 May 2003.

4. Ibid.
5. Judith Miller. "Iraqi scientist tells of illicit arms" *The New York Times* 21 March 2003.
6. Whitaker and McCarthy, op.cit.
7. Michael White, Ewen MacAskill and Richard Norton-Taylor. "Downing St admits blunder on Iraq dossier; Plagiarism row casts shadow over No 10's case against Saddam". *The Guardian*, 8 February 2003.
8. Richard Norton-Taylor. "MI 6 led protest against war dossier". *The Guardian* 30 May 2003.
9. Ibid.
10. Phone interviews done by Jim Wolf of Reuters. "US insiders say Iraq intel deliberately skewed". *Reuters* 30 May 2003.
11. Ibid.
12. He thus implicitly confirmed what Nicholas Kristoff had written in the *New York Times*. op. cit. See Chapter 14 footnotes.
13. "Bush Plays Down Iraq WMD Hunt". *Reuters*, St Petersburg, 1 June 2003.
14. Ibid.
15. "US Senate opens Iraq weapons probe". *BBC News* 3 June 2003.
16. Warren Hoge and Don Van Natta Jr. "Blair heads for the US, trailing controversy over Iraq". *The New York Times* 17 July 2003.
17. Beth Gardiner. Memo: "Blair urged to defend War in Iraq". Associated Press. 23 August 2003.
18. David S. Broder. "Black Thursday for Bush". *The Washington Post*. 15 July 2003.
19. Robert Scheer. "Bush was all Too Willing to believe Émigrés' lies". *The Los Angeles Times*, 2 September 2003.
20. Walter Pincus. "Report casts doubt on Iraq-Al Qaeda connection". *The Washington Post* 22 June 2003.
21. Gaby Hinsliff, Kamal Ahmed and Ed Vuillamy. "Blair stakes his political future on beating Iraq". *The Observer* 16 February 2003
22. Warren Hoge and Don Van Natta Jr. *The New York Times* 17 July 2003. op. cit.
23. E.J Dionne Jr. "Behind the Failure". *The Washington Post* 22 August 2003.
24. The White House: Text of Bush' speech on Iraq. Associated Press. 7 September 2003.
25. US Department of Defense. News Briefing, 16 July 2003.
26. Tareq Al Issawi "Sabotage knocks out power in Iraqi town". Associated Press, 20 June 2003.

27. Robert Fisk. "And the truth the victors refuse to see". *The Independent* 1 June 2003.
28. Lauren Sandler. "Veiled and Worried in Baghdad". *The New York Times*, 16 September 2003.
29. Medea Benjamin. "Open Arms May Turn into Fire Arms, Says Iraqi Soldier Turned Taxi Driver". Occupation Watch Center—Iraq website. http://occupationwatch-conditionsinIraq.htm 4 August 2003.
30. Elizabeth Bumiller. "US names Iraqis who would face war crimes trial". *The New York Times* 16 March 2003.
31. E.A.Khammas. "10 million unemployed: The forgotten issue". *International Occupation Watch Center* 9 August 2003.
32. David L. Phillips. "Listening to the Wrong Iraqi". *The New York Times* 20 September 2003.
33. Khaled Yacoub Oweis. "US troops ambushed in Iraq as new raids launched". Reuters, 15 June 2003.
34. Charles J. Hanley. "US Compound at Baghdad Hotel Attacked". Associated Press, 27 September 2003.
35. Kamal Ahmed. "Party ready to turn on PM . *The Observer* 28 September 2003.
36. "Bush Defiant as polls show him losing over Iraq". *Times of India* 24 September 2003.
37. Giovanni Arrighi. *The Long Twentieth Century* op. cit. p.27.
38. Ibid.p.28-9.
39. "Bush: UN must lift Iraq sanctions". *The Guardian* 17 April 2003
40. "UN lifts sanctions on Iraq". Agencies *The Guardian* 22 May 2003.
41. Larry Elliott and Michael White: Chirac tries to make the best of a bad job. *The Guardian* 4 June 2003.
42. "Evian down the drain". *Guardian* 5 June 2003.
43. The Pew Research Center: "Views of a Changing World 2003. War with Iraq further divides Global Politics" http://people-press.org/ 3 June 2003.

6

The Real Story

On 2 October 2003, David Kay, the chief of the Iraq Survey Group, the team of 1,200 weapons inspectors that the US and UK assembled to find Iraq's weapons of mass destruction, submitted an 'interim' to the intelligence committees of both houses of the US Congress, that the Group had not found any weapons and probably there were no weapons to be found. Given the importance of the finding and the high level of public interest in the subject, one would have expected the meeting to have been an open one. But it was declared a closed session. The gist of the ISG's finding was, however, leaked to *The Washington Post* by the administration the previous day. Here is the spin the Bush administration gave to its findings:

> With no chemical or biological weapons yet found in Iraq, the US official in charge of the search for Saddam Hussein's weapons of mass destruction is pursuing the possibility that the Iraqi leader was bluffing, pretending he had distributed them to his most loyal commanders to deter the United States from invading. Such a possibility is one element in the interim

report that David Kay, who heads the 1,200-person, CIA-led team in Iraq, will describe before the House and Senate intelligence committees on Thursday, according to people familiar with his planned testimony".[1]

The BBC went one better the next day:

> Saddam Hussein may have been pretending to possess weapons of mass destruction, the US Congress is expected to be told by the man in charge of the US-led hunt for Iraqi weapons. David Kay will tell the intelligence committees of both Houses of Congress that Saddam pretended his battlefield commanders had chemical weapons, in order to deter invasion, according to *The Washington Post*. At closed briefings on Thursday, he is also widely expected to say that so far no weapons have been found".[2]

This was the first ever public report from a highly controversial inquiry group, set up in circumstances that constituted a direct rebuke to the United Nations, its weapons inspectors and their chairman, Hans Blix. Its principal finding did nothing less than invalidate the entire case for war. But in the two news reports, this became incidental—mentioned virtually as an afterthought. Instead both focussed on the *speculation* that Kay *might* make before the Congress, that Saddam *might* have pretended to have WMD in order to discourage an invasion. The purpose was obvious: if Saddam had done that, then Bush and Blair and the entire intelligence agencies of the two superpowers would be exonerated for having been taken in. The destruction of Iraq was therefore *still* Saddam Hussein's fault. All would have been well if only he had not lied!

It takes only a moment to see that the proposal is absurd. Saddam had not been able to intimidate the US in 1991 when he actually possessed WMD. He would have had to be unhinged to believe that he could intimidate the US with a bluff 12 years later. But the purpose of 'spin' is not to convince but to sow doubt. Once that is done, the proposition sounds less preposterous the next time it is aired, and even less so the time after that. With a sufficient number of repetitions, and with sceptical comment carefully screened out, what was once preposterous becomes truth.

In the case of Iraq the truth was buried from the very beginning in layer upon layer of 'spin'. Can it be unearthed now? 'Truth' is always relative, but from the analysis of events given in the previous chapters it is possible to construct another version of Iraq's tragedy.

In 1979, when he came to power, Saddam Hussein was not a stranger to the US intelligence agencies. On the contrary, having worked with him in their abortive attempt to assassinate Gen. Abdel Karim el Kassem, the CIA had a fair idea of the kind of man he was. Saddam's summary execution of all the members of the Ba'ath leadership who could remotely pose a threat to him in the future could not have caught them entirely by surprise. On the contrary, Washington remembered Saddam as a former ally in the struggle against communism. It had little difficulty in looking the other way. This may partly account for the speed with which the US reestablished relations with Iraq when confronted by the Khomeini regime and the American hostages crisis in Iran.

The revelations contained in the official transcript of the US Ambassador April Glaspie's last meeting with Saddam Hussein, strongly suggest that not only did the US side with Iraq after the war began, but it also encouraged Iraq to attack Iran. No other construction can be put upon the two countries' decision to keep the resumption of relationship, broken in 1967, secret. Saddam's reference to their common desire 'to avoid misinterpretation' two months before the war began only makes sense if the US knew that the war was already on the way. The fact that US AWACs based in Saudi Arabia jammed Iraqi radar for a full three days before Iraq launched its assault on the Fao peninsula also shows that intelligence cooperation had been planned well before the war started. That made the US an ally of Iraq during the war. Only that can explain the strength of the relationship, revealed in the transcript, that Saddam believed he had with the US. Saddam therefore had some reason to feel let down when the US refused to intercede on its behalf with Kuwait and the UAE, to write off or reduce its debts, raise the price of oil, or at least stop Kuwait from pilfering Iraqi oil.

Ambassador Glaspie's awareness of Iraq's status as a covert ally in 'stabilising' the Middle East, also explains the deferential tone of her remarks to him and the complete absence of confrontation. On the contrary, her remarks were very much in the spirit of allies trying to prevent a misunderstanding on an important issue.

Saddam's over-estimation of the strength of that past alliance was almost certainly the consideration that tipped the balance in favour of invading Kuwait. In the end, he simply could not bring himself to believe that the threats the Bush administration was making were real.

After Iraq lost the 1991 war, Saddam Hussein had no option but to agree to abide by the Security Council's Resolution 687. But he was determined to save as much of Iraq's weapons, and its research and production programmes, as was possible. His motives for doing so could hardly have been to attack even Israel, let alone Europe, Britain or the USA, as Bush, Blair, Colin Powell and their spokespersons maintained to justify their invasion of Iraq twelve years later. Exhausted and decimated by two wars, and bled by economic sanctions, he could scarcely have contemplated crossing the entire width of Jordan (even if that country was willing to let him) to take on an Israel armed with nuclear weapons and backed to the hilt by the US. The purpose of his deception was almost certainly to preserve a minimum deterrent capability. Iraq had been attacked by Israel in 1981, and could be attacked again. It had launched an unprovoked attack on Iran. Iran could pay it back in the same coin. With his army all but destroyed, Saddam had to rely disproportionately upon the fear that his weapons of mass destruction evoked in his neighbours. The spectre of Scud missiles loaded with biological weapons, his advisers must have calculated, would make both Iran and Israel pause and reconsider any offensive plans they might develop.

Saddam probably also calculated that the Bush (Sr.) Administration would allow him, tacitly, to retain a minimum deterrent capability. The fact that it stood by and allowed him to crush the Shia revolt in Southern Iraq, showed that it too did not want Iraq to be dismembered, for that could only strengthen Iran. Almost by definition, therefore, it did not want Iraq to become so weak as to virtually invite an invasion by Iran. In this he was wrong, for the US began to foment a military coup from late 1991, and a failed coup attempt did take place in July 1992. But UNSC 687 had taken both Iraq and the UN into new territory, and no one knew then precisely how high the bar of compliance would be raised, or how effective UN inspections would be.

The High-level Concealment Committee that Saddam set up was given the task of deciding which weapons to destroy and which to conceal. With the benefit of hindsight, we can surmise that he decided to destroy his chemical and biological weapons and to declare most, if not all, of the research facilities but tried to conceal his nuclear weapons and missile development programmes. In this he was violating not only UNSC 687 but also the Nuclear Non-Proliferation Treaty, of which Iraq was a signatory. But in view of Israel's possession of nuclear weapons this was hardly an irrational, or even aggressive, endeavour.

But Saddam once again misjudged the US. By the end of 1992, Wolfowitz's paper on 'Defense Planning Guidelines' had been circulating within the administration and Congress for several weeks, had built an elaborate case for preemptive action against Iraq, and had deeply influenced thinking in both the political parties. The Clinton administration was therefore caught in the cusp of two competing doctrines for the establishment of an international order. The first was the old Westphalian doctrine which respected the sovereignty of nations, enjoined them not to intervene in the internal affairs of other countries, strictly separated domestic from international policy, and relied upon deterrence to maintain peace. The second was the emerging neo-conservative vision of a world governed by the US on the basis of overwhelming and ever increasing military power, without any reference, let alone subordination, to the UN. In this world the US would be policeman, prosecutor and judge, ever vigilant, on the lookout for any incipient rebellion, which it would ruthlessly crush.

By degrees, the Clinton administration settled for a 'middle path' that in the end only paved the way for the acceptance by most Americans of the neo-conservative doctrine of unilateral supremacy. US foreign policy would henceforth be far more intrusive than it had been in the Cold War. It would aim at identifying potential threats not only to US territory but also to American interests anywhere in the world, and would seek to head these off through early action. Since American interests were global after the Cold War; since these required the maintenance of the market system and above all, since war was the worst enemy of the market, their defence could be brought under the rubric of peacekeeping. In this, the US was prepared to work *with* the United Nations, with NATO, but not *under* either. When such cooperation was not forthcoming, it would reserve the right to act on its own to defend its interest.[3]

When applied to Iraq, this shift to a half-way house between the old and the new meant a drastic change of policy. Iraq had to kept in a condition where it could never again acquire the strength to thwart any US design for the Middle East. The alternatives were to remove Saddam, a 'nationalist' leader of the Cold War era mould and replace him with someone like King Abdullah of Jordan, or to keep the economic sanctions on indefinitely. Whatever willingness there might have been earlier to keep the bar of compliance low, vanished. Instead, by 1994 the Clinton administration had publicly backed away from its commitment to lift the sanctions once Iraq was declared free of weapons of mass destruction.

Saddam's effort to hide some of his WMD and research and production facilities made the prolongation of sanctions very easy. Till 1996 fresh revelations kept the inspectors busy . It was only after (as it turned out) just about everything had actually been unearthed and destroyed that the US' dilemma became acute. Shortly after the outgoing UNSCOM chairman Rolf Ekeus' last report in April 1997, in which he said that Iraq had mainly to account for some of the materials that it had possessed before 1991 and claimed to have destroyed, Iraq began asking for a time-bound programme to complete the inspections and lift sanctions as promised by paragraph 22 of Resolution 687. When it found that the US had no intention of allowing the sanctions to be lifted it resorted to the only strategem that was left to a weak and desperate country. It began to withdraw cooperation from UNSCOM and to make an agreement to resume cooperation, conditional upon a promise that these would lead to the lifting of sanctions. In February 1998, Kofi Annan gave Iraq that assurance. This was followed by three months of excellent cooperation. During Butler's June visit to Baghdad, a two-month work programme was drawn up, whose conclusion was for the first time specifically linked to the lifting of economic sanctions.

That was when the US used its Aberdeen laboratory report on the possible presence of VX degradation and detergent residues on fragments of warheads to derail the process that Butler had agreed upon with the Iraqi government. Since the warheads in question *had already been destroyed*, their existence could not be made an issue. What remained possible was to claim that Iraq had lied when it said that it had not filled them with VX gas. It was essential to damage Iraq's credibility because only then could the US and UNSCOM insist upon a truly exhaustive accounting of every last weapon that Iraq had destroyed in the pre-July 1991 period. Butler put the argument for total disbelief in his 15 December 1998 letter to the Security Council as follows:

> In response to the Commission's requests for relevant documents, Iraq has repeatedly claimed that they no longer exist or cannot be located, *a claim which very often has been shown to be false, either because inspection activities have in fact located precisely such documents or because Iraq has reversed its stated position and then produced relevant documents* (emphasis added).[4]

Iraq had indeed lied in the past. But by 1998 most its proscribed weapons and all of its nuclear and its biological research and production facilities had been destroyed. With each UNSCOM discovery, the damage that successful concealment could do, and for that matter the gains to Iraq from such concealment, had dwindled. Butler needed to concede this, as Kofi Annan had done, draw up a final programme of work and when that was completed to recommend the lifting of the sanctions. Instead, in August 1998, he presented the Iraqis with a new list of demands for documents based upon the Aberdeen 'discovery', that fell outside the June programme of work, and refused to accept their contention that they could not supply most of them because the documents no longer existed. This left Iraq with no option but to go back to the only coercive strategy that remained open to him: stop UNSCOM's work and extract a fresh commitment to lift sanctions after a time limited inspection. In February 1998, Annan gave him that assurance. In December Clinton bypassed the UN and chose to bomb Iraq into submission, instead.

The way in which the Clinton administration used the VX warheads issue is notable not only for its manipulation of the media, which was extensively described in Chapter 3, but also for the emergence of the Iraqi National Congress. Set up in Vienna in 1992 by two rival Kurdish parties—the Kurdish Democratic Party and the patriotic Union of Kurdistan—and a moderate leader of the southern Shias, virtually handpicked by the US, the INC's executive council was chaired an Iraqi Shia financier, Ahmed Chalabi, who had headed the Petra bank in Jordan and later left for the US in questionable circumstances. Initially the INC had claimed to have approximately 40,000 fighters, 35,000 of them Kurd. But a succession of splits, mainly between the two Kurdish parties, put an end to its effectiveness as an instrument against Saddam in 1994. For the next two years the US backed the Iraqi National Accord, a group of ex-military officers who were given sanctuary and a base of operations in Jordan. But the Iraqi intelligence penetrated the INA and in June 1996 Saddam Hussein executed or arrested more than 200 of its key members.

Following that debacle, by March 1998 the US administration had turned its attention back to the INC, now minus many of its original constituents.[5] Washington's decision to leak the Aberdeen Testing laboratories report to the Washington Post through the INC may have been one of the early examples of the new cooperation. This was the relationship that blossomed into full-fledged intelligence and propaganda cooperation during the run-up to the invasion of Iraq.

The connection between the Clinton administration and the INC strengthened after UNSCOM withdrew from Iraq. As the former senior weapons inspector, Scott Ritter, had unambiguously confirmed, the CIA had planted its agents in UNSCOM as far back as in 1992.[6] Thus when UNSCOM pulled out, the US lost its eyes in Iraq. Its paranoia, about what Saddam was up to, was therefore heightened. To fill the gap in its intelligence it was compelled to rely on the Iraqi opposition, and in particular the Iraqi National Congress. It is now clear that, especially after 9/11, the INC saw a heaven-sent opportunity to prosecute its own agenda of toppling Saddam, using the paranoia of the US as its guided missile. The 'intelligence' it provided was, to put it mildly, 'inflated'.[7] Yet Bush, and with him Blair, swallowed it lock, stock and barrel, and cited informants on the ground in Iraq, "people who had risked their lives" to collect the information contained in the two countries' WMD reports, to prepare their case for invasion.

The US–INC link became watertight, however, after 9/11. In the Defense Department, Rumsfeld set up the 'Office of Special Plans' whose sole purpose was to collate intelligence and formulate programmes for the "war on terror". The INC gave this office exactly what it wanted to hear. So cosy did the relationship become and so complete the dependence of the Office of Special Plans on the INC that the latter virtually took over all key aspects of planning for a new Iraq after the war. So great was its influence that, having set up a 'Future of Iraq' project in 2002, which drew upon the Defense Department and 17 other federal agencies, the Pentagon consistently ignored its recommendations on all key political issues and accepted the advice of the INC. David Phillips, Chairman of the Democratic Principles Working Group, described the role the INC was playing as follows:

> On security, the participants envisioned a key role for reformed elements of the Iraqi Army. They insisted on the dissolution of agencies involved in atrocities—like military intelligence and the secret police (the Mukhabarat)—and proposed setting up a body to investigate war crimes, prepare a "most wanted" list, and prosecute war criminals. They envisioned a military council vetting and then taking steps to professionalize the armed forces.
> Representatives of the Iraqi National Congress, however, claimed to control a vast underground network that would rise in support of coalition forces to assist security and law

enforcement. They insisted that the entire Iraqi Army be immediately disbanded. The Pentagon agreed, in the end leading many Iraqi soldiers who might otherwise have been willing to work with the coalition to take up arms against it. Chalabi's promised network didn't materialize, and the resulting power vacuum contributed to looting, sabotage and attacks against American forces.

The working group also emphasized winning (the) hearts and minds of average Iraqis, largely through improving living conditions. It urged cooperation with Iraq's existing technocracy to ensure the uninterrupted flow of water and electricity. Though civil servants and professionals for the most part were required to be Ba'ath party members, the working group maintained that not all Ba'athists were war criminals. The group proposed so-called lustration laws to identify and remove officials who had committed atrocities. On the other hand, the Iraqi National Congress was adamant that all former Ba'ath party members were inherently complicit in war crimes. Siding with Chalabi, the coalition provisional authority decided that the Ba'ath party would be banned, and dismissed many party members from their jobs. As a result millions of Iraqis are still without electricity and fresh water, necessities they could at least count on under the criminal regime of Saddam Hussein.

Most important, the working group insisted that all Iraqis needed a voice in the transition to a stable, democratic Iraq. Participants agreed that exiles alone could not speak for all Iraqis, and endorsed discussions with leaders inside and outside the country as the basis for constituting a legitimate and broadly representative transitional structure.

Before the London Opposition conference in December, Chalabi lobbied the United States to appoint a government in exile, dominated by his partisans, to be installed in Baghdad at the moment of liberation. Concerned about legitimacy, the Bush administration ultimately rejected this proposal. Still, Chalabi's supporters in Washington—particularly civilians in the Pentagon—relentlessly promoted him as Iraq's future leader. Exceptional treatment included airlifting Chalabi and his American-trained 700-man paramilitary force to Nasariya in the middle of the war. He is now a member of the Iraqi Governing Council, serving as its president this month.[8]

The role played by Chalabi's men in toppling Saddam's statue in Firdous Square, and subsequently bringing out poor Shias from Saddam City, Baghdad's poorest suburb, to rejoice at their freedom for the benefit of the television cameras, showed that the INC had remained an integral part of the US government's attempt to manufacture consent through propaganda and deceit.

The INC's success in bringing down Saddam Hussein's government in Iraq by fanning the paranoia of the world's only superpower, is disturbing because it would be relatively easy to emulate. The US has minorities from all over the world. Many of their members fled to the US to seek refuge from political persecution, and dream of the day that they can return as conquering heroes to their own countries. The INC's success is likely to act as a beacon for them and greatly intensify the onslaught on the nation state and the disintegration of the Westphalian order.

The death throes of a nation state

The rest of Iraq's story is short, but tragic. For an entire year as the US and UK relentlessly built up their propaganda campaign to justify an invasion of Iraq, they made sure, with the assistance of the international media, that everything Iraq said and did was viewed with intense suspicion. Baghdad's every action was interpreted as a stalling tactic designed to buy time, or a propaganda exercise to win the sympathy of other nations and split the permanent members of the Security Council. The starting point of every chain of reasoning was that Iraq *had* WMD, and that its every action was designed to protect them and give it time to increase their number or make them more lethal. In those twelve months, and especially in the six months that preceded the war, when the buildup was the main news story on every major television network every hour, not one news anchor, and not one commentator, ever questioned this assumption.

The failure to find a single proscribed weapon, other than two missiles that were capable of flying a few kilometres beyond the permitted 150 kms, albeit without their guidance systems, reveals the monstrous injustice that was done to this country. Attempts to justify the injustice by raking up Saddam Hussein's record of expression and torture only compound it, for they seek to turn a gross infringement of international law into a precedent for further infringements.

Throughout this time, Iraq was telling the truth. If anyone was lying—'sexing up' worthless 'intelligence' data, or simply making it up—it was the US and the UK. This realisation casts a totally different light on all that Iraq did in the nine months that preceded the invasion. What was once portrayed, and accepted, as stalling tactics by a dictator who was beyond the pale of international law, appears as what it really was—a desperate last-ditch effort to do each and everything required of it, to persuade a heavily indoctrinated world to believe what it was saying.

From 1999 till early in 2002, Iraq had continued to use the only strategy left open to it—of insisting that inspection should resume where it was disrupted by Butler's abrupt change of stance in August 1998, i.e. with the drawing up of a list of tasks and an explicit commitment to lift sanctions once these were completed. When Iraq realised, probably in April 2002, that the US was serious about invading it, it hastened to invite the inspectors back in, but still wanted an assurance from the UN Secretary General that paragraph 22 of Resolution 687 would be honoured. The US did everything it could to sabotage the talks that followed, once again using calculated leaks to the media. When Iraq struck an agreement with the UN it (along with the UK) used its power in the Security Council to delay the start of inspections still further.

When the inspections finally began, they did everything they could to lift the requirements for compliance to an impossibly high level in order to make sure that the Council found Iraq in 'further material breach of its obligations'. They did so not only in the Security Council and subsequent pronouncements, but also by putting immense pressure on Hans Blix to render an unfavourable judgment.[9] In the end the pressure worked. For in his anxiety to remain strictly impartial, and to present a report that no one could reject out of hand, thereby destroying its value, Blix stated in his 27 January report that Iraq had not been forthcoming in offering cooperation 'in substance' (as distinct from process). This gave the US and UK the fig leaf that they wanted for an invasion. Blix may have realised this and regretted it. For five months after the war ended, in an interview to Australian Radio, Blix said that he had come to the conclusion that Iraq had destroyed most of its WMD (other than nuclear, which was the domain of the IAEA) in the summer of 1991, i.e. within the time span for autonomous destruction that resolution 687 had given it.[10]

There is an aura of fatalism, reminiscent of Greek tragedy, about the last days of Saddam Hussein's Iraq. On the streets of Baghdad people knew that an invasion was coming, knew they were powerless to stop it and simply shut it out of their consciousness. Instead with dread in their hearts they went to work, went out to restaurants, put up plays, and rehearsed for Western classical music concerts. In the UN and in its dealings with UNMOVIC, Iraq stretched itself frantically to meet each and every demand of the US, UK and UN. That desperate effort has already been described, but we need to hear it one more time in the Iraqis' own words. Throughout the media coverage of the build-up to war, the only voice the world did not hear was that of the intended victim. Although the international news channels televised the Security Council debates live, worldwide, none of them were fair-minded enough to beam the statement of Iraq's permanent representative to the UN, Mahmoud Al Doury, as he defended his country and told the council what Iraq had done to comply with the wishes of the Council. Here is what he had to say:

> I have listened very carefully to the presentation by Dr. Blix, the chairman of the United Nations Monitoring, Verification and Inspection Commission and Dr. El Baradei, the director general of the IAEA, as well as the esteemed members of the Security Council, and I should like to point out the following.

Iraq accepted to deal with Resolution 1441 based on the fact that this is the means to reach a solution to the so-called issue of the disarmament of Iraqi weapons of mass destruction. Following three rounds of technical negotiations with the United Nations, following the return of inspectors to Iraq, Iraq indeed provided all that may fall within the concept of a proactive Iraqi cooperation.

And I should like to point to the following. Iraq submitted the declaration required under paragraph 3 of Resolution 1441 in record time. The declaration contained many documents on previous Iraqi programs in the nuclear, chemical, biological and ballistic fields.

We continue to believe that these documents require in-depth study by the relevant authorities, because they contain updated information responding to many questions. We have the right to wonder has the declaration been subjected to study with due diligence and depth or should the declaration be reconsidered as a whole by the relevant authorities? We should like the file to be reconsidered in total.

Second, Iraq's doors were open to the inspection teams without restrictions or conditions. And the world—the entire world—was surprised at this level of unprecedented cooperation. We know that some states were not very happy with this cooperation; in fact, some would have wished Iraq had obstructed inspections or locked some doors. However, this did not and will not happen because Iraq has genuinely decided to prove that it is free of weapons of mass destruction and to lift any doubt in that regard.

And let me mention what Drs. Blix and El Baradei stated this morning: 675 inspections have taken place so far within Iraq. In this short of period of time, the inspectors have found no evidence contradicting Iraq's declarations or bolstering the allegations asserted by the United States and the United Kingdom on the proscribed weapons programs or, indeed, the weapons alleged by the distinguished representative of the UK this morning.

Now, concerning interviews with Iraqi scientists, the government of Iraq continues to encourage those scientists to accept interviews. Additional lists of names containing other scientists have been submitted following the requests by Drs. Blix and El Baradei. Other lists are on their way, as they know. Four, Iraq did agree to over-flights by U-2 aircraft, by Mirage aircraft and by Antonov 2 aircraft in Iraqi airspace for surveillance purposes. It is logical and reasonable that while these aircraft are undergoing their missions, it is reasonable and logical for British and US warplanes to cease air strikes, because this will affect the security. Thus, inspectors have six levels of aerial surveillance, beginning with satellites, followed by high-altitude surveillance aircraft, the U-2, then medium-level aircraft, the Mirage aircraft, then low-level aircraft, Antonov 2, followed by helicopters and other means for aerial surveillance.

As for the issue of the Iraqi penal legislation that some have considered among the important elements of Iraqi's cooperation, Iraq had not had a negative position in this regard. We had technical considerations.

At any rate, the decree was enacted today in order to end the controversy surrounding this matter. I was surprised to hear some say that this decree was unimportant or late in coming. Concerning other issues, UNMOVIC, following its establishment, adopted a process that includes merging outstanding disarmament issues within the reinforced monitoring system, and this was referenced in its report to the Security Council S-2292. However, in order to facilitate UNMOVIC's mission in identifying these issues and resolving them, Iraq in its full, comprehensive and updated declaration of 7 December 2002, provided full details on these outstanding issues and the means to resolve them. Nevertheless, Iraq has begun to proactively cooperate with UNMOVIC, having lately agreed to discuss these issues with Iraq. And we have provided 24 documents pertaining to many of the outstanding issues.

Two commissions have been set up, made up of high Iraqi

officials and scientists to consider these issues and to provide all the information thereon. And this has been requested by Drs. Blix and El Baradei on more than one occasion.

After all that, we continue to face allegations by some that Iraq not only has not cooperated, but rather that Iraq is in material breach of 1441. Our question is, where is this material breach? Is it as asserted in the allegations made by the United States of America at the previous session, which did not gain acceptance by many states in the world or is the matter related to the concept of proactive cooperation required of Iraq? Many in this forum have called for proactive cooperation. What is this proactive cooperation? If it means that Iraq is to show weapons of mass destruction, we would respond saying: Mr. President, by an Arab proverb I hope will be interpreted correctly, an empty hand has nothing to give. You cannot give what you don't have. If we do not possess such weapons, how can we disarm ourselves of such weapons? Indeed, how can they be disarmed when they do not exist? At any rate, we join the cause of those who do believe that the best means to resolve these issues is continuing proactive cooperation with the inspectors. We do not stand with those who want failure for the inspection work.

And I would refer to the quote in *The Washington Post* from members of the US Senate, and I quote, "We, the US government, have undermined the inspectors."

As for the missile issue, I should like to point out, distinguished ministers and ambassadors, that Iraq—and I say that to the uninformed—Iraq declared these missiles in its biannual declaration and in its full declaration to the Security Council. They were not uncovered by the inspectors. Iraq continues to stress that these missiles, delivered to our armed forces, do not have a range of over 150 kilometres. The issue was lately discussed with the UNMOVIC experts.

Iraq believes that this issue can be taken up toward a technical solution, and therefore it is not logical to accuse Iraq that it is going beyond the permitted range so long as Iraq is dealing with these issues in full transparency, so long as its establishments and test areas are open and under oversight. Iraq would suggest in this regard that test-firings can be undertaken through a random choice of missiles in order to ascertain the range. However, the option of dialogue is open between technical parties in Iraq and within UNMOVIC in order to reach a satisfactory solution to this issue.

Mr. President, when it comes to VX and anthrax, which were also mentioned, Iraq has put forward practical proposals to resolve these issues among other outstanding issues. These are related to VX, to anthrax, as well as some chemical precursors, as well as information on growth media. Iraq suggested that one could ascertain the amount of VX and anthrax destroyed through measuring the dissolved quantities of VX and anthrax in the unilateral destruction sites. And that there is a means to extrapolate the quantity destroyed through scientific investigation and comparing that with Iraq's declaration. And therefore, the issue needs perseverance because it is a difficult subject.

Mr. President, in conclusion, at a time when voices in the world are rising, calling on the United States and Great Britain to heed reason and to respect international legitimacy, the United States of America and the United Kingdom continue to mass forces against Iraq in an unjust cruel campaign, believing that this vast media campaign will make the world silent.

We would like to stress that Iraq has chosen the path of peace. We want to reach solutions that satisfy the international community. We are prepared to provide all means to assist in clarifying the real picture to avoid the objectives of those who are ill-intentioned, who wish to ignite a war in Iraq with incalculable consequences toward clear colonial objectives. We wish the Security Council to follow the wish of the vast majority of member-states in the United Nations. It is to give the inspectors their full role by undertaking their tasks through the path of dialogue and proactive cooperation leading certainly to peace and not war. We would also seriously call on the Security Council to consider lifting the unjust embargo imposed on Iraq and to rise to its commitments by respecting Iraq's sovereignty, independence and territorial integrity. We call upon it to continue to work toward the elimination of all weapons of mass destruction in the Middle East in implementation of paragraph 14 of Resolution 687."

The world listened and agreed with Al Doury. But the US and UK did not.

Notes

1. Walter Pincus and Dana Priest. "Hussein's weapons may have been a bluff". *The Washington Post* 1 October 2003.
2. "Saddam 'may have bluffed' on WMDs. "BBC News 2 October 2003.
3. Anthony Lake's Speech at Georgetown University, Washington on 6 March 1996. Lake was Clinton's National Security Adviser.
4. Letter from the Secretary General to the Security Council. S/1998/1172. 15 December 1998.
5. Kenneth Katzman. "Iraqi opposition Groups". CRS issue brief. http://www.fas.org/irp/crs/crs-iraq-op.htm#11
6. Philip Shenon. "CIA Was With UN in Iraq for Years, Ex-Inspector Says". *New York Times,* 23 February 1999
7. Julian Borger. "Pentagon cools on finding weapons". *The Guardian* 29 May 2003.
8. David L. Phillips. "Listening to the Wrong Iraqi". *The New York Times,* 20 September 2003.
9. Helena Smith. "Blix: I was smeared by the Pentagon". *The Guardian* 11 June 2003. Smith reported Blix as saying: "But towards the end the [Bush] administration leaned on us," he conceded, hoping the inspectors would employ more damning language in their reports to swing votes on the UN Security Council.
10. Reuters. "Blix: Iraq destroyed WMD ten years ago". 17 September 2003. "I'm certainly more and more to the conclusion that Iraq has, as they maintained, destroyed almost all of what they had in the summer of 1991," Blix said.

Epitaph for Saddam

Saddam Hussein was finally captured at 8.30 pm local time, on December 13 in the little town of Adwar, a few kilometres outside his home town of Tikrit. The Coalition Provisional Authority in Baghdad is claiming the capture of Saddam Hussein as a great success. In language worthy of his President, Paul Bremer announced to a hurriedly assembled press conference, "We've got him". An army general who gave an extensive illustrated briefing of the capture described him as having been 'caught like a rat'. But Saddam's capture was not a great victory. By the time it occurred, it was at most a footnote in history. Had Saddam been skillfully masterminding the attacks on the American forces in Iraq it might still have been a significant footnote. But as the circumstances of his capture showed, all he had been doing for eight months was to hide in one small hole after another dug for him by close members of his tribe. Throughout this time he had been in touch with almost no one. So the question of masterminding a continuing guerrilla war did not even arise. Instead what the world saw on TV was a tired, haggard old man, who had lost hope long ago but did not lose his dignity even when forced to open his mouth before the world's TV cameras, in order to have a DNA sample taken.

As has been described in the preceding chapters, the British and American governments, aided by a complaisant international media, have done so thorough a job of demonising Saddam Hussein that few have dared to say even a word in his support. Yet history demands of us a small amount of courage and honesty, if for no other reason than to keep alive our capacity for scepticism and independent thought in a brainwashed world.

Saddam Hussein was a cruel and ruthless dictator. As a result he inspired only fear and no love. But he was not the evil Hitlerian creature that the western media have portrayed. On the contrary, he was a rather run-of-the-mill dictator, a product of the history and culture of his country, and the circumstances of its creation. He was also, from his earliest days a pawn of the west, which used him and then discarded him like a bag of trash.

Saddam did not create an Iraq that contained three distinct and powerfully self-assertive ethnic minorities. That Iraq was casually created by the British who betrayed their promises to the Arab national movement in 1918 and drew straight lines on the map that bisected the ethnic groups of the region, leaving it to others to hold the truncated bits together. So whoever ruled Iraq had to do it by force. Saddam not only did not have a choice—there simply was no other way.

The Kurds, of course bore the brunt of Iraqi repression. But was Saddam's repression of them any worse than that of the Turks or the Shah of Iran? The answer is, almost certainly not. 'Ah, but what about the gassing of the Kurds, as at Halabja? The Turks and Iranians only imprisoned, tortured and killed the Kurds. They did not use poison gas against them'. Not true: as was shown in chapter 4[1], even before Iraq's invasion of Kuwait in 1990, the US administration was in possession of a report written by its own military intelligence that the bulk if not all of the Kurds killed in Halabja had died as a result of cyanide and not mustard gas. Cyanide gas was used by the Iranians but not the Iraqis. However, the Bush senior administration buried the report when it became necessary to rally a coalition against Saddam.

But was not Saddam an indefatigable warmonger? Did he not attack Iran? Yes, but who encouraged him to do so, entered into a clandestine agreement with him just two months before the attack, and then supplied him with all the battlefield radar and satellite intelligence on Iran to wage the war? Why the US, of course.

'But look how he attacked tiny Kuwait. And that too so soon after the war with Iran!' True again. But Saddam believed, and the Kuwaitis and the UAE and the Americans led him to believe, that he was fighting Iran to protect his 'Arab brothers'. What Saddam could not foresee in 1980 was the crash in oil prices in 1985. By the time the war ended Iraq was left with a $41 billion debt that none of these countries was prepared to help alleviate. Kuwait even stole Iraqi oil throughout the war by digging laterally into its oil reserves from across the border. All this did not justify the invasion of Kuwait, but Saddam did appeal to the US to help him to make Kuwait and the UAE see sense. On July 25, 1990 he told US Ambassador April Glaspie in some detail what he intended to do if the Kuwaitis were not reasonable. He thus gave the US a full seven days' warning of his plan to attack if Kuwait did not come even minimally to its aid, but the US did nothing.

What about Saddam's brutal treatment of the Shias of southern Iraq? Of all the accusations that have been levelled against him, this is by far the most justified. Western estimates of the numbers he killed, which range from 100,000 to 300,000 are probably highly exaggerated, but the testimony of the mass graves that have been unearthed and of Shia notables whose family members disappeared at the whim and fancy of the *Mukhabarat*, is incontrovertible. However, it also needs to be remembered that to preserve the integrity of Iraq Saddam had to counter the powerful pull of the Shia revolution in Iran. Given Iraq's history, repression was the only way Saddam could go.

What is more, the worst atrocities occurred when Saddam crushed the revolt of the marsh Arabs and other Shias in the south after the Kuwait war. But most of this slaughter would not have occurred had the US not first systematically incited the Shia leaders of the area to revolt against the Ba'athist regime and then left them completely in the lurch without access even to the arms captured from the fleeing Iraqi soldiers, to be butchered by Saddam when he had time to draw his breath once again.

In any case, faced with a revolt, what was Saddam expected to do? What would any other country have done? What did the Federal government of the USA do in 1861, when faced by the secession of the South? It is worth remembering that till the first world war, the bloodiest conflict the western world had known was the American civil war.

But what about Saddam's weapons of mass destruction? By playing cat and mouse with the UN over their disclosure, did he not himself force the Security Council to prolong the economic sanctions and condemn his people to penury and children to death? Did he not use oil revenues to build palaces, restart his WMD programmes and rearm his military while his people starved?

The complete failure of a 1400–man team of weapons inspectors appointed by the US to unearth more than a vial of botulinum toxin in a scientist's home refrigerator and some laboratory–scale projects connected with chemical and biological weapons, gives us the answer to that question. What the world now has to face, as Chief UN Weapons Inspector Hans Blix was honest enough to say in an interview on, is that it was Iraq that had been telling the truth all along and the US and UK that had been lying.[2] UNSCOM had indeed destroyed all of Iraq's WMD making facilities by 1995. By 1997 there was little it did not know about Iraq's WMD programme. All that was left was to sort out important accounting discrepancies. It was the US and UK that, by setting impossible standards of accounting and disclosure, prevented the sanctions from being lifted for six more years, bombed Iraq once more into ruins and, having pulled out UNSCOM from the country, gave in to rising waves of paranoia that ended in the unilateral invasion of a defenceless country in defiance of majority opinion in the UN Security Council and unprecedented world opposition.

Even that is not the full measure of US' disregard for international law. As the *New York Times* disclosed in November 2003, in the last days before the war Saddam made desperate efforts to contact the US and invite it to send its own weapons inspectors into Iraq to make sure for themselves that the WMD did not exist. But instead of jumping at the opportunity the US rejected Saddam's offer with contempt. The conclusion is unavoidable: by then the US was bent upon 'regime change' at any cost.

But when the trauma is over, isn't Iraq going to emerge a better, a happier, a more democratic and a freer country? In theory anything is possible. But a December 12, 2003 report by a human rights organisation Occupation Watch leads one to doubt whether this will happen. Between December 1 and 7, 2003, Occupation Watch took a delegation to Iraq consisting of parents of US soldiers serving in Iraq, including the father of one who had died there, along with some Vietnam and Gulf war veterans. Here are some of their findings:

> We found a country with millions of people out of work and with no means to support for their families. Electricity remains intermittent; telephone exchanges destroyed during the war had still not been fixed; the water is not safe to drink; many hospitals lack basic equipment and medicines such as antibiotics; schools have no heat, lights or books; garbage is piled up in the streets; and in a country floating on oil, mile-long gas lines involving five to seven hour waits snake through the cities. ...Many Iraqis report rude and even violent treatment from US soldiers at checkpoints or in home searches. Women told of their great shame at having soldiers barge into their bedrooms during a raid. But much more tragic is the number of cases we heard of Iraqi civilians being shot at by US troops at check points or while driving by in patrols. We heard so many heart-breaking stories of soldiers mistakenly shooting civilians, and these mistakes in turn lead to hatred of our troops and a desire for revenge.
> We visited the Abu Ghraib prison on the outskirts of Baghdad, a prison once run by the former regime under brutal conditions. Today, the prison is overflowing with people detained by the US occupying forces. On the day we visited, the parking lot was full of family members trying to find information about their detained relatives. We talked to a woman with two young children whose husband was arrested without charges; a poor woman crying uncontrollably because her son—the sole breadwinner of the family—had been held for four months; an elderly man looking for his son. They all had one thing

in common: none of their family members had been charged with a crime. Most had no access to lawyers because they couldn't afford the services, but even the lawyers we met said there was little to do for their clients since the prisoners were held without charges and no trials had been set. This prison alone is said to house over 5,000 prisoners.[3]

Saddam's capture has not reduced the intensity of resistance in Iraq. If anything, the opposite has happened. In all forty-two American soldiers were killed in Iraq in December 2003. Twenty-four of them died after December 13[4].

Notes

1   P. 129
2   Reuters: *Blix: Iraq destroyed weapons 10 years ago.* September 17, 2003.
3   Occupation Watch: Report from the Military Families' delegation to Iraq, December 12, 2003.
4   www.usnewslink.com/uscasualties.htm

INDEX

AIDS, 188–189
Abdullah, King, 199
Aberdeen labratory report on VX gas, 44–46, 51, 200–201
Abizaid, John, 178
Abu Dhabi T.V., 158
Adenauer, Geeman Chancellor, 181
Afghan War, 72
Aflaq, Michel, 3
Ahani, Ahmed Samir, 80
al-Bakr, Ahmed Hassan, 7
al Baradei Mohamed, 90, 102, 107, 109, 140, 206–209
Al Doury Mohamoud, 206, 211
Al Fatoxin production, 34
Al Kasem Gen Abdel Karim, 4–5
Al Maraghi, Dr article in the Middle East Review of International Affairs, 170
al-Qaeda, Iraqlinks, ix, 59, 69, 79–82, 101, 104, 106, 127, 128, 130–131, 167
al Saadi, Gen Amir, 169
al Zarqawi, Abu Musah, 106
Al Jazeerah, 157–160
Albright, Madeleine, 39, 41, 47–48, 57

American Embassies in Nairobi and Dar-es-Salaam attack, (1998), 70
American Enterprise Institute, 76–77, 81
American foreign poly, 76–79
American hegemony boss of, 186–191 pew survey, 190–191 struggle, 127
American hostages crisis in Iran, 10, 196
American Intelligence Agency (CIA), 4–5, 7, 32–33, 39, 69, 79, 81, 91, 130, 168, 171, 201
American Intelligence Agency (CIA), 7, 32–33, 39, 69, 79, 81, 91
American media anthrax mail to, 80
American soldiers attack, 184 death tool, ix, 185 Saudi Arabia attack, 70
Ammagh, Dr Huda, 169
Annan, Kofi, 41–42, 49–51, 55, 57, 90, 172, 200
Augar-ul-Islam, 106

220 • Index

Anthrax, 8, 33, 37, 80, 83, 210 estimate,106, 173 production, 34
Anti-Soviet Baghdad Pact, 4
Arab Independence, 2
Arab nationalism, 3–4
Arab nationalist movement, 1
Arab revolt, 2
Atta, Mohammed, 80–81
Aziz, Tariq, 43, 48, 50–51

Ba'ath Party (Arab socialist) Foundation of, 3
Ba'ath Party, 5, 56–58, 132, 184, 203 coup, 7 hunting down, 7 secret intelligence apparatus, 7
Baathism, 3
Barber, Benjamin, 181
Barton, Rod, 34
Biological and Toxin Weapons Convention Iraq signatory, 33
Biological warfare agent, 37 burrial of, 169 false allegations, 168
Blair, Tony, 11, 35, 90, 96, 113, 127–128 131, 161, 167, 170–171, 174, 175–176, 185–186, 197, 202
Blix, Hans, 90, 94, 102–104, 107–108, 111–113, 127, 140, 195, 206–209
Bitar, Salah, 3
Bolton, John, 78
Botulenum toxin production, 134 estimate, 173
Botulism, 8
Boucher, Richard, 133
Bowen, Jeremy, 137
Bradley Institute, 77
Bremer, L Paul, 182
British Joint Intelligence Committee Report on WMD, ix
Brooks, General Vincent, 149

Bruckheimer, Jerry, 154
Bush (Jr), George W, 11, 19, 31, 48, 54, 71, 78, 82, 104, 107, 112, 126, 128, 135, 137, 139, 161, 167, 170, 172–175, 181, 185, 188–189, 197, 200
address to the nation, 128–129
Graduation Day speech, 84–85
Press Statement, 107
UN General Assembly, speech, 87–89, 91–92, 94–96
Bush, George (Sr), 30, 38, 73, 76
Butler, Richard, 42–47, 50–53, 55–60, 200

Cannistraro, Vince, 171
Centre for Security Policy, 77
Chalabi, Ahmad, 130, 157, 171, 183–184, 201, 203
Chemical bombs estimate, 106
Chemical Weapons Convention Iraq signatory, viii
Cheney, Dick, 73, 76, 81, 172, 176
Cheney, Lynn, 76
Chirac, 189–190
Chomsky, Noam, 143
Christopher, Warren, 39
Churchill, Winston, 2
Clarke, Gen Wesley, 186
Clinton, 34, 53–56, 76–77, 198
Closlridium per finger reagent test kits revealing of, 50
Cold War, xiii, 4, 21, 38, 70, 75, 77, 85, 134, 176, 199
Concept of proactive cooperation, 209
Conway, Lt Gen James, 172
Copeland, Miles, 5–6
Craig, Rear Admiral, 160
Creel Commission, xi
Crimean war, 134

Cuban Missile crisis, 85
Cyanide gas use, 129
Cyclosarin estimate, 33

Dana, Mazen Killing of, 160–161
Darwish, Adel account of, 5–7
Daschle, Tom, 80
Decter, Midge, 79
Defence Intelligence Report, 129, 168
Dhamapala, Jayantha, 42
Disarmament issues, 208
Doctrine of deterrence, 72, 85
Doctrine of preeemption, 72, 125
Doctrine of prevention (re-labbead pre-emption), 85
Down, Black Hawk, 154
Duelfer, Charles, 40
Dulles, Allan, 5
Dyke, Greg, 142

Economy, 13–15 Dinnar value, 182
infrastructure shattered, 138
oil reserves, 182
per capita, 37, 138
War impact, 14
Egypt invasion (1956), 4
Eichelherger, Jim, 6
Ekeus, Roef, 36, 39
El-Hasimi, Akila assassination, 185
el Kassem, Abdel Karim, 196
Empty munitions estimate, 106
Ethnic awarness of, 3 groups, 132–134
Ethnicities suppression of, 3–4
European Broadcasters Union, 158

Fahd, King, 17–18
Faisal, Emir, 2
Farid, Cap Abdel Maguid, 6
Federation of ethnic nationalities creation of, 2
Feith, Douglas, 78

fideyeen, 132, 145, 147, 178
Fisk, Robert, viii, 142, 159
Frankfurter Allegemeine Zeitung study, 139
Frontieres, Sans, 159
Future of Iraq Project setting up, 183

Gaffney, Frank, 79
Gasoline Supply, 178–179
General Amnesty, 185
Germ bombs destruction of, 36
Germ warheads, 36
Gilligan, Andrew, 127, 173
Gingerich, Newt, 76
Glaspie, April, 10, 13–21, 134, 196
Government's 139 public buildings destruction of, vii
G-8 Summit, Evian, 188–189
Gulf wars, viii, x, 33–34, 38, 54, 76, 97, 105, 134–135, 137, 156, 180, 186

Habibou, Allele, 109
Halahta, 134, battle between the Gramans and the Iraquis, 129
Halabja (Kurdish village) Chemical weapons attack, 128–129
Hemoud, 150
Hergh, Seymour, 127
High-level Concealment Committee, Iraq setting up, 198
Hijacking, 71
Hirohito, Emperor, 181
Hezbullah, 79
Houssona, Dr Harith, 150, 152
Hudson Institute, 77
human rights record, xii–xiii, 97, 128, 176
Huntington, Samuel, 77
Husain, Sharif, 1
Hussein, King, 18

Hussein, Saddam
  another Adolf Hitler, 20, 135
  assassination plan, 6, 38–39, 54
  Beirut, 6
  CIA Connection, 4–9
  Clinton efforts to depose, 75
  collapse of his government, 133
  cross into Syria, 6
  Saddam crusade, 138
  escape to Tikrit, 6
  frequent visits to the American Embassy, 6
  Glaspie meeting, 18–21, 134–135, 196–197
  head of Al-Jihaz-e-Khas, 7
  Kofi Annan meeting, 41–42
  US 18 Co-signatories letter to Clinton to take diplomatic and military action, 75–76
  US strategy of removal, 30, 39, 74–76, 79, 169
  Wolfowitz attack on Clinton policy, 75–76
Hussein, Uday, 150

Imams alleigiance to the monarch, 3
Ingram, Adam, 171
International Atomic Emergy Agency (IAEA), 33, 81, 98–100, 102, 104, 107–110, 140, 188, 206
Iran pursues weapons and export terror, 83
US policy, x
US warning, 79
Iran-Contra-Israel scandal, 78
Iran's Communist Killing of, 7
axis of evil, Bush allegation, 138
boundaries, 2
British plan of imposing colonial rule, 2
ethnic divides, 2

Infant mortality rate, 37, 68, 138, 176
Kristol open letter to Bush, 79, 82
back of timely medicine, 69
lack of safe drinking water and sanitation facilities, 37, 68, 138
living on food handouts, 69
military coup of 1991 failure, 198
neo conservate arguments, 79
poverty line, 37, 68
respiratory and gastro intestinal diseases, 68–69
ruler death killing or exile, 3
Shias and Sunnis fight, 3
under Saddam and after war, 178–182
urban infrastructure destruction, 37
US intervention in internal affairs, 4
US threat, 4
Iraq biological warfare programme, 42 false allegation, 168
Butler's reports, 55–56
Iraq biological weapons discovery of, 36, 50
doubt over, 102–103
Iraq's cooperation with UNSCOM failure, 55
Security Council Condition, 31
UNSCOM discovery, 33, 36, 46–47
Iraq explosive training camp Powell allegation, 131
Iraqi defence facilities American Inspectors spying, 40
Iraq Implossive devices possession Albright vi CWS, 47–48
Butler mission, 47
IAEA refute charge, 47
Iraq withdraw cooperation with UNSCOM, 47

UNSCOM's charge, 47
Iraq long-range missile programme, 42
Iraq MI6, 169–170, 177
Iraq missiles guidance system and propellants destruction of, 36
UNSCOM panel, 51
Iraq National Congress, xii, 177, 183–184, 201–204
Iraq nuclear weapons performance, viii
US allegations and IAEA disapproval, 81
Iraq Policemen running the government, 182, 185
Iraq Power Plant boming during Kuwait War, 31
Iraq radar system, Basra destruction of, 90
Iraq Scud missle propellants discovery, 34–36 distruction of, 53
Iraq war Anglo-Saxon failing to get second security Resolution, 140–141
Anglo-Saxon Joint operations, vii, ix
Anglo-Saxon moral case, 128–129
Anglo-Saxon propaganda, 124–127
Anglo-Saxon troops resistance, 132–133, 177–178
anti-war movement, 131
Blair justification, 131–132, 175–177
British Parliament support, 127
British peace marchers, 175–176
Bush justification, 176–177
eminent international Jurists appeal to Security Council, 125
example of Al Amriya bombing and number of women and children killers, 135
Iraq defeat, ix
Kristol and Kagan warning to US administration, 93–94
legal sanction from own attorney's general, 141
manufacturing Congent Campaign, 125–126
small protest in Britain, 124, 131–132
neo-conservative policy, 92
official version, viii
opinion polls survey, 107, 124
opposition, 124
preparation, 87–90
Ranonett article in Le Moude Diplomalique illegal aggression, 125
Robert Fisk's description, viii
Rumsfield responsible, 168
UN Security Council voting, 126
US Air Force bombing on Basra, 90
US Congress resolution, 127
US facing a classic guerrilla campaign, 178
US loss of hegemony, 188
Washinton post-poll survey, 127
Iraq Weapons of Mass Destruction, 36, 39
al Baradeis report, 94, 102, 108–110
Amorim Report, 46, 102
Anglo-Saxon strategy, 101–102
Anglo-Saxon unable to find out, 68
Annan intervention, 41–42
Annan report, 42
Annan talks to Naji Sabri, 90
Blix mission, 90
Blix reply, to Colin Powell's statement, 107–108
Blix report 94, 102, 111–112
British Intelligence report, 95, 98, 169
Bush accusation, 174–175

224 • Index

Bush UN speech, 94–96
Butler mission, 42–46
Butler report, 49, 55–60
Colin Powell report to UN, 104–106
complaints against UNSCOM's inspectors, 42
cooperator with UNMOVIC, 94
criticism of CIA report, 171–172
details of the return of the Inspectors, 90
discovery of documents, 56
Ekens report, 39, 198
hide and seek role with U.N. inspectors, ix, 32, 130
IAEA Chief visit, 90
IAEA's findings, 33
Iraq agrees to inspect Presidential palaces, 42
Iraq violation of UN resolutions, 54
Military Intelligence report, 169, 171
National Intelligence estimate, 175
Saddam blocks UN inspections, 40, 76
sites verifications, 168
Survey Group Report, 174–175
12,000 page document to UNMOVIC, 100–101
UN team to Baghdad, 40
UNSCOM demand access to Presidential palaces, 40–41
UNSCOM's report, 34–35, 102–103
UNSCOM role, 32–33
UNMOVIC inspection, 69
UNMOVC Inspection Completion, 188
UNMOVIC failure of discover, 130–131
UNSCOM withdrawal, 201
US and UK technology, 8

US false allegations, 167–168
UN resolutions, 42, 97–100
Vienna talks, 90
Violation of UN Security Resolution, 44
Voting in the Security Council, 188
Waxman letter to Bush, 173
Weapon inspectors report, 194–195
Iraqi Army crippling, 130 lack of modern weapons, 138
proposal of disbandment, 183
remnants of, vii
Iraqi Installations Desert Fox operation, 53–54 US air Force targetting, 40
Iraqi National Accord US backing, 201
Iraqi National Guardsmen CIA provide sub-machine gun-toting, 7
Iraqi National Standards Laboratory inspection of, 50
Iraqi Scientists interview, 169, 208
Iraq's Communist hunting down, 7
Iraq-Kuwait war, viii, 9, 11–21, 29–31, 34–37
Iraq's oil refineries blown up, 3
Iraq's Presidential palaces inspection of, 50
Iraq's Special Security Organisation document from, 50
Iraq-Iran War, viii, 7–11, 33, 46, 73, 129
Iraq-US relations, 8–9

Jackson, Glenda, 170
Jewish Institute for National Security Affairs, 77–78
John M. Institute for Strategic Studies, Harvard University, 77

Jordanian Embassy bombing of, 185
Journalism rule of, 139
Journalist Caste system, 158
Cameramen death, 158, 160–161
Casualities, 158, 161
death of ITN Crew, 158
death rate, 158
repeated attacks, 158
slaying in Palestine Hotel and attack, 158–159
US-military Killing, 158
War correspondents number, 160

Kagan, Robert, 79, 93
Kamel, Hussein, 53
Kasem killing, 7
Kay, David, 174, 194
Keller, Bill, 82
Kelly, David British scientist suicide, 170–174
Kennedy, John F, 7
Khalaf, Roula, 56
Khomeini, Ayatollah, 7, 196
Kidnapping, 179
Killing estimate, viii, 7
Knightley, Philip, xii, 159–160
Krauthammer, Charles, 79
Kristoff, Nicolas, 127
Kristol, William, 75, 77–79, 82, 93
Kristol's *Weekly Standard* organ of the neo-congervatives, 77, 79, 93
Kurdish Democratic Party, 201
Kurdish Parties Split, 201
Kurds, 2–3, 30, 157 casualities, 128 Iraq use chemical weapons, viii, 33
poison gas use, 8–9, 128 revolts, 39

Long, Patrick, 171

Lawrence, T.E, his mission and report, 1–2
Ledeen, Michael, 78
Looting, vii, 133, 179
Lott, Trent, 76
Kristol *Weekly Standard*, 79, 93
Kristol, will open letter to Bush, 79
Kristol, Williams, 77
Kristol, 93
Kristol *Weekly Standard*, 93
Kagan, Robert, 93 Kristol open letter to Bush, 82
Khomeini, 196
Kristol, coil, 82
killings, 7
looting, 179

McGovern, Ray, 172
Manufacturing conigent media and, 133–135 pharase, xi, 125–126
Media bias role, 139 coverage, 134–144
instructions, 141–142
Israeli lobby in the US infiltration, xii
murder of journalist, 146
pool system, 135–136, 143
pressure on, 175
role, 133–137
tools of propaganda, xi–xii
Menarol, Robert, 159
Middle East Forum, 77
Military Field Information Centre, 158
Milroie, Laurie, 81
Missile issue dissension with UNMOVIC experts, 209
Mobile laboratories US report, 168
Monarchy coup, 4 fall, 3
Morris Roger, 5, 7
Mubarak, 16, 18–19

Murder, 179 political, 1 rate, vii
Murdoch, Rupert, 77, 142–143
Mustard gas estimate, 33, 106 use, 129

Naets, Tony, 158
Nasserism, 3–4
Nasser, Gamal Abdel, 3–5
Nasiriyah refcul mission details of, 149–150
National Archaelogical Museum destination of, vii–viii, 133, 179
National sovereignty concept of, 172
Nehru, Jawaharlal, 3
Nehruvian socialism, 3
New citizenship project, 77
New-conservative doctrine of unilateral supremacy, 198
Neo-conservative movement, 76–77
NATO, 82, 96, 141, 167, 190, 199
North Korea arming with missiles and WMD, 83 US warning, x
Nuclear Non-Proliferation Treaty Iraq signatory, viii

Office of Special Plans setting up, 202
Oil discovery of, 2
Oil Industry, 4
Oil prices, 13–14
Oil reserves of the world US reaction, 30
OPEC Ministerial Council Meeting Geneva, 12, 15
Opposition Conference, London, 2002, 184, 203–204
Operation "Desert Fox", 48, 53–54, 59, 68, 92–93, 96

Osama bin Laden, ix, 78–81, 107
Ottoman Empire, 2

Palestine Hotel attack, 159
Paris Peace Conference, 2
Patriotic Union of Kurdish, 201
Pelletiere, Stephen, 129
Pentagon, 34, 153, 171, 177, 203 report, 73 war plan leak by, 90 Iraq National Congress Infiltration, xii
Perle, Richard, 79
Persian Gulf oil US interest, 31, 74
Phillips, David L, 183, 202–203
Pilger, John, xii
Podesta, John, 57–58
Poison gas Iraq use of its own people, 83–84
Pool system experience, 143–146
Powell, Colin, 92, 101, 103–106, 112, 126, 131, 170, 172, 197
Power Supply, 179
Presidential Palaces Inspection of, 90–91
Private Jessica Lynch's rescue story accounts, 146–154
Project for the New American Century (PNAC), 77, 79, 93
Public hanging, 1

Ramonet, Ignacio, 125
Razak, Dr Mudhafer, 151, 153
Reagan, Ronald, 9–10
Records and fills destruction of, vii
Reeve, William, 159
Riad-al-Qayzi, 53
Religions Identity awareness of, 3
Rich and middle classes houses ransack of, vii
Rioting, vii
Ritter, Scott, 40, 49, 201
Rubin, James P, 52

Rumsfield, Donald, 75, 78–79, 159, 168–169, 171–172, 202
Russert, Tim, 176

Schmitt, 80–82
Senators anthrax mail, 80 draft document, 74–75
Shah, Prakash, 43, 56
Sharon, Ariel, 155
Sheikhs alligiance to the monarch, 3
Shia revolts, 39
Shinah, Kalida, 152–153
Sissons, Peter, 137
Smart sanctions, 69
Smith, Ian Duncan, 174
Spertzed, Richard, 50, 91
Spin Importance, xiii
Straw, Jack, 101, 112
Statue of Saddam Hussein destructionof, vii, 154–157, 204
Suez Canal, nationalisation of, 4
Sunni Arabs and Shia Arabs religious division, 4
Survey Group Report, 174–175, 194–195
Sutherland, Alan, 157
Syria US warning, x US policy, 79

Taha, Dr Rihah, 169
Taliban, 176, 179
Teicher, Howard, 9
Television Coverage, 134–144
Terrorism Casualties, 71 goal, 69–70
network, 131
Threats to US citizens from, 74
US war, 71–72
Terrorist Camps shutting down plan, 83
Trans–Jordan (Modern Jordan) Foundation, 2

Trevan, Tim, 170
Saad, Sheik, 19
Sabri, Naji, 90
Sale, Richard, 4
Samhrook, Richard, 143, 145–146
Sanctions, viii, 36, 38, 40–41, 48–49, 51, 54, 58, 69, 83, 132, 178, 188, 190
Sandler, Lauren, 179
Sarin estimate, 33, 173
4–2 planes, shooting down, 40

Uday, Dr Anmar, 150
United Arab Republic (1958) Formation of, 4
UN Kuwait member, 29
UN Charter Violation of Article, 29
UN headquarters devastating svicide bombing, ix
UN National Security Division Directive, 9
United Nations Monitoring and Verification Commission, (UN MOVIC), 69, 90–91, 102–103, 105, 109, 111–112, 130, 140, 168, 188, 208–210
UN Security Council differences between permanent members, 40
UN Security Resolutions viii, 29–32, 36, 38–39, 42, 69, 90–94, 97–100, 103, 109, 141,173, 191, 197, 199, 207, 211
United Nations Special Commission (UNSCOM), 31–36, 40–47, 49–52, 55–60, 68, 91, 96–100, 112–133, 130, 199–201
UN's Oil for Food Programme, ix, 178, 188–189

UAV (Unmanned aerial vehicle) devlopment, 106
US bio warfare research centre, Fort Detrick, 8
US Committee to Protect Journalists, 160
US Defence Planning Guidance Paper, 73, 198
US National Security Council, 69, 71, 81
US National Security Strategy, 85–87
USS Cole in Yemen waters (1999) suicide bombing, 70
US-Iraq relations, xii, 11–14, 175

VX nerves gas 37, 51, 53, 83, 173, 210 Aberdeen Report, 44–45, 51 Amorin report, 46 estimate, 33 French and Swiss scientists findings, UNSCOM discovery, 43–44
Villepin, Dominique, 112
Violence, 1, 3 factors, 4

War Council, 79
warheads categories destruction, 65
Washington Institute for Near East Policy, 77

Watson, Neville, 156
Watson, Reverend, 157
Watts, Susan, 173
Waxman, Henry, 173
Weapons of Mass Destruction (WMD) UN verification, viii–ix
Westphalian State System principles, 55, 72, 94, 127, 132, 134, 141, 198
Wilson, Woodrow, xi
Wolfowitz, Paul, 72, 76, 78, 81, 198
Woman ceased to go out, vii, insecure, 179–180
World Food Programme, 69, 138
World Trade Centre (WTC) attack, x, 48, 59, 69–72, 78–81, 86, 89, 154

Yantis Lt Col Ryan, 153
Youh, Tarek, 158
Youssef, Ramzi, 81

Zaid, Sheik, 18
Zalheim, Dov, 78

RD/2144/2/06